u.r.s. josé zuber
Moser Graphic Design Team

MAYA
ZUVUYA
AGENDA
2021

Diese Agenda ist allen indigenen Völkern dieser Erde gewidmet,
besonders den mesoamerikanischen, welche uns das Wissen über
die «Natürliche Zeit» für die Zeitenwende hinterlassen haben,
in der wir uns befinden.

«Ayum Hunab Ku. Evam Maya E Ma Ho»
Möge sich Harmonie und Frieden in unserem Geist ausbreiten.

....

This agenda is dedicated to all the indigenous peoples of the world,
especially the Mesoameric peoples, who have left us the knowledge of
«natural time» for the new era of consciousness in which
we find ourselves.

«Ayum Hunab Ku. Evam Maya E Ma Ho»
May harmony and peace spread in our minds.

VORWORT

Als am 12. Oktober 1492 Christoph Columbus seinen Fuss auf den amerikanische Kontinent setzte und später darauf viele andere Eroberer aus Europa, begann ein beispiellose Zerstörung von Menschen, Kultur und Natur. Tausende von Schriften un Büchern der Maya und anderen Hochkulturen (Azteken, Inkas, Olmeken, etc.) wurde verbrannt und Jahrtausende altes Wissen ging verloren.

Die Eroberer staunten nicht schlecht, als man feststellte, dass die Maya nicht nur Meist der Zeit und deren Zyklen waren, sondern Berechnungen angestellt hatten die um etlich Kommastellen genauer waren als die Europäischen.

Daher liess Papst Gregor XIII den bisherigen «Julianischen Kalender» optimieren un verordnete ihn 1583 als «Gregorianischen Kalender» überall, wo die Kirche präsent wa Damit wurde gleichzeitig die Entwicklung der «mechanischen Zeit» (oder auch küns lichen Zeit) eingeläutet, die auf dem unnatürlichen Verhältnis von 12:60 (12 Monat Stunden und 60 Minuten/Stunde) basiert. Unsere moderne Technologie ist auf diese unharmonischen Verhältnis aufgebaut, welches zu den zerstörerischen Folgen führt, d wir heute auf der ganzen Welt erleben.

Nach der ersten grossen Wirtschaftskrise in Amerika versuchte der berühmte Georg Eastman (Gründer von Kodak/Fotofirma) mit vielen anderen Geschäftsmännern, ein Kalenderreform einzuleiten, basierend auf einem harmonischen 13 Monde Kalend (13 Monde à 28 Tage + ein Tag).

Es war der Vatikan, der diese Reform abwürgte, weil es letztlich um die Basis sein weltweiten Macht und Kontrolle ging. Immer noch schlagen zu jeder vollen Stund weltweit Tausende von Kirchenglocken, um die Menschen an die kirchliche Institution z erinnern. Weitere Versuche in den 70er Jahren (UNO) scheiterten ebenfalls am Einspruc des Vatikans.

Es war schliesslich der berühmte und inzwischen verstorbene Mayaforscher Dr. Jos Argüelles (1939–2011), der weltweit eine neue Kalenderreform auslöste. Er erkann jedoch, dass dieser erneute Versuch an der Basis beginnen musste.

Inzwischen folgen Millionen von Menschen seinem «13 Monde Kalender», der mit d Natur und zahlreichen kosmischen Zyklen verbunden und synchronisiert ist.

Diese Kalenderreform läuft weiter und jeder Mensch, der diesem neuen Rhythmus folg lässt die Macht des «Gregorianischen Kalenders» schmelzen, bis es eines Tages sowe ist, dass sich Argüelles Vision erfüllen kann: Die weltweite Einführung des «13 Mond Kalenders» als universeller Ausdruck für den Frieden.

Möge diese «Zuvuya Agenda» viele Menschen dazu inspirieren, über die Zeit, insbeso dere die eigene «Lebenszeit» nachzudenken, und bewusst eine neue Wahl zu treffen

«Ayum Hunab Ku. Evam Maya E Ma Ho»
Möge sich Harmonie und Frieden in unserem Geist ausbreiten

FOREWORD

When Christopher Columbus set for the first time his foot at the 12th of October 1492 on the American continent, and later after him a lot of other conquistadores, an unequaled destruction of human beings, culture and nature occurred. Thousands of scriptures and sacred books of the maya and other high developed cultures (e.g. Aztecs, Incas, Olmecs, etc.) have been burned to ashes and wisdom of millennia has been lost.

The conquerors were indeed puzzled when they realized, that the Maya were not only masters of time and its cycles, but even used more precise calculations in their solar calendars than the ones used in Europe (the Julian calendar at this time).

Therefore pope Gregor XIII called out for the best astronomers and mathematicians at his time and optimized the Julian calendar. With a decree the «Gregorian Calendar» was put in motion everywhere and this very act was also the beginning of the «mechanic time» (also known as «artificial time») based on the unnatural ratio 12:60 (12 month/12 hours/60 minutes). Our whole modern technology is built upon this unnatural and wrong ratio of time which has led to all the massive destructions we see everywhere on this planet.

Instead of connecting us with nature and the universal cycles (movements of the sun/planets/etc.) it has led to machines which separate us from each other and support the exploitation of the resources of mother earth. All the social media (internet/cell phones/etc.) just create a virtual connection and all the war machines are the other extreme of this development.

After the first big financial crisis in America the famous George Eastman (Founder of Kodak) among other great thinkers tried to establish a calendar reform, based on the harmonic 13 moon calendar (13 moons à 28 days = 364 + 1 free day) which was used all over the planet in ancient cultures.

It was the Vatican who finally brought down this first attempt, because the «Gregorian Calendar» is like a powerful tool to control the «rhythm of civilization». Still today on every full hour millions of church bells beat powerfully and loudly to remember the people to the christian religion. Even further attempts to change the calendar in the 70's (UNO) have been blocked by the Vatican.

Nevertheless in the meantime millions of human beings follow the «13 moon cycles» which are synchronized with nature and the cosmic cycles.

This calendar reform is ongoing and every person who joins this new (old) cycles frees himself from a slave rhythm and supports the vision of Dr. José Argüelles: The worldwide acceptance of the global «13 Moon Calendar» as an expression for world peace.

May this «Zuvuya Agenda» support this vision and inspire people to think about time in general, but especially about the own «Lifetime» in order to make everyday a new conscious choice: what do I really want to have in my life and how can I create it?

«Ah Yum Hunab Ku, Evam Maya E Ma Ho»
May peace and harmony prevail in our spirits

INHALTSVERZEICHNIS | CONTENTS

6	**Editorial**	56	Rote Erde *Red Earth*
7	Editorial	57	Weisser Spiegel *White Mirror*
		58	Blauer Sturm *Blue Storm*
10	**Einleitung**	59	Gelbe Sonne *Yellow Sun*
13	Introduction		
		60	**13 Töne der Schöpfung**
16	**Synchronisation**	62	13 Tones of Creation
18	Synchronization		
		64	**Wellentexte**
21	**Heart Brain Coherence**	64	Wavespells
23	Heart Brain Coherence		
		65	**Early Bird Gutschein**
26	**Das Geburtsorakel**	65	Early Bird Voucher
28	The Birth Oracle		
		66	**13 Monde Kalender**
30	**Dein Geburtsorakel**	66	13 Moon Calendar
30	Your Birth Oracle		
		72	**Xocolatl Rezept**
32	**Anleitung**		
33	Tutorial	**74**	**Wo finde ich was?**
		76	Where do I find what?
35	**Der Tzolkin**		
35	The Tzolkin	**78**	**Together to One**
		80	Together to One
37	**Zahnräder**		
37	Toothed Wheels	**82**	**Jahresübersicht 2021**
		82	Year Overview 2021
38	**Die 20 galaktischen Spielfiguren**		
39	The 20 galactic game characters	**83**	**Jahresübersicht 2022**
		83	Year Overview 2022
40	Roter Drache *Red Dragon*		
41	Weisser Wind *White Wind*	**84**	**Jahresplaner 2021**
42	Blaue Nacht *Blue Night*	84	Year Planner 2021
43	Gelber Same *Yellow Seed*		
44	Rote Schlange *Red Snake*	**86**	**Jahresplaner 2022**
45	Weisser Weltenüberbrücker *White Worldbridger*	86	Year Planner 2022
		88	**Agenda**
46	Blaue Hand *Blue Hand*		
47	Gelber Stern *Yellow Star*	**232**	**Vision – Wie weit wollen wir springen?** | Vision – How far do we want to jump?
48	Roter Mond *Red Moon*		
49	Weisser Hund *White Dog*		
50	Blauer Affe *Blue Monkey*		
51	Gelber Mensch *Yellow Human*	**234**	**Adressverzeichnis und Notizen** | Address directory and Notes
52	Roter Himmelswanderer *Red Skywalker*		
53	Weisser Magier *White Wizard*	**244**	**Impressum**
54	Blauer Adler *Blue Eagle*		
55	Gelber Krieger *Yellow Warrior*		

EDITORIAL

....

Alles ist eins – Einer für alle

Das inzwischen recht bekannte und legendäre **«The Global Consciousness Project»** der Princeton University in den USA hat bereits mehrfach bestätigt, was die Quantenphysik seit dem Verleih des Nobelpreises im Jahre 1919 weiss: Dass erstens alles mit allem verbunden ist und daher alles auf alles einen Einfluss hat, ob wir das bewusst erfahren oder erkennen oder auch nicht!

Und ja, eine weitere Erkenntnis, die für fundamentalistische Wissenschaftler der alten, newtonschen Schule so etwas wie ein geistig*intellektuelles K.O. darstellt, ist die Tatsache, dass die ZEIT alles andere als linear verläuft. Im Gegenteil, die drei wichtigsten Eigenschaften der «natürlichen Zeit» (im Gegensatz zur «mechanischen, linearen Uhrzeit») sind:

1. Zeit ist zyklisch
2. Zeit ist radial
3. Zeit ist fraktal

Während wir die erste Eigenschaft ohne weiteres nachvollziehen können und seit unserer Geburt in uns eingeprägt ist (Tag/Nacht, Jahreszeiten, Wochen-Jahres-Rhythmen, Herzrhythmus, Atemrhythmus, Gehirnrhythmen, etc.), sind die beiden weiteren Eigenschaften bereits ein bisschen herausfordernder.

Die zweite Eigenschaft bedeutet, dass jedes Ereignis in unserer sogenannten physischen (3D) Realität Wirkungen in alle (Zeit-) Richtungen auslöst, wie ein Stein, der ins Wasser fällt und damit konzentrische Wellen auslöst. Auf die Zeit bezogen bedeutet das, dass zukünftige Zeit*Potentiale (noch nicht realisiert, aber potenziell sehr wahrscheinlich) ihre Ereigniswellen auch in die Gegenwart hinaussenden. Das ist für einen linearen Geist kaum nachvollziehbar, aber es erklärt so ziemlich alle «spooky» Phänomene, die von der newton'schen Wissenschaft schlichtweg nicht erklärbar sind. Darüber gibts in meinem Buch («Einführung ins Zuvuyasurfen») eine «kleine Geschichte der Zeit» über den russischen Forscher Nikolay Kozyrev und seine Entdeckung, was Zeit wirklich ist!

Aber jedes Kind versteht, wenn ich ihm erkläre, dass die kommende Weihnachten (Geburtstag, Ostern etc.) bereits eine vorzeitige Wirkung auf die Gegenwart haben, denn erstens wächst die Vorfreude auf das kommende Geburtsfest von Jesus Christus, und zweitens beginnt fast jedes Kind bereits WoOooOoOOochen im Voraus den Eltern seine (meist mehrere Posten umfassende) Wunschliste zu übergeben, natürlich mit Unschuldsaugen, wie es nur Kinder hinkriegen :-)

Auch wir Erwachsenen müssen doch alle eindeutig zugeben, dass für die meisten von uns ein bevorstehendes Geschäftsevent, Geburtstag, Ferien oder vielleicht sogar ein sich näherndes «Sabbaticaljahr» seine Wellen in die Gegenwart wirft und wir uns bereits irgendwie darauf vorbereiten!

Als ich 20 Jahre alt war und gerade mein Abitur gemacht hatte, wachte ich damals auf und hatte einen Traum, in welchem ich hohe Geschäftshäuser und Wolkenkratzer wie Dominosteine einstürzen sah. Es war klar, dass es sich um Banken und alle möglichen Finanzinstitute handelte. Als ich davon erzählte, hiess es lediglich: Alles kann zusammenbrechen, aber ganz sicher nicht das Bankensystem!

Nun, fast 20 Jahre später war es dann tatsächlich soweit mit der Lehmann-Brothers Bank, die ein regelrechtes Zusammenkrachen wie Dominosteine auslöste.

Der damalige Traum unterschied sich von den anderen, indem er viel intensiver und gefühlsmässig sehr kraftvoll war. Ich habe es damals sogar physisch wahrgenommen, aber eben, das Problem hatte schon Nostradamus: Bei Visionen hängt meistens kein «Event Datum» dran ...

Und daran litt ich einen Grossteil in meinem Leben, dass mir Bilder der Zukunft geschenkt wurden, die jeweils so stark waren, dass ich da

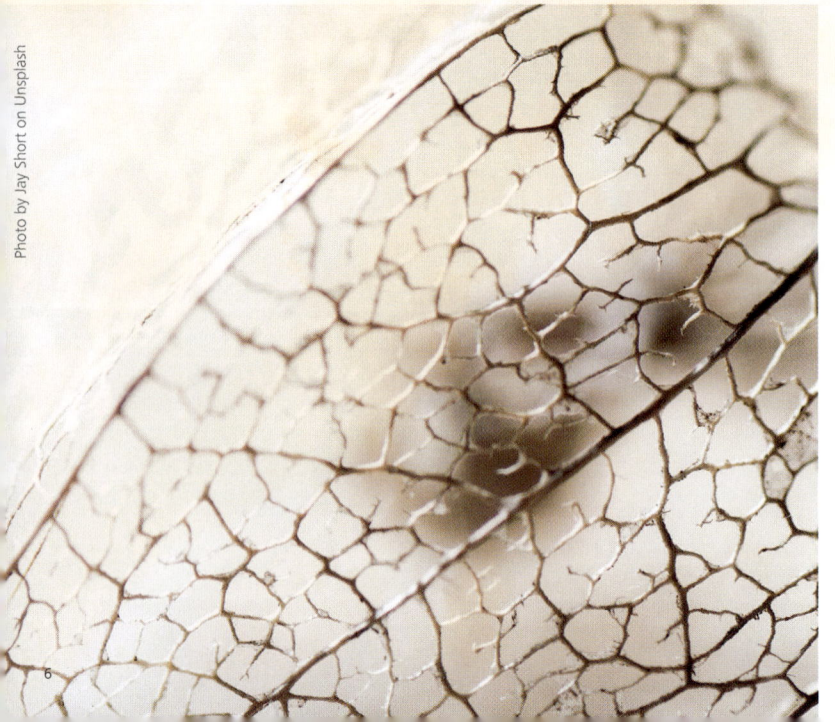

Photo by Jay Short on Unsplash

Gefühl hatte, dass sie demnächst eintreffen werden, was jedoch meistens erst Jahre später der Fall war. Daher glaubte mir damals auch keiner :-)

Inzwischen nehme ich das alles viel gelassener und bin einfach dankbar, wenn ich als visuell veranlagter Mensch ab und zu solche Bilder sehen darf.

Als ich jedoch Ende Herbst 2019 in einer längeren Meditation (über das kommende Jahr 2020) auf einmal das Gefühl hatte, dass ein Tsunami über mich hineinbrechen werde, war ich gelinde ausgedrückt, etwas «verunsichert», weil ich damals noch keine Ahnung hatte, um was es geht und ob dieses Tsunami alleine mir galt!

Jetzt, 9. Juni 2020, nachdem die Weltbevölkerung einen «Fuckdown» (man verzeihe mir meine Wortschöpfung!) hinter sich hat, der wohl einmalig in der Geschichte der jüngeren Menschheit ist, ist mir klar, was ich da im Voraus gespürt habe.

Als ich dann noch die Voraussichten meiner persönlichen Schweizer-Astroqueen Silke Schäfer » www.silke-schaefer.ch las, war mir definitiv klar, da rauscht etwas ganz Intensives auf uns zu. Sie zeigte Ende 2019 auf, dass wir im 2020 eine regelrechte Serie von ganz speziellen Konstellationen haben werden. Eine davon fand zum letzten mal statt, als das Römische Reich gefallen ist (Jupiter/Pluto), und eine grosse Konjunktion von Saturn und Jupiter findet Ende 2020, exakt am 21. Dezember 2020 (Wintersonnenwende) statt.

Warum ich das hier alles schreibe? Weil mir gerade die Corona*Krise einmal mehr gezeigt hat, dass «Ereignisse mit hoher Wahrscheinlichkeit und einer gewaltigen Energieverdichtung» im Quantenfeld bereits Tage, Wochen oder sogar Monate im Voraus wahrnehmbar sind, bevor sie sich auf unserer kollektiven Zeitlinie manifestieren!

Damit möchte ich die Brücke schlagen zu der vierten Ausgabe unseres magischen Zeit*Kompasses, unserer **«Zuvuya Maya Agenda 2021»**, welche uns nicht nur dabei unterstützen soll, unser persönliches Geburtspotential (basierend auf dem heiligen Kalender der Mayas «Tzol'Kin») zu erkennen und in die Welt zu bringen, sondern auch kollektive Zeitpotentiale wahrzunehmen, damit wir uns bereits im Voraus damit synchronisieren können. Dann werden wir von solchen Zeitwellen nicht überrollt, sondern wir surfen im wahrsten Sinne des Wortes auf oder mit ihnen!

DAS ist die hohe Kunst jeder Zuvuya*SurferIn: selbst die höchsten Zeitwellen zu surfen und keinen Schiffbruch zu erleiden.

Das und noch viel mehr wünsche ich mir von meinem Kind, meinem Herzprojekt und meiner Lebensaufgabe: Die «Gesetze der Zeit» auf einfache, spielerische, kreative Weise zu vermitteln, auf dass sogar Kinder und Jugendliche mit diesem Wissen mitspielen können.

Jetzt wünscht dir unser ganzes Zuvuya*Team ein spannendes Jahr mit vielen magischen und synchronen Momenten. Und wenn du etwas erlebst, das du gerne teilen möchtest, schreib mir auf:

» urs@zuvuya-agenda.ch

In lak'ech * Dein anderes Du

u.r.s. jOsé
Weisser elektrischer Magier KIN 94

Photo by Silas Baisen on Unsplash

EDITORIAL

....

Everything is one * One for all

The now quite well-known and legendary **«The Global Consciousness Project»** of Princeton University in the USA has already confirmed on several occasions what quantum physics has known since it was awarded the Nobel Prize in 1919: That firstly, everything is connected with everything else and therefore everything has an influence on everything, whether we consciously experience or recognize it or not!

And yes, another insight that represents something like a mental*intellectual knockout for fundamentalist scientists of the old, Newtonian school is the fact that TIME is anything but linear. On the contrary, the three most important properties of «natural time» (as opposed to «mechanical, linear (clock) time») are

1. time is cyclical
2. time is radial
3. time is fractal

While we can easily comprehend the first quality and it is imprinted in us since birth (day/night, seasons, week-year rhythms, heart rhythm, breathing rhythm, brain rhythms, etc.), the two other qualities are already a bit more challenging. The second characteristic means that every event in our so-called physical (3D) reality triggers effects in all (time) directions, like a stone falling into water and causing concentric waves. In terms of time, this means that future time*potentials (not yet realized, but potentially very likely) send their event waves out into the present. This is hardly comprehensible for a linear mind, but it explains pretty much all «spooky» phenomena that are simply not explainable by Newtonian science.

But every child understands when I explain to him that the coming Christmas (birthday, Easter, etc.) already has a premature effect on the present, because first of all the anticipation of the coming birth of Jesus Christ is growing, and secondly almost every child starts already weeks in advance to give his (usually several items encompassing) wish list to his parents, of course with innocent eyes, as only children can do. :-)

Even we adults have to admit that for most of us an upcoming business event, birthday, holidays or maybe even an approaching «sabbatical year» throws its waves into the present and we are already somehow preparing for it!

When I was 20 years old and just graduated from high school, I woke up and had a dream in which I saw tall office buildings and skyscrapers collapse like dominoes. It was clear that they were banks and all kinds of financial institutions. When I spoke about it, all I heard was: Everything can collapse, but certainly not the banking system!

Well, almost 20 years later, the Lehmann-Brothers Bank did indeed collapse like dominoes.

The dream at that time was different from the others in that it was much more intense and emotionally very powerful. I even noticed it physically at that time, but the problem had already Nostradamus: With vision there is usually no "event date" attached to them ...

And from that I suffered a large part of my life, that I was given pictures of the future, which were so strong in each case that I had the feeling that they will arrive soon, but mostly it was the case only years later. Therefore nobody believed me at that time :-)

In the meantime I take it all much more relaxed and I am simply grateful if I, as a visually inclined person, can see such pictures from time to time.

However, when I suddenly had the feeling at the end of autumn 2019 in a longer meditation (about the coming year 2020) that a tsunami was about to hit me, I was, to put mildly, a bit «insecure», because at that time I had no idea what it was

Photo by Jay Short on Unsplash

all about and whether this tsunami was only for me!

Now, June 9th, 2020, after the world population has gone through a «Fuckdown» (forgive my coinage!), which is probably unique in the history of younger mankind, I realize what I felt in advance.

When I read the predictions of my personal Swiss astro-queen Silke Schäfer » www.silkeschaefer.ch, it was definitely clear to me that something very intense was rushing towards us. At the end of 2019 she showed that in 2020 we will have a real series of very special constellations. One of them took place for the last time when the Roman Empire has fallen (Jupiter/Pluto), and a great conjunction of Saturn and Jupiter will take place at the end of 2020, exactly on December 21, 2020 (winter solstice).

Why am I writing all this?

Because just the Corona*Crisis has shown me once again that «events with a high probability and a huge energy compression» in the quantum field can be perceived days, weeks or even months in advance before they manifest themselves on our collective timeline!

With this I would like to build a bridge to the fourth edition of our magical time*compass, our «Zuvuya Maya Agenda 2021», which should not only help us to recognize and bring into the world our personal birth potential (based on the sacred calendar of the Mayas «Tzol'Kin»), but also to perceive collective time potentials, so that we can synchronize ourselves with them in advance. Then we will not be overrun by such time waves, but we will literally surf on or with them!

THIS is the high art of every Zuvuya*Surfer: to surf even the highest time waves and not to suffer a shipwreck.

This and much more is what I want from my child, my heart project and my life's work: to convey the "laws of time" in a simple, playful, creative way, so that even children and teenagers can play along with this knowledge.

Now our whole Zuvuya*Team wishes you an exciting year with many magical and synchronous moments. And if you experience something you would like to share, write me at » urs@zuvuya-agenda.ch

... because sharing is caring ...

In lak'ech * Your other . magical You

u.r.s. jOsé
White Electric Wizard KIN 94

EINLEITUNG

«Next Level» im Spiel mit der Quantenzeit

Egal ob du mit dieser Agenda zum ersten Mal die Wellen der Zeit zu surfen beginnst oder schon ein langjähriger und erfahrener «Zuvuya*SurferIn» bist, mit dieser vierten Ausgabe möchte ich erneut einen Schritt weitergehen und dich (und deine Mitmenschen, falls du sie zum Mitmachen inspirieren kannst) dazu einladen, ab und zu, aber am besten regelmässig und zyklisch, bei Übungen, Experimenten, Taten, Gedanken, etc. mitzumachen.

Das im Editorial erwähnte **«The Global Consciousness Project»** der Princeton University in den USA hat wissenschaftlich empirisch (durch eine überwältigende Anzahl von Daten/Statistiken) bestätigt:

Dass alles mit allem verbunden ist und daher alles auf alles einen Einfluss habt.

» www.noosphere.princeton.edu/index.html

Diese Erkenntnis ist nicht nur uralt (die Grundlage von fast allen indigenen Völkern, die im Einklang mit der Natur, Erde und dem Kosmos lebten), sondern vor allem eins: EXTREM WICHTIG für jeden Menschen!

Denn wenn wir wirklich, wirklich verstehen, dass wir nicht nur alle aus der gleichen **«Quanten-UR-Suppe»** stammen (Bewusstsein, welches sich als Mensch (Materie) materialisiert hat), sondern dass jeder Gedanke, jedes Gefühl, jedes Wort und jede Tat, die wir ausführen eine unmittelbare Wirkung auf das GANZE QUANTENFELD (!) hat, dann wird jeder einsehen müssen, dass die Gesetze der Liebe, die uns Jesus Christus vor rund 2000 Jahren gelehrt hat, tatsächlich stimmen. Diese «Quantengesetze» sind so entscheidend, dass sie unser Grosser Bruder immer und immer wieder erzählt hat, stets in neuen, metaphorischen (Wort-)Bildern. Eines der bekanntesten ist: **«Liebe deinen nächsten wie dich selbst»** (oder umgekehrt)!

Warum ich immer mal wieder Bezug auf **Jesus Christus** nehme, ist weniger, weil ich ein überzeugter Bibelleser bin, sondern weil für mich klar ist, dass er vor 2000 Jahren einen machtvollen **«geistigen, fraktalen Zeitsamen»** ins Bewusstsein (Quantenfeld) eingespiesen hat, der nun langsam aufgeht und seine ersten Früchte trägt.

Mir ist zwar noch kein Meister begegnet, der im wahrsten Sinne des Wortes **«Berge versetzen»** kann, aber das ist wohl auch nicht immer sinnvoll! Denn es gilt, nur weil wir rein theoretisch etwas/alles können, heisst das noch lange nicht, dass auch alles sinnvoll ist. Daher glaube ich, dass die Wunder, die von Jesus überliefert sind, einfach ein Hinweis sind, was alles möglich ist.

Und ja, auch hier gebe ich ganz ehrlich und offen zu, ich glaube wirklich zutiefst daran, dass wir Wasser in Wein umwandeln und auf Wasser wandeln können. Aber wohl erst, wenn wir als allererstes die Tatsache akzeptieren, dass es rein theoretisch wirklich möglich ist!

Und zahlreiche, unglaubliche Experimente im Bereich der Quantenphysik zeigen ganz klar auf, dass wir mit (spezifischen) Schwingungen (singen, tönen, summen, vibrieren, etc.) Unfassbares verwirklichen können (z.B. DNS-Umwandlung von einer Spezies in eine andere durch elektromagnetische Beeinflussung).

Das Problem dabei ist jedoch, dass wir als einzelner Mensch gegen ein starkes Quantenfeld ankämpfen müssen, in welchem das erst ganz wenige Menschen überhaupt in Erwägung ziehen. Dann muss man eben wirklich ein vollendeter **«Jesus Christ Superstar»** (tolles Musical/Film übrigens!) sein, wenn man diesen **«Gegenwind»** im kollektiven Quantenfeld überwinden möchte :-)

Zum Glück gilt jedoch **«das Prinzip des 100. Affen»,** von welchem sicher etliche bereits gehört haben. Auf Wikipedia wird schon seit Jahren vieles, das uns die Quantenphänomene erklären würde, entweder krass

verunglimpft oder sogar als **«Verschwörungstheorie»** denunziert, dazu gehört auch diese Geschichte, die dort als «Mythos» bezeichnet wird. **Wikipedia-Gläubige** werden jedoch von der professionellen Art und Weise, wie dort geschummelt wird, komplett getäuscht, wie ich früher auch, überzeugt von der **«Schwarmintelligenz»** (übrigens auch ein Quantenphänomen). Doch diese wurde zunehmend ausser Gefecht gesetzt. Wer jedoch mehr dazu wissen möchte, gibt auf Youtube einfach **«Wikipedia Lüge»** ein und erhält diverse Dokus über diese üblen Machenschaften.

Hier in Kurzform die Geschichte: Vor Jahrzehnten hat man auf einer japanischen Insel beobachtet, wie auf einmal ein Affe begann, die Kartoffeln im Seewasser zu reinigen, bevor er sie verspeiste. Kurze Zeit darauf taten es alle Affen auf dieser Insel, was bereits erstaunlich war. Doch das eigentliche spektakuläre war, als nochmals kurze Zeit darauf auch die Affen auf dem Festland die gleiche Handlung ausführten. Wie konnte das geschehen, ohne Telefon, Handy und Fax :-)

Die **«Theorie des 100. Affen»** war geboren! Wenn eine gewisse Anzahl Tiere oder Menschen die gleiche Handlung (oder auch Gefühle, Gedanken, Worte!) ausführt, ist diese Idee (Programm/Muster/etc.) im Quantenfeld genügend stark verankert, dass sie auf einfache Weise auch von anderen Menschen/Tieren (meistens intuitiv) aufgegriffen werden.

Der berühmt-berüchtigte englische Biologe **Rubert Sheldrake**, entwickelte in den 70er Jahren diese Theorie weiter und nannte sie **«Morphogenetische Felder»**, welche übrigens ebenfalls seit Jahrzehnten empirisch bewiesen sind, auch wenn das immer wieder bestritten wird.

Warum ich dies hier alles so genau beschreibe?

Ganz einfach, weil dieses Wissen uns ermächtigt, bewusst dem Pfad von Jesus zu folgen und ebenfalls Wunder zu bewirken (wir müssen ja nicht sogleich mit «Toten erwecken» beginnen, es reicht für mich, gutes Wasser in edlen Wein zu verwandeln.

Kleiner Werbespot in eigener Sache
» www.aquariurs.ch

Und ja, wir können es drehen oder wenden wie wir wollen, aber es gibt auf dieser Erde (Kosmos) Kräfte, die nicht wollen, dass wir unsere göttlichen und schöpferischen Kräfte bewusst einsetzen, um einen friedlichen, grünen und gerechten Planeten für alle, statt für sehr wenige, zu erschaffen, weil ihnen das sehr ungelegen kommt.

Im Internet tobt im Hintergrund ein Informations- und Zensurkrieg, den leider nur diejenigen mitbekommen, die sich die ZEIT nehmen, um das herauszufinden, aber auch hier gilt: **«wer sucht, der findet»!**

Und es gilt, dass uns nur die Wahrheit wirklich frei macht! Zurzeit wird es jedoch nicht nur immer anspruchsvoller, die Wahrheit von der Lüge (Halbwahrheiten, Fake News, Manipulationen, Zensur, etc.) zu unterscheiden, sondern auch, diese Wahrheit überhaupt erstmal zu finden!

Doch zurück zum eigentlichen Thema. Eine der ersten Ebenen dieses Zuvuya*Projektes ist das Synchronisieren. Damit ist in erster Linie gemeint, dich selbst mit deinem Geburtspotential (basierend auf dem **«Tzol'Kin»**) zu verbinden/synchronisieren und als zweites, dich mit deinen Mitmenschen. Eine weitere Ausdehnung ist dann die Synchronisation mit den kosmischen Zyklen, ab dann wirds dann definitiv sehr spannend :-)

Doch egal ob «Newbie» oder langjährige.r Surfer*In, am besten Schritt für Schritt und in einem Tempo, bei welchem ein Grossteil mit Leichtigkeit mitmachen kann :-)

Daher führen wir in dieser vierten Ausgabe verschiedene, neue Symbole **(Tiere)** ein, welche euch einladen, an einem bestimmten Tag (allenfalls sogar Tageszeit) eine **spezifische Handlung** auszuführen mit dem Ziel, euch nicht nur mit der Tagesenergie (Tages*KIN) zu synchronisieren, sondern gemeinsam ein starkes Feld innerhalb des groOossen Quantenfeldes zu erschaffen, verbunden über die **«Quantenzeit»,** welche nicht linear, sondern zyklisch, radial und fraktal arbeitet und wirkt.

Wenn die **«natürliche ZEIT»** tatsächlich ein universelles, alles miteinander verbindendes PRINZIP ist, dann muss es – per Definition – überall, jederzeit und unter allen Umständen anwendbar sein!

Doch anstatt noch länger hier darüber zu schreiben, biete ich euch ein ganzes Jahr lang zahlreiche Möglichkeiten an, selber zu erleben/erfahren, wovon ich hier schreibe und was mich persönlich seit meinem 11. Lebensjahr begleitet, seit ich mit Tagebuchschreiben begonnen habe (meinem weisen Patenonkel sei Dank!): Das magische Dreieck von ZEIT * SYNCHRONISATION * FLOW! Wer diesen **«Flow»** dank zahlreicher Synchronisationen im Leben einmal erlebt hat, sucht eigentlich nur noch mehr davon! Und das ist auch selbstverständlich, denn laut C.G. Jung, der den Begriff Synchronizität geprägt hat, sind dies alles Zeichen vom Universum, sogenannte harmonische Rückkoppelungen / Reflektionen aus dem Quantenfeld, welche aufzeigen, dass wir unserer ganz individuellen Lebensspur folgen. Dieser Kreislauf der Erinnerung, dieser einzigartige Seelenpfad wird von den Maya **«Zuvuya»** genannt.

Synchronizitäten tauchen auf, wenn wir unsere **Zuvuya kreuzen** und häufen sich, wenn wir mehr und mehr synchron mit ihr unser Leben navigieren. Dafür haben wir diesen magischen **Zeit°Kompass** geschaffen.

Doch jetzt möchten wir weitergehen und herausfinden, WAS wir alles GEMEINSAM ERSCHAFFEN können, wenn wir uns zeit.gleich mit gleicher Absicht/Ausrichtung (Gedanke, Gefühle, Worte, Taten) synchronisieren. Einen Anfang machte vor Jahrzehnten (1993) das berühmte Mediations-Experiment, während dessen Verlauf die Verbrechensrate in New York signifikant (= wissenschaftlich mess- und nachweisbar) gefallen ist. In den Jahren 2007–2010 wurde eine neue Studie im Auftrag der **Mahrishi University** durchgeführt. Während diesen vier Jahren sanken zum Beispiel die jährliche Tötungsrate (Homizidrate) auf nationaler Ebene, während auch die städtische Gewaltkriminalität um über 21 % sanken (5.3 % pro Jahr). Ja, mehr noch, die Tötungsrate (Tötungsdelikte) war vor dem **«Maharishi Experiment»** sogar am Steigen. Forscher schätzen, dass rund 8'157 Tötungsdelikte verhindern werden konnten! Der Clou war jedoch, dass diese Zahlen VOR DEM EXPERIMENT bereits prognostiziert wurden und dann tatsächlich so eintrafen. Wer sucht, der findet im Netz Informationen, hier eine von vielen Quellen: » www.bit.ly/2Ye9CeG

Eine wichtige Formel, die aufgrund von Langzeitforschungen in diesem Bereich der Quantenphysik gemacht wurden, ist:

Die Quadratwurzel von 1% der Bevölkerung reicht aus, um signifikante Veränderungen zum Wohle ALLER zu erreichen!

Diese Tatsache wurde inzwischen in zahlreichen **«peer-reviewed»** (von Fachleuten nachgeprüfte und wiederholte Experimente mit gleichem Ergebnis) bestätigt worden. Aber nochmals, statt noch mehr Daten und Beweise anzuhäufen, gilt im neuen **«Goldenen Zeitalter»** (des universellen Friedens und des Quantenbewusstseins): **«Probieren geht über Studieren»**, wie mein geliebter Papa (Baufachlehrer im verdienten Ruhestand) stets zu sagen pflegte.

Daher, mitmachen und selbst erfahren, was wir als Einzelne und dann als **Kollektiv** erschaffen können. Lass uns das Jahr 2021 zum «besten Jahr so far» machen, lass uns gemeinsam die Zukunft kreieren, die wir uns alle so sehnlichst wünschen und die vor langer Zeit bereits angekündigt worden ist, wenn wir die Zeitschwelle 21.12.2012 passieren, ohne uns vorher in die Luft zu jagen.

Das haben wir bereits geschafft, halleluja! Aber jetzt sind alle gefordert zum Mitmachen! Denn zu wissen, dass wir am Beginn eines neuen, goldenen Zeitalters (von den Maya «Quinto Sol» genannt) stehen, heisst nicht, dass alles wie von allein geht! Im Gegenteil, wir sind diejenigen, auf die wir gewartet haben! Ob ZuvuyasurferIn, LichtkriegerIn, Heilerin, NeO*Schamane, Wundertäter und TransfOrMator, die **Zeit der EinzelkämpferInnen ist vorbei,** vernetztes und synchronisiertes Handeln im Quantenfeld zeigt JETZT die grösste Wirkung. Und je höher (wahrhaftiger, liebevoller, friedlicher, etc.) schwingender unsere Ideen, Absichten, Gedanken, Worte, Taten, desto rascher werden wir das Gewünschte kreieren, weil es völlig synchron mit den harmonischen Zeitwellen vibriert, die seit Jahren zunehmend von der Sonne her auf unseren Planeten (und das ganze Sonnensystem) einströmen/einwirken.

Mit dem **«Tzol'Kin»** hast du einen holografischen Kompass und Massstab für die kleinen, mittleren und gigantischen Zyklen der Zeit, in welche wir als **«Zeit*Wesen»** verwoben sind. Wer diese kennt (Gesetze der Zeit), navigiert nicht nur durch anspruchsvolle Gewässer, sondern manifestiert sogar während **globalen Stürmen** (2020: Corona*Wahn) Harmonie, Frieden, Licht, Liebe und Harmonie in sich und um sich herum für seine Mitmenschen. Dies ist bereits ein machtvoller und wichtiger **Akt der Schöpfung.**

Ja, unser Projekt lebt mehr und mehr davon, dass wir uns nicht nur einseitig miteinander verbinden (von uns zu euch über die Agenda/Website/Videos/etc.), sondern vor allem über einen kreativen Dialog. Daher gibt es inzwischen die **«Zuvuya Online Gatherings»,** wo wir uns im «virtuellen» Quantenraum persönlich begegnen können. Ob Austausch vor Erfahrungen und Wissen, dem Teiler von magisch.synchronen Erlebnissen, für eine gemeinsame Meditation oder gegenseitiges inspirieren ...

Falls du interessiert bist, schreib mir einfach auf:
» urs@zuvuya-agenda.ch
Denn **«sharing is caring»** ...

Ps.: Zahlreiche Forscher haben inzwischen diese Meditationsexperimente auf verschiedene Länder und Kulturen ausgeweitet, unterstützt vor privaten Institutionen.

Wir arbeiten mit Susanne Trine und ihrem Quantenprojekt 12–21 zusammen.

INTRODUCTION

....

«Next Level» in the game of quantum time

No matter if you start surfing the waves of time for the first time with this agenda or if you are already a longtime and experienced «Zuvuya*Surfer», with this fourth issue I would like to go one step further and invite you (and your fellow surfers, if you can inspire them to join in) to join in from time to time, but preferably regularly and cyclically, in exercises, experiments, actions, thoughts, etc.

The **«Global Cinsciousness Project»** of Princeton University in the USA, mentioned in the editorial, has scientifically confirmed empirically through an overwhelming amount of data/statistics) that everything is connected to everything and therefore everything affects everything.

» www.noosphere.princeton.edu/ndex.html

This realization is not only ancient the basis of almost all indigenous peoples who lived in harmony with nature, earth and the cosmos), but above all one thing: EXTREMELY IMPORTANT for every human being!

Because if we really, really understand that we not only all come from the same **«quantum-UR-soup»** consciousness that has materialized as a human being (matter)), but that every thought, every feeling, every word and every deed we perform has an immediate effect on the WHOLE QUANTUM FIELD, then everyone will have to realize that the laws of love that **Jesus Christ** taught us about 2000 years ago are indeed true. These **«quantum laws»** are so crucial that our Big Brother told them over and over again, always in new, metaphorical (word) images. One of the best known is: **«Love your neighbour as yourself»** (or vice versa)!

Why I refer to Jesus Christ from time to time is not so much because I am a convinced Bible reader, but because it is clear to me that 2000 years ago he injected a powerful **«spiritual, fractal time seed»** into consciousness (quantum field), which is now slowly rising and bearing its first fruits.

Although I have not yet met a master who can **«move mountains»** in the truest sense of the word, this is probably not always useful! Because just because we can do something/all in theory, it doesn't mean that everything makes sense. Therefore I believe that the miracles handed down by Jesus are simply a hint of what is possible.

And yes, also here I honestly and openly admit that I really deeply believe that we can change water into wine and walk on water. But probably only if we first of all accept the fact that it is purely theoretically really possible!

And numerous, incredible experiments in the field of quantum physics clearly show that we can use (specific) oscillations (singing, sounding, humming, vibrating, etc.) to realize unbelievable things (e.g. DNA conversion from one species to another by electromagnetic influence).

The problem here, however, is that we as individual humans have to fight against a strong quantum field in which only very few people even consider. Then you really have to be an accomplished **«Jesus Christ-Superstar»** (great musical/film by the way!) if you want to overcome this **«headwind»** in the collective quantum field :-)

Fortunately, however, **«the principle of the 100th monkey»** is valid, of which surely quite a few have already heard. On Wikipedia many things that would explain quantum phenomena to us have been either blatantly denigrated or even denounced as **«conspiracy theory»** for years, including this story, which is called a myth there. Wikipedia believers, however, are completely deceived by the professional way of cheating there, just like me, convinced of the **«swarm intelligence»** (by the way, also a quantum phenomenon). But this was increasingly put out of action. But if you want to know more about it, just enter **«Wikipedia lie»** on Youtube and you will receive various documentaries about these evil machinations.

Here is the story in short form: Decades ago, on a Japanese island, a monkey suddenly started to clean the potatoes in sea water before eating them. A short time later all monkeys on this island did it, which was already astonishing. But the really spectacular thing was when a short time later the monkeys on the mainland did the same thing again. How could this happen without telephone, mobile phone and fax :-)

The **«theory of the 100th monkey»** was born! If a certain number of animals or humans perform the same action (or also feelings, thoughts, words!), this idea (program/pattern/etc.) is anchored sufficiently strongly in the quantum field that it can easily be picked up by other humans/animals (mostly intuitively).

In the 1970s, the notorious English biologist Rubert Sheldrake developed this theory further and called it **«Morphogenetic Fields»**, which, by the way, have also been empirically proven for decades, even if this is repeatedly denied.

Why am I describing all this so precisely?

Quite simply because this knowledge empowers us to consciously follow the path of Jesus and also to perform miracles (we don't have to start with «raising the dead» right away, it is enough for me to turn good water into noble wine.

And yes, we can turn it or turn it any way we want, but there are forces on this earth (cosmos) that do not want us to consciously use our divine and creative powers to create a peaceful, green and just planet for everyone, instead of for very few, because it is «very inconvenient» for them.

On the Internet, a war of information and censorship is raging in the background, which unfortunately only those who take the TIME to find out about it are aware of, but here too the motto is: **«he/she who searches finds»!**

And it applies that only the truth really sets us free! At present, however, it is not only becoming more and more demanding to distinguish the truth from the lie (half-truths, fake news, manipulations, censorship, etc.), but also to find this truth in the first place!

But back to the actual topic. One of the first levels of this Zuvuya*project is **synchronisation.** This means first of all to connect/synchronize yourself with your birth potential (based on the **«Tzol'Kin»**) and secondly, to connect/synchronize yourself with your fellow human beings. A further extension is then the synchronization with the cosmic cycles, from then on it will definitely be very exciting :-)

But no matter if you're a «newbie» or a long-time-surfer, it's best to do it step by step and at a speed that most people can easily join :-)

Therefore, in this fourth issue we introduce various new symbols **(animals),** which invite you to perform a specific action on a certain day (or even time of day) with the goal of not only synchronizing with the energy of the day (day*KIN), but also to create a strong field within the huge quantum field, connected via **«quantum time»,** which is not linear, but works and acts cyclically, radially and fractally.

If the **«natural TIME»** is indeed a universal PRINCIPLE connecting everything, then it must – by definition – be applicable everywhere, anytime and under any circumstances!

But instead of writing about it here for even longer, I offer you a whole year long numerous possibilities to experience/experience for yourself what I am writing about here and what has personally accompanied me since I was 11 years old, since I started writing a diary (thanks to my wise godfather!): The magic triangle of TIME*SYNCHRONISATION*FLOW! Whoever has once experienced this **«flow»** thanks to numerous synchronizations in life, is actually only looking for more of it! And this is a matter of course, because according to C.G. Jung, who coined the term **«synchronicity»,** these are all signs from the universe, so called **«harmonic feedback/reflections from the quantum field»,** which show that we follow our very individual path of life. This cycle of memory, this unique soul path is called **«Zuvuya»** by the Maya.

Synchronicities appear when we cross our Zuvuya and accumulate as we navigate our lives more and more synchronously with it. For this we have created this magical time compass.

But now we want to go further and find out WHAT we can CREATE COMMONLY when we synchronize ourselves with the same intention/alignment (thoughts, feelings, words, actions). Decades ago (1993) the famous mediation experiment made a start, during the course of which the crime rate in New York fell significantly (= scientifically measurable and verifiable). In the years 2007–2010 a new study was conducted on behalf of Mahrishi University. During these four years, for example, the annual homicide rate («homicide rate») at the national level fell, while urban violent crime also fell by over 21% (5.3% per year). Yes, even more so, the homicide rate was actually on the rise before the **«Maharishi Experiment».** Researchers estimate that about 8'157 homicides could be prevented! The trick was, however, that these numbers had already been predicted BEFORE the experiment and then actually happened. If you are looking for information, you will find it on the net, here is one of many sources:
» www.bit.ly/2Ye9CeG

An important formula that has been made on the basis of long-term research in this field of quantum physics is:

The square root of 1% of the population is sufficient, to achieve significant changes for the benefit of EVERYONE!

This fact has now been confirmed in numerous **«peer-reviewed»** (peer-reviewed and repeated experiments with the same result) experiments. But once again, instead of accumulating more data and evidence, in the new «Golden Age» (of universal peace and quantum consciousness): **«The proof of the pudding is in the eating»,** as my beloved dad (a well-deserved retired teacher of construction) used to say.

Therefore, participate and experience for yourself what we can create as individuals and then as a collective. Let's make 2021 the «best year so far», let's create together the future we all wish for so eagerly and which was announced a long time ago when we cross the time threshold 12/21/2012 without blowing ourselves up first.

We have already achieved that, hallelujah! But now everyone is called upon to participate! Because to know that we are at the beginning of a new, golden age (called «Quinto Sol» by the Maya) does not mean that everything will go by itself! On the contrary, we are the ones we have been waiting for! Whether Zuvuyasurfer, Light Warrior, Healer, NeO*Shaman, Wonderworker and TransfOrMator, **the time of lone warriors is over,** networked and synchronized action in the quantum field shows the greatest effect NOW. And the higher (truer, more loving, more peaceful, etc.) our ideas, intentions, thoughts, words, deeds vibrate, the faster we will create what we want, because it vibrates completely synchronized with the harmonic time waves, which have been increasingly influencing our planet (and the whole solar system) from the sun for years.

With the **«Tzol'Kin»** you have a holographic compass and scale for the small, medium and gigantic cycles of time in which we as **«time*being»** are interwoven. Those who know these (laws of time) not only navigate through challenging waters, but even during global storms (2020: Corona*Madness) manifest harmony, peace, light, love and harmony within and around themselves for their fellow human beings. This is already a powerful and important **act of creation.**

Yes, our project lives more and more from the fact that we not only connect with each other one-sidedly (from us to you via the agenda/website/videos/etc.), but above all via a creative dialogue. That's why there are now the **«Zuvuya Online Gatherings»,** where we can meet personally in the «virtual» quantum space. Whether exchange of experiences and knowledge, sharing magical synchronous experiences, for a common meditation or mutual inspiration …

If you are interested, just write me:

» urs@zuvuya-agenda.ch

Because **«sharing is caring»** …

Ps.: Numerous researchers have now extended these meditation experiments to different countries and cultures, supported by private institutions.

This year we have integrated the magical and powerful project of Susanne Triner and the Code 12–21. More Informations on page 80/81.

SYNCHRONISATION

....

Probieren geht über studieren

Eigentlich wollte ich diese Idee erst in 2–3 Jahren einbringen, aber die Corona*Zeit hat mir aufgezeigt, dass es JETZT gilt, unsere Zukunft nicht nur zu erträumen, zu visualisieren, sondern diese im wahrsten Sinne des Wortes ins Netz, ins Feld, in die Matrix einzuweben. Und das geht am besten mit synchronisierten, ausgerichteten gemeinsamen Aktionen. Sei es über eine gemeinsame, kurze **«Heart Brain Coherence®» Meditation,** einer Yoga-Asana (Figur) die wir ausführen, ein paar tiefen Atemzügen oder weiteren Handlungen, die nicht nur uns selbst nützen, sondern uns mit zahlreichen anderen zeitreisenden «Zuvuya*SurfernInnen» verbinden und dazu führen, dass wir bewusst ein Feld innerhalb des grossen Quantenfeldes kreieren.

Das ist ein höchst kraftvoller Schöpfungsakt und ich bin mir sicher, dass wir dies nicht nur spüren werden, sondern dass wir alle gemeinsam auch davon profitieren können.

Wir sind diejenigen, auf die wir gewartet habe! Diese ZEIT ist JETZT!

Symbole zum Einsteigen und mitmachen

Mein tolles Zuvuya Design Team in Bern hat ein paar Tiere erschaffen, welche als Auslöser, als Triggersymbole über die ganze Agenda verstreut dich einladen, während einigen Minuten täglich oder wöchentlich mitzumachen, unsere kollektive Zukunft in eine friedliche, wohlwollende Richtung zu lenken.

Bist du bereit? Dann ready, steady, floOow ***

**Symbol 1:
Fuchs
meditierend**

Der Fuchs ist die Einladung an dich, dir heute mal Zeit zu nehmen für eine 5–10-minütige **Meditation**, wir empfehlen natürlich die «Heart-Brain Coherence®» Meditation.

Und falls du eine magische Zeit wählen möchtest, hier einige Vorschläge:

10.23h | 10.23h | 11.11h | 12.03h | 12.30h | 13.02h | 13.20h (mein Favorit) | 20.13h | 20.31h | 21.03h | 21.30h | 23.01h | 23.10h | 01.23h | 01.32h ... du kannst natürlich auch selber eine «magische Zeit» wählen, die für dich stimmig ist und allenfalls ein paar Freunde inspirieren, dich mit «deiner» Zeit zu synchronisieren.

**Symbol 2:
Flamingo
Yogameister**

Der Flamingo, welcher grad in der «Baum Asana» (Vrksasana) steht, ist die Einladung, tagsüber 1–3 **Yoga Asanas** (zum Beispiel deine drei Lieblingsasanas) zu praktizieren oder auch etwas anderes körperliches auszuführen, z.B. Qi Gong, Tai Chi, allenfalls auch eine Atemübung. Vielleicht packt dich auch die Lust auf einen Spaziergang in die Natur oder sogar ein bisschen Joggen. Der Storch möchte dich einfach daran erinnern, dass unser Körper unser Raumanzug, unser Fahrzeug und unser Tempel ist, mit dem wir achtsam umgehen und pflegen sollten.

Symbol 3: Tapir Künstler

Das malende Tapir ist unsere Einladung, die berühmte Zeitformel {Zeit = Kunst} von Dr. José Argüelles immer mal wieder anzuwenden und deinem **inneren Künstler** Raum zu geben. Kunst zu machen bedeutet nicht, wie Leonardo da Vinci anatomisch korrekte Zeichnungen anzufertigen, sondern einfach Stift und Papier vor dich hinzulegen und ein paar Linien, Kreise, Symbole und Worte draufzuschreiben. Vielleicht kennst du das Mind Mapping oder die noch junge, russische Weiterentwicklung (inklusive Quantenfaktor!), die sogenannte «Neurografik®» von Pavel Piskarev, Ph. D. oder du entwickelst eine kreative Freundschaft zu den «Zentangles®», die ebenfalls einen hohen Suchtfaktor entwickeln können :-)

Nimm dir an diesem Tag ca. 10–20 Min. Zeit für deinen kreativen Ausdruck. Als ehemaliger Gestaltungslehrer kann ich dir garantieren, dass wir alle einen äusserst kreativen Kern besitzen, der sich jedoch nur zeigen kann, wenn wir ihm auch einen gewissen «Zeit°Raum» geben in unserem Leben.

Und ja, «Sharing is caring»! Tolle Zeichnungen, Neurografiken, Mindmaps oder Kunstwerke à la da Vinci, alles ist herzlich willkommen und wird nach Möglichkeit auf unserer Projektwebsite publiziert.

**Symbol 4:
Springender
Fisch**

Der springende Fisch ist unser Symbol für «Auszeit» oder «Ferienzeit» oder «Me*time», eine Zeitphase nach beliebiger Länge, in welcher du einfach genau DAS machst, worauf du JETZT Lust hast. Denn wir sind uns so gewohnt in diesem Hamsterrad für andere Menschen zu arbeiten, dass wir uns oftmals nicht nur straflässig vernachlässigen, sOndern gar nicht mehr spüren, WAS genau wir jetzt benötigen.

«... fish are jumping, and the cotton is high ...» ist eine berühmte Zeile aus dem Lied **«Summertime»**, welches wiederum aus dem ersten Musical «Porgy and Bess» stammt. Obwohl es eine traurige Geschichte ist, das erwähnte Schlaflied hat etwas Herzberührendes und auch Mutmachendes, dass mich dieses Lied auch heute noch in eine «erhöhte Frequenz» versetzt und mich daran erinnert, meine Flügel auszustrecken und loszufliegen.

Falls du eine Inspiration benötigst, bei jedem Text zu den 20 Symbolen/Zeichen der Zeit haben wir ein paar Ideen unter «Guter Tag für ...» aufgeführt. Mit diesen kannst du nicht falsch liegen und du kannst sie gerne weiterentwickeln und uns deine Ideen zurücksenden, damit wir den Text für zukünftige Surfeinsteiger erweitern können.

**Symbol 5:
Singender Vogel**

Wie du mit Sicherheit schon bemerkt hast, geht es in diesem Projekt sehr stark um Schwingungen, Frequenzen, Rhythmen und Zyklen und das möglichst harmonisch und kreativ.

Eine weitere Möglichkeit, das Quantenfeld wirklich sehr, sehr stark zu harmonisieren, ist über den **Klang und unsere Stimme.**

Es gibt immer noch ganz viele Menschen, die glauben, dass sie erstens nicht singen können und weiter, dass sie es auch nicht lernen können. Nichts ist falscher als dieser Irrglaube! Wir alle sind ein vibrierendes, schwingendes, klingendes Quantenwesen höchster Güte. Hinter den Kulissen sind bereits Quantenmessgeräte entwickelt worden, mit welchem nicht nur unser elektromagnetisches Feld gemessen werden kann, sondern auch die Lichtquanten, die wir abstrahlen.

Leider sind viele der Menschen, die diese Geräte entwickelt haben, gar nicht so interessiert, diese publik zu machen, weil dann alle sehen könnten, dass sie zu den Menschen gehören, die nicht wollen, dass wir uns auf eine höhere, friedlichere und liebevollere Schwingung eintunen.

Trotzdem fühlen mehr und mehr Menschen, wer einem selbst guttut. Auch wenn viele Menschen noch nicht den Mut haben, zum Beispiel einem langjährigen Freund, der seit Wochen auf der DeproOowelle (z.B. wegen Coronapanik) surft, glasklar mitzuteilen, dass wir an dieser Energie nicht mehr interessiert sind, spüren jedoch immer mehr Menschen, dass genau dies der nächste Schritt in ihrer persönlichen, spirituellen Entwicklung ist.

Hilfreich sind Tage, welche uns in dieser Absicht unterstützen. Mit dem Weissen Wind haben wir die Zeitqualität der Kommunikation, des Geistigen. An einem Blauen Affen Tag sind wir sicher gut in der Lage, die Botschaft so kreativ zu verpacken, dass uns das Gegenüber danken wird, dass wir so ehrlich mit ihm sind.

Doch zurück zum singenden Vogel. Ich freue mich auf den Moment, wo meine individuelle Stimme wieder völlig frei und authentisch Lieder anstimmen wird.

Aber auch ich bin traumatisiert worden in der Schule, damals, als ich den Stimmbruch hatte und mich die Gesanglehrerin vor allen blossstellte, was sie mit allen pubertierenden Jungs machte. Auch spätere Bemerkungen sorgten dafür, dass in meiner Adoleszenz die Singstimme in ihrer Entwicklung und Transformation gehemmt und gestört wurde.

Ich wende daher seit Jahren die «Politik der kleinen Schritte» an. Zuerst war es einfach nur Summen. Später kam dann das Tönen dazu (z.B. Aum), ein Freund, der mir sehr nahesteht, brachte den magischen Obertongesang in mein Leben, das ich sporadisch am üben bin. Und jetzt schleichen sich die Mantras über zahlreiche Freunde in mein Leben. Obwohl ich sie seit Jaaaaahren geniesse (Mein Favorit: Gayatry Mantra von Deva Premal), kommt jetzt der nächste Schritt: Mitzusingen – nicht schüchtern, sondern selbstbewusst.

Was auch immer du an diesem Tag machst, sei dir bewusst, dass du mit deiner Stimme, mit deinem einzigartigen **KLANG*BILD** die Matrix zum Vibrieren bringst. Mach vorher noch eine «Heart Brain Coherence®» Meditation und gehe mit hoher Absicht ans Summen, Tönen, Singen, Lachen, ... und man wird dich auf der Venus spüren!

QUO VADIS ZUVUYA FLOW?

Mit der Agenda 2021 gelangen wir vom vierten Jahr ins fünfte, die «Oberton» Frequenz im 13'er Zyklus. Damit kommt ein grösserer Drive ins Projekt, welches sich an einer dreizehnjährigen Welle (Wavespell) orientiert. Im vierten Jahr sind wir daran, stabile Strukturen (4 = selbstbestehende Frequenz) aufzubauen, damit wir mit der Beschleunigung im fünften Jahr mithalten können.

Unsere magischen Tools, um euch alle zu unterstützen, euren ganz individuellen und von Gott*der Göttin höchstpersönlich abgesegneten Lebenspfad zu gehen, sind zurzeit:

1. Die alljährliche **«Zuvuya Maya Agenda 2020»** (limitierte Auflage)

2. Der alljährliche **«13 Monde Wandkalender»** (limitierte Auflage)

3. Unser Videokanal: **www.vimeo.com/zuvuya** (vBlogs, kostenlose Kurse, etc.)

4. Unsere Projektwebsite: **www.zuvuya-agenda.ch** (Blogs, Ressourcen, etc.)

5. Unser magischer Shop: **www.shop.zuvuya-agenda.ch** (Agenda, Bücher, Cacao, etc.)

6. Unsere **Zuvuyaflow App** » Diese entwickeln wir laufend weiter!

7. Meine **Kurse, Workshops, Cacao-Zeremonien, Online Gatherings, Zuvuya*Readings**, etc.

Unsere Vision ist es, **eine Million Menschen** zu inspirieren, zu berühren oder in irgendeiner kreativen Art und Weise das Leben zu bereichern. **Jede kreative Unterstützung ist herzlich willkommen.** Denn genau wie das Zuvuya*Projekt wächst, wächst auch die galaktische Crew, die diese Mission vorantreiben.

Ich freue mich auf dich! Entweder im virtuellen Space oder bei einer Gelegenheit an einem Workshop oder einem **magischen Event.**

In lak'ech * dein anderes magisches DU *

SYNCHRONIZATION

The proof of the pudding is in the eating

Actually, I didn't want to introduce this idea until 2–3 years, but the Corona* time showed me that NOW it is not only necessary to dream, to visualize our future, but to literally weave it into the net, into the field, into the matrix. And this is best done with synchronized, aligned joint actions. Be it a short **«Heart Brain Coherence®» meditation,** a yoga asana (figure) that we perform, a few deep breaths or other actions that not only benefit ourselves, but connect us with numerous other time traveling «Zuvuya*surfers» and lead us to consciously create a field within the big quantum field.

This is a very powerful act of creation and I am sure that we will not only feel this, but that all of us can benefit from it.

We are the ones we have been waiting for! This TIME is NOW!

Symbols to enter and Participate

My great Zuvuya design team in Bern created a couple of animals which, as triggers, as trigger symbols scattered all over the agenda, invite you to join in for a few minutes every day or week to steer our collective future in a peaceful, benevolent direction.

Are you ready? Then ready, steady, floOow ***

Symbol 1: Fox meditating

The Fox is an invitation to you to take some time today for a 5–10 minute meditation, we of course recommend the «Heart-Brain Coherence®» meditation.

And if you want to choose a magical time, here are some suggestions:

10.23h | 10.23h | 11.11h | 12.03h | 12.30h | 13.02h | 13.20h (my favorite) | 20.13h | 20.31h | 21.03h | 21.30h | 23.01h | 23.10h | 01.23h | 01.32h ... of course you can also choose a «magic time» that is right for you and maybe inspire a few friends to synchronize with «your» time.

Symbol 2:
Flamingo
yoga master

The flamingo, which is currently in the «Tree Asana» (Vrksasana), is the invitation to practice 1–3 **Yoga Asanas** (for example your three favourite Asanas) during the day or to do something else physical, e.g. Qi Gong, Tai Chi, at best also a breathing exercise. Maybe you also feel like taking a walk in the nature or even a little jogging. The stork simply wants to remind you that our body is our space suit, our vehicle and our temple, which we should handle and care for with care.

Symbol 3:
Tapir Artist

The painting tapir is our invitation to apply the famous time formula {Time = Art} of Dr. José Argüelles from time to time and to **give space to your inner artist.** Making art does not mean making anatomically correct drawings like Leonardo da Vinci, but simply putting pen and paper in front of you and writing a few lines, circles, symbols and words on it. Maybe you know the Mind Mapping or the still young, Russian development (including quantum factor!), the so-called «Neurografik®» by Pavel Piskarev, Ph. D. or you develop a creative friendship with the «Zentangles®», who can also develop a high addiction factor :-)

On this day, take about 10–20 minutes for your creative expression. As a former design teacher I can guarantee you that we all have an extremely creative core, which can only show itself if we give it a certain amount of «time» in our lives.

And yes, «Sharing is caring»! Great drawings, neurographs, mind maps or artwork à la da Vinci, everything is welcome and will be published on our project website if possible.

Symbol 4: Fish are jumpin'

The jumping fish is our symbol for «time-out» or «holiday time» or «Me*time», a time phase of any length, in which you simply do exactly WHAT you want to do NOW. This is often easier said than done. Because we are so used to work for other people in this hamster wheel that we often neglect ourselves not only punishably, but also don't even feel WHAT we need now.

«... fish are jumping, and the cotton is high ...» is a famous line from the song **«Summertime»,** which in turn comes from the first musical «Porgy and Bess». Although it is a sad story, the lullaby mentioned has something heart-touching and also encouraging about it, that this song still puts me in a «high frequency» and reminds me to stretch out my wings and fly away.

In case you need inspiration, for each text about the 20 symbols/ characters of the time, we have listed a few ideas under «Good day for ...».

You can't go wrong with these and feel free to adapt or develop them further and send us your ideas back so we can expand the text for future surfing beginners.

Symbol 5:
Singing bird

As you have certainly noticed, this project is very much about vibrations, frequencies, rhythms and cycles, and as harmoniously and creatively as possible.

Another way to harmonize the quantum field really very, very strongly is through sound and our voice.

There are still many people who believe that they cannot sing and that they cannot learn to sing.

Nothing is more wrong than this mistaken belief! We are all a vibrating, oscillating, sounding quantum being of the highest quality. Behind the scenes, quantum measuring devices have already been developed, with which not only our electromagnetic field can be measured, but also the light quanta that we emit.

Unfortunately, many of the people who have developed these devices are not so interested in making them public, because then everyone could see that they are among those people who do not want us to tune into a higher, more peaceful and loving vibration.

Nevertheless, more and more people feel who does good to themselves. Even if many people do not yet have the courage, for example, to tell a long-time friend who has been surfing the DeproOo wave for weeks (e.g. because of Coronapanik) in a crystal clear way that we are no longer interested in this energy, more and more people feel that this is exactly the next step in their personal, spiritual development.

Helpful are days which support us in this intention. With the White Wind we have the time quality of communication, the spiritual. On a Blue Monkey Day we are certainly well able to wrap the message so creatively that the person opposite will thank us for being so honest with him.

But back to the singing bird. I look forward to the moment when my individual voice will once again sing songs completely freely and authentically.

But I was also traumatized at school, back when I had my voice broken and the singing teacher exposed herself to everyone, which she did with all pubescent boys. Later remarks also ensured that in my adolescence the singing voice was inhibited and disturbed in its development and transformation.

Therefore I have been using the «policy of small steps» for years. At first it was simply humming. Later on I added humming (e.g. Aum), a friend who is very close to me brought the magic overtone singing into my life, which I am sporadically practicing. And now the mantras sneak into my life through numerous friends. Although I have been enjoying them for years (my favourite: Gayatry Mantra by Deva Premal), now the next step is coming: Singing along – not shyly, but confidently :-)

Whatever you do on this day, be aware that with your voice, with your unique SOUND*PICTURE you make the Matrix vibrate. Do a **«Heart Brain Coherence®»** meditation first and go with high intention to hum, sound, sing, laugh, ... and you will be felt on Venus!

QUO VADIS ZUVUYA FLOW?

With the Agenda 2021 we move from the fourth year to the fifth, the «overtone» frequency in the 13th cycle. This brings a greater drive into the project, which is based on a thirteen-year wave (Wavespell).

In the fourth year we are in the process of building stable structures (4 = self-existing frequency) so that we can keep up with the acceleration in the fifth year.

Our magical tools to support you all to follow your very individual and God*Goddess personally blessed path of life are currently:

1. the annual **«Zuvuya Maya Agenda 2020»** (limited edition)

2. the annual **«13 moons wall calendar»** (limited edition)

3. our video channel: **www.vimeo.com/zuvuya** (vBlogs, free courses, etc.)

4. our project website: **www.zuvuya-agenda.ch**

5. our magic shop: **www.shop.zuvuya-agenda.ch** (agenda, books, cocoa, etc.)

6. our **Zuvuyaflow app**
» We are constantly developing it further!

7. **my courses, workshops, cocoa ceremonies, online gatherings, Zuvuya*Readings, etc.**

Our vision is to inspire, touch or in any creative way enrich the lives of one million people ...

Any creative support is welcome. Just as the Zuvuya* project is growing, so is the galactic crew that drives this mission.

I look forward to seeing you! Either in virtual space or at an wokshop or magical event.

In lak'ech* your other. magical you

HEART BRAIN COHERENCE

Quantenverschränkung mit «Heart Brain Coherence»

Als ehemaliger (Gestaltungs-) Lehrer gebe ich mir die grösste Mühe, alle Informationen möglichst einfach nachvollziehbar, spür- und erlebbar und vor allem auch spielerisch und kreativ zu vermitteln.

Das ist zum Teil eine Herausforderung, aber nicht, weil die Informationen und Erkenntnisse aus der **Quantenphysik** so kompliziert sind, ... Im Gegenteil! Sie sind anspruchsvoll, weil unser **Geist/Bewusstsein** über Jahrhunderte (wenn nicht sogar Jahrtausende) so eingeschränkt, manipuliert und zum Teil sogar verkrüppelt wurde, dass dieses faszinierende Wissen uns als komplette **«Science Fiction»** erscheint!

Aber genau diese Erfahrung haben bereits unzählige Generationen vor uns auch durchgemacht. Wer hätte vor einigen hundert Jahren gedacht, dass die Menschheit irgendwann «fliegen» werden kann, geschweige, auf dem Mond landen. Auch das ganze Internet, Social Media, welches jeden mit jedem jederzeit in Echtzeit verbindet! Selbst unsere Grosseltern, die mit Radio und Fernsehen aufgewachsen sind, wurden von dieser technologischen Lawine regelrecht überrollt, weil die Fortschritte so riesig waren innert weniger Jahren.

Aber jetzt stehen wir vor einem wirklich wichtigen, globalen und unvermeidlichen Sprung! Im wahrsten Sinne des Wortes einem **«Quantensprung»**, denn es geht um nichts weniger als die Auseinandersetzung, was denn eigentlich «Bewusstsein» ist, aus dem letztlich alles entstanden ist. Auch wenn es immer noch ein paar unvergängliche, Newton'sche Wissenschaftler-Fundamentalisten gibt, die tatsächlich glauben, dass zuerst die Materie da war und erst dann das Bewusstsein (irgendwie entstanden, kein Mensch weiss woher). Andere glauben sogar, dass es nur ein **«Epiphänomen»** ist, ein Nebenprodukt unseres Denkens!

Das **tragisch*komische** daran ist, dass eines der Quantenprinzipien besagt, dass wir uns mit unserem Denken (Fühlen und Handeln) unsere eigene **«Realität»** (eigentlich «Realitätsblase») erschaffen. Das bedeutet daher: Wer nicht an die Quantenphysik und damit an diese **«Wunder»** glaubt, der erzeugt genau diese Realität, in welchem er auch keine solchen Erfahrungen machen wird!

Wer jedoch offen ist, oder sogar ganz fest davon überzeugt, dass wir tatsächlich unsere Realität in jedem einzelnen Augenblick erschaffen, ja, der übernimmt nicht nur die totale Verantwortung für jeden Gedanken, Gefühl, Wort und Tat, sondern ermächtigt sich damit den Weg zu gehen, der von **«Jesus Christ Superstar»** vor rund 2000 Jahren vorgespurt wurde. Wie hat er doch gesagt? «Dies und noch viel mehr werdet ihr auch tun!»

Und meine Interpretation seiner Aussage, dass er in etwa 2000 Jahren zurückkehren wird, ist, dass er durch uns hindurch kommen wird, jeder von uns hat das Potential, ein Heiler und Lichtbringer zu sein.

Wir sind diejenigen, auf die wir gewartet habe! Diese ZEIT ist JETZT!

Da ganz vieles, vielleicht sogar alles, in und um dieses Projekt herum mit der Quantenphysik zu tun hat, ist es mir ein groOosses Anliegen, in der Agenda (und zukünftig auch vermehrt in meinen Video*BLOGS, Podcasts, etc.) darauf aufmerksam zu machen und eine leicht verständliche Einführung zu geben, die jedoch alles andere als einen Anspruch auf Vollständigkeit hat. Dazu ist dieses Gebiet schlichtweg zu unendlich gross und von ewiger Natur, ein Umstand, den unser beschränkter, linearer und polarer Verstand schlichtweg nicht verstehen kann.

Daher betone ich mehr und mehr, dass es wichtig wird, dass wir alles persönlich erleben und fühlen/erfahren können. Denn was wir mit unseren Sinnen erlebt und gefühlt haben, ja, das kann uns so rasch niemand mehr nehmen ...

Heart Math Institute in Kalifornien

Im Jahr 1991 von Doc Childre gegründet im warmen Kalifornien, wo bereits seit den 70er Jahren eine groOosse Aufbruchsstimmung und Offenheit für Neues herrscht, hat das Heart Math Institute inzwischen tausende von wissenschaftlichen Versuchen durchgeführt. Diese zeigen empirisch und auch messbar (Kardiogramm, EEG, Feldstärke Messgeräte, etc.) auf, wie unsere Gedanken (z.B. Meditation), unsere Gefühle (z.B. Gebete, Freude, Wut, etc.) und unsere Handlungen sich unmittelbar auf unser **elektrOMagnetisches Feld** des Herzens und des Gehirns auswirken.

Die Forscher am Heart Math Institute waren es auch, die herausgefunden haben, dass das elektromagnetische Feld des Herzens ca. 6'000 Mal stärker (!) ist als dasjenige des Gehirns.

Damit ist doch eigentlich alles gesagt: Das Gehirn ist da, um mitzudenken, zu unterstützen, aber die wahre Führung unterliegt dem Herzen. Und sie wissen sicher schon, dass es in unserem Herzen ca. 40'000 Neuronen gibt, die ein eigenständiges und vom Gehirn und autonomen Nervensystem unabhängiges Netzwerk bilden.

Obwohl wir mit unserem Geist im wahrsten Sinne alles Mögliche erdenken können, aber ohne die Kraft des Herzens bleibt es im wahrsten Sinne des Wortes eine **«Kopfgeburt».**

Daher freut es mich riesig, dass Rolling McCraty, Ph. D. am Heart Math Institute mit anderen Koryphäen der Bewusstseinsforschung die berühmte **«Heart Brain Coherence»** Meditation entwickelt haben, die uns in wenigen Minuten in einen völlig kohäränten (synchronen) Zustand versetzen können. In diesem Zustand gibt das Herz den Takt vor, das Gehirn schwingt synchron mit und der Körper blüht zu Höchstleistungen auf!

Egal ob Selbstheilung, erhöhte kognitive Leistungen oder ein grosses Einfühlungsvermögen (Empathie), dieser kohäränte Modus ist eigentlich unser gottgebener **«Normalzustand»,** welcher uns hilft, die notwendigen Bewusstseinssprünge zu machen, die jetzt anstehen.

Daher möchte ich euch hier kurz die **«Herz Gehirn Kohärenz»** Meditation aufzeigen und euch einladen, im Internet, besonders natürlich auf der
» www.heartmath.org
Website zu recherchieren und euch in diesem Bereich weiterzubilden, es lohnt sich!

Heart-Brain-Coherence® Meditation

In einem Online-Panel hat uns Rolling McCraty in nur fünf Minuten in diesen kohärenten Zustand hineingeführt. Wenn ihr mal darin seid, werdet ihr mit Sicherheit den Wunsch verspüren, diesen Zustand möglichst laaaaaange aufrechtzuerhalten. Die hohe Kunst ist natürlich, diese Übung im Alltag mit offenen Augen anwenden zu können.

1. Eine **Hand aufs Herz** legen und Augen schliessen. Durch den leichten Druck und die Wärme, die ihr auf Herzhöhe dank der Hand verspürt, sorgt ihr dafür, dass bereits ein Teil eurer Aufmerksamkeit auf die Herzregion gelenkt wird.

2. Verstärkt diesen Fokus nun, indem ihr eure **Atemfrequenz** mit jedem Ein- und Ausatmen verlangsamt, bis ihr locker ca. 5 Sekunden ein/ausatmet, allenfalls mit einer kleinen Atempause dazwischen. Damit signalisiert ihr euch selbst, dass ihr euch geborgen und sicher fühlt (tiefe Atmung/geschlossene Augen).

3. Jetzt stellt euch zusätzlich vor, wie ihr durch das Herzen ein- und ausatmet. Wie ein Blasebalg atmet ihr nun auch Luft durch euer Herz ein und aus und fühlt dabei die Wärme oder das Kribbeln im Herzbereich auf den ganzen Körper auszudehnen. Es gilt: **If you can't make it – fake it!** Falls ihr also das Gefühl noch nicht überall im Körper wahrnehmt, stellt euch einfach vor, dass es so wäre.

4. Denkt nun an etwas **Positives,** Aufbauendes, an Freude, Dankbarkeit, Wertschätzung euch selbst oder einen Menschen oder Situation oder Ort gegenüber und versucht dies nun zu fühlen. Viele Menschen denken über Gefühle nach, fühlen jedoch nicht wirklich. Das kann also ein Weilchen dauern, bis wir wirklich Gefühle fühlen können. Gebt euch Zeit, auch hier gilt: Fake it until you make it!

5. Jetzt gilt es nur noch, dieses **Gefühl über euren Körper auszudehnen,** wie eine Kugel, deren Mittelpunkt euer Herz ist. Diese Kugel dehnt sich aus, umfasst den Raum, der euch umgibt, dann das Haus, eure Stadt, euren Kanton/Bundesland, das ganze Land, Kontinent, Erdkugel und ja, gerne bis an den «Rand» unseres Sonnensystems.

Fühlt die Verbundenheit mit allem, dem umgebenden Raum, der Natur, der Tierwelt, dem Planeten (Pachamama), dem Weltall, Mond, Planeten, Sonne ... und geniesst dieses Gefühl der Einheit.

Wenn ihr dann irgendwann die Augen wieder öffnet, gilt es, diesen Zustand möglichst lange aufrecht zu erhalten und auch zu lernen, diese Übung im Bus, in einer Sitzung, im Kino, ja, überall und jederzeit mit offenen Augen zu erreichen.

Damit leistet ihr bereits einen riesigen Beitrag für den kommenden universellen Frieden, der sich uns unaufhaltsam nähert. Und ja, jeder der mitmacht sorgt dafür, dass er etwas früher eintreten wird und wir als Weltbevölkerung etwas zu feiern haben, dass es so wohl noch nie auf diesem Raumschiff Erde gegeben hat.

Abschliessend möchte ich noch folgendes erwähnen: Im Buch **«Der Welt-Geist»** von Roger D. Nelson dem Mitbegründer des «Global Consciousness Projekt» und natürlich enger Freund von Rolling McCraty, zeigt er auf, dass sich unser kohärentes Herz-Gehirn-Feld automatisch mit dem elektromagnetischen Feld der Erde synchronisiert. Wenn DAS nicht der Burner ist!

Aber eben, nicht wirklich neu unter der Sonne, es bestätigt nur, was die indigenen Völker und unsere Vorfahren alle bereits wussten: Dass wir nicht nur ein Teil der Natur sind, sondern mit ihr verbunden sind, ja, sogar mit ihr synchron und harmonisch schwingen, wenn wir bewusst wieder in diesen Schwingungszustand der Liebe und des Friedens eintreten.

Das Buch **«Der Welt-Geist»** ist übrigens in unserem Shop erhältlich, leicht und verständlich geschrieben und höchst inspirierend und bewusstseinserweiternd im wahrsten Sinne des Wortes.

» www.shop.zuvuya-agenda.ch/produkt-kategorie/buecher

HEART BRAIN COHERENCE

Quantum entanglement with «Heart Brain Coherence»

As a former (design) teacher, I make every effort to make all information as easy to understand, to feel and experience and above all to communicate in a playful and creative way.

This is partly a challenge, but not because the information and findings from **quantum physics** are so complicated, ... On the contrary! They are demanding because our **mind/consciousness** has been so restricted, manipulated and sometimes even crippled over centuries (if not thousands of years) that this fascinating knowledge appears to us as complete **«science fiction»**!

But this is exactly what countless generations before us have experienced. Who would have thought a few hundred years ago that mankind would one day be able to «fly», let alone land on the moon.

Also the whole internet, social media, which connects everyone with everyone at any time in real time! Even our grandparents, who grew up with radio and television, were literally overwhelmed by this technological avalanche, because the progress was so enormous within a few years.

But now we are facing a really important, global and inevitable leap! A **«quantum leap»** in the truest sense of the word, because it is about nothing less than the debate about what actually is «consciousness» from which everything has ultimately emerged. Even if there are still a few immortal, Newtonian scientist fundamentalists who actually believe that first the matter was here and only then the consciousness (somehow created, nobody knows where from).

Others even believe that it is only an **«epiphenomenon»**, a by-product of our thinking!

The tragic*comical thing is that one of the quantum principles says that we create our own «reality» (actually «reality bubble») with our thinking (feeling and acting). That means therefore: Who does not believe in quantum physics and therefore in these «miracles», creates exactly this reality, in which he will not have such experiences!

But whoever is open, or even firmly convinced that we actually create our reality in every single moment, yes, not only takes total responsibility for every thought, feeling, word and deed, but also empowers himself to follow the path that was foretold by **«Jesus Christ Superstar»** about 2000 years ago. What did he say after all? «You will do this and much more!»

And my interpretation of his statement that he will return in about 2000 years is that he will come through us, each of us has the potential to be a healer and a bringer of light.

We are the ones we have been waiting for! This TIME is NOW!

Since a lot of things, maybe even everything, in and around this project has to do with quantum physics, it is a great concern of mine to draw attention to it in the agenda (and in the future more and more in my video*BLOGS, podcasts, etc.) and to give an easy to understand introduction, which however has anything but a claim to completeness. This area is simply too infinite and of eternal nature, a fact that our limited, linear and polar mind simply cannot understand. Therefore I emphasize more and more that it becomes important that we can personally experience and feel/experience everything. Because what we have experienced and felt with our senses, yes, nobody can take that away from us so quickly ...

Heart Math Institute in California

Founded in 1991 by Doc Childre in warm California, where there has been a great spirit of optimism and openness to new things since the 1970s, the Heart Math Institute has since conducted thousands of scientific experiments. These show empirically and also measurably (cardiogram, EEG, field strength measuring devices, etc.) how our thoughts (e.g. meditation), our feelings (e.g. prayers, joy, anger, etc.) and our actions have a direct effect on our electro-magnetic field of the heart and brain.

It was also the researchers at the Heart Math Institute who found out that the electromagnetic field of the heart is about 6000 times stronger (!) than that of the brain.

This says it all: The brain is there to think, to support, but true leadership is subject to the heart. And you probably already know that there are about 40'000 neurons in our heart, which form a network independent of the brain and autonomous nervous system.

Although we can literally conceive all kinds of things with our mind, but without the power of the heart, it remains literally a **«head birth»**.

Therefore I am very pleased that Rolling McCraty, Ph. D. at the Heart Math Institute, together with other luminaries of consciousness research, have developed the famous **«Heart Brain Coherence»** meditation, which can put us into a completely coherent (synchronous) state in a few minutes. In this state, the heart sets the pace, the brain resonates synchronously with it and the body blossoms into peak performance!

No matter whether it is self-healing, increased cognitive performance or a great empathy, this coherent mode is actually our God-given «normal state», which helps us to make the necessary leaps of consciousness that are now pending.

Therefore I would like to show you here briefly the «Heart Brain Coherence» meditation and invite you to research on the Internet, especially of course on the
» www.heartmath.org
website and to educate yourself in this area, it is worth it!

Heart-Brain-Coherence® Meditation

In an online panel, Rolling McCraty guided us into this coherent state in just five minutes. Once inside, you will certainly feel the desire to maintain this state for as long as possible. The high art, of course, is to be able to use this exercise in everyday life with your eyes open.

1. put a **hand on your heart** and close your eyes. By the light pressure and warmth you feel at heart level thanks to the hand, you ensure that part of your attention is already directed to the heart region.

2. reinforce this focus by slowing down your **breathing** rate with each inhalation and exhalation until you inhale and exhale loosely for about 5 seconds, with a small pause in between if necessary. In this way you signal to yourself that you feel safe and secure (deep breathing/closed eyes).

3. now additionally imagine how you inhale and exhale through your heart. Like a bellows, you now inhale and exhale air through your heart and feel the warmth or tingling in the heart area spreading to the whole body. The motto is: **If you can't make it – fake it!**

So if you don't feel it all over your body yet, just imagine that it is.

4. think now of something **positive,** constructive, joy, gratitude, appreciation for yourself or a person or situation or place and try to feel it now. Many people think about feelings but do not really feel them. So it can take a while before we can really feel feelings. Give yourselves time, also here applies: Fake it until you make it!

5. Now it is only to extend this feeling over your body, like a ball whose center is your heart. This sphere expands, encompasses the space that surrounds you, then the house, your city, your canton/state, the whole country, continent, globe and yes, even to the «edge» of our solar system.

Feel the connection with everything, the surrounding space, nature, the animal world, the planet (Pachamama), the universe, moon, planets, sun ... and enjoy this feeling of unity.

When you open your eyes again at some point, it is important to maintain this state for as long as possible and also to learn to achieve this exercise in the bus, in a session, in the cinema, yes, anywhere and anytime with your eyes open.

In doing so, you are already making a huge contribution to the coming universal peace that is approaching us inexorably. And yes, everyone who participates will make sure that it will happen a little earlier and that we as a world population will have something to celebrate that has probably never been seen before on this spaceship Earth.

In conclusion, I would like to mention the following: In the book «The World Spirit» by Roger D. Nelson, the co-founder of the «Global Consciousness Project» and of course close friend of Rolling McCraty, he shows that our coherent heart-brain field automatically synchronizes with the electromagnetic field of the earth. If THIS is not the burner!

But just, not really new under the sun, it only confirms what the indigenous peoples and our ancestors already knew: That we are not only a part of nature, but are connected to it, even synchronously and harmoniously vibrating with it, when we consciously re-enter this vibrational state of love and peace.

By the way, the book «The World Spirit» is a book i highly recommend to read. It summarizes quite a lot of studies in the field of consciousness and inspires you how to activate your own conscious power.

Ausschnitt aus u.r.s. jOse privatem Tagebuch

DAS GEBURTS-ORAKEL

Basierend auf dem Dreamspell von Dr. José Argüelles

Die Schamanen der Mayas besassen Kenntnis über zahlreiche Kalenderzyklen und Rhythmen. Sie waren die Tageshüter und wussten immer, welche Tagesqualität am Wirken war und wie man sie am besten für das individuelle und kollektive Wachstum nutzen konnte.

Daher könnte man die alten Mayas auch als erste Kultur bezeichnen, die professionelles «Human Ressources» betrieben, da sie bei jeder Geburt die Tagesqualität (das Tages°KIN) als Fundament für das ganze Leben des neugeborenen Kindes betrachteten.

Kam ein Kind an einem Schlangentag (Rote Schlange) zur Welt, war den Tageshütern klar, dass dieses Kind über eine stabile und starke Körperstruktur verfügte und für Arbeiten geeignet war, wo Kraft und Ausdauer nötig waren (z. B. Maisanbau, Städtebau, etc.). Weiter wussten sie auch, dass solche Menschen über die Gabe verfügten, das Körperliche/Irdische zu transzendieren und die unteren Chakras (mit der aufsteigenden Kundalinikraft) mit den oberen zu verbinden. Wenn dies eintraf, hatte man einen Menschen vor sich, der nicht nur über physische, sondern auch psychische Energien verfügte, die zum Wohle aller eingesetzt werden konnten. Daher konnte es gut sein, dass ein Bauarbeiter auf einmal als Schüler eines Schamanen angenommen wurde, der seine Weiterentwicklung förderte und begleitete.

Die Mayas sorgten mit ihrem Wissen über die Zeitqualitäten dafür, dass jeder Mensch im Volk seine Fähigkeiten möglichst optimal einsetzen und zur Blüte bringen konnte. Das sorgte nicht nur für zufriedene und glückliche Menschen, sondern brachte die ganze Mayakultur zum Erblühen.

Auch wenn es immer noch Geschichtsforscher und Anthropologen gibt, die unsere eigene blutrünstige Vergangenheit auf andere Kulturen wie die Mayas projizieren; die Mayas wären mit Sicherheit keine Hochkultur geworden, wenn sie tatsächlich die ganze Zeit nur Kriege geführt und massenhafte Blutopfer durchgeführt hätten.

Das Gegenteil ist der Fall: Wir müssen lediglich einen Blick auf die noch rund 6.1 Millionen Maya werfen, die in Mexico, Guatemala, Honduras, etc. noch fast genau so leben, wie vor hunderten, wenn nicht sogar tausenden von Jahren. Sie pflanzen Reis, Gewürze und Cacao an, stellen beeindruckende Kleider her und folgen immer noch den uralten Kalendersystemen ihrer Vorfahren. Auch ihre Sprache und Schrift haben sie erhalten und geben dieses Wissen stets an ihre Kinder weiter.

Ich bin sicher, wenn die Spanier um 1511 nicht in Vera Cruz (Yocatán) gelandet und mit grosser Waffenkraft und Gewalt die Einheimischen massakriert hätten, hätten die Ureinwohner Mesoamerikas nie zu den Waffen greifen müssen und wir würden wohl heute eine völlig andere Welt antreffen.

Doch zurück zum Tagesorakel. Die alten Mayas kannten also das Tagessiegel des Kindes und die aktuelle Welle, in welche das Tageszeichen eingebettet ist. Dies war für die damaligen Schamanen mehr als genug Information, um die Weichen für die Zukunft stellen zu können. Und noch ein Hinweis: Das Mayasystem ist alles andere als ein Kastensystem, wie wir es von Indien her kennen, wo die untersten Kasten (die Unberührbaren) sogar tiefer als die Tiere stehen und als Form der Unterdrückung angesehen werden kann.

Bei den Mayas ging es um die maximale Entfaltung des individuellen und kollektiven Geistes. Die Mayas wussten, dass alles zusammenhängt, ja, jeder ein Teil des anderen ist. Ihr noch heute gebrauchter Gruss «In lak'ech a la KIN» bedeutet übersetzt:

«Ich bin dein anderes Du!»

Damit ist eigentlich schon alles gesagt, oder nicht?

Dank der Weiterentwicklung des Maya-Wissens (basierend auf ihrer Mathematik, ihren Kalendersystemen, ihrer Kosmologie, etc.) von Dr. José Argüelles, haben wir nicht nur das Geburts°KIN und die Welle als Information zur Verfügung, sondern sehr viel, viel mehr!

Je länger wir uns mit dem Thema «Zeit» auseinandersetzen, desto mehr erkennen wir, dass wir in ein Fass ohne Boden, respektive, in ein Wurmloch gefallen sind, das kein Ende nehmen und uns in neue Welten führen wird.

Aufgrund ein paar simpler Additionen hat Dr. José Argüelles zusätzlich einen Analogen Partner (Unterstützung), einen Antipodalen Partner (Herausforderung) und einen Okkulten Partner (versteckter Schatz) berechnet, und ausserdem noch eine Führungskraft (in der gleichen Farbe wie das Tages°KIN), welche das Geburtszeichen zusätzlich mit Informationen aus den höheren Ebenen (Intuition / höheres Selbst / Akasha) versorgt.

Diese vier Zeichen ermöglichen, herauszufinden, welche Menschen und welche Tage eher unterstützend und welche eher herausfordernd sein können.

Wenn du beginnst, dein Umfeld (Eltern, Geschwister, Freunde, Bekannte, etc.) zu berechnen (ihr Geburts°KIN), wirst du mit groOosser Sicherheit ein paar spannende Überraschungen erleben und weisst zukünftig auch viel besser, mit WEM (Archetyp) du es eigentlich zu tun hast.

Als «Weisser Magier» kommuniziere ich ganz anders als das darauf folgende Zeichen des «Blauen Adlers». Während der Magier aus einem Samenkorn eine ganze Geschichte spinnen kann (Schlüsselfähigkeit) möchte es der Archetyp des blauen Adlers «kurz und knackig», auf den Punkt gebracht oder «reduced to the max».

Wenn man das weiss, kann man viel achtsamer und verbindender miteinander kommunizieren. Der Weisse Magier schweift nicht so weit aus und der Blaue Adler ist allenfals bereit, anstatt ein klares «Ja» oder «Nein» eine kleine Geschichte zu hören. Das schafft Verbindung, Vertrauen, Nähe, Freundschaften und vieles mehr, was man unter dem Begriff «Frieden» oder «Liebe» zusammenfassen könnte.

Auf der nächsten Doppelseite kannst du mit nur drei Zahlen (Geburtsjahr, Geburtsmonat und Datum) dein Geburts°KIN berechnen. Ausserdem findest du auch rasch heraus, in welche Welle du hineingeboren bist, denn das wird zu deinem zentralen Lebensthema, während dein Geburts°KIN so etwas wie deine «Spielfigur» (Avatar) ist, die du für das «Spiel des Lebens» gewählt hast, mit all ihren Licht- und Schattenseiten (siehe detaillierte Beschreibung der 20 Siegel).

Für das ganze Orakel (Führung, Analog, Antipode, Okkult) brauchst du am Anfang ein bisschen Zeit und Geduld. Wenn du das Berechnen mal im Griff hast, brauchst du keine Tabellen mehr dazu. Wenn du jedoch mal grad keine «Zeit» hast, dann empfehlen wir dir die Website www.maya.at wo du unter KIN-INFO ganz einfach das Geburts°KIN berechnen kannst. Und dann gibts noch jede Menge Maya-Apps, mein Favorit (iPhone) ist: **13:20:Sync** (App Store) für nur CHF 2.–. Und ja, wir sind ebenfalls daran, unsere eigene «Zuvuya Surf App» herzustellen (kostenlos). Falls du dich in unserem Newsletter eingetragen hast, wirst du rechtzeitig über alles Neue informiert (wärmstens empfohlen).

Jetzt aber viel Spass beim Ausrechnen/Decodieren deines und vieler anderer Geburtstage …

PS: Wenn du bei deinen Kontakten (macOS) noch das Geburtsdatum eingibst, kann die 13:20:Sync App darauf zurückgreifen und zeigt dir für alle deine Kontakte (mit Geburtsdatum) das Geburtsorakel an. Sehr aufschlussreich :-)

THE BIRTH ORACLE

Based on the Dreamspell by Dr. José Argüelles

The Mayan shamans had knowledge of numerous calendar cycles and rhythms. They were the guardians of the day and always knew what the quality of the day was and how best to use it for individual and collective growth.

Therefore, the ancient Mayas could also be described as the first culture to practice professional «human resources», as they regarded the quality of the day (the day°KIN) at birth as the foundation for the whole life of the newborn child.

When a child was born on a serpent day (red serpent), it was clear to the day minders that this child had a stable and strong body structure and was suitable for work where strength and endurance were needed (e.g. maize cultivation, urban planning, etc.). They also knew that such people had the gift to transcend the physical/earthly and to connect the lower chakras (with the ascending Kundalini force) with the upper ones. When this happened it was clear that this person had not only physical but also psychic energies that could be used for the benefit of all. Therefore, it could well be that a construction worker was suddenly accepted as a disciple of a shaman who encouraged and accompanied his further development.

With their knowledge of the qualities of time, the Mayas ensured that every human being of their culture could use his abilities as optimally as possible and bring them to bloom. This not only ensured satisfied and happy people, but also brought the whole Mayan culture to bloom.

Even if there are still historians and anthropologists who project our own bloodthirsty past onto other cultures such as the Mayas, the Mayas would certainly not have become a high culture if they had actually fought wars and made mass blood sacrifices all the time.

The opposite is the case! All we have to do is take a look at the 6.1 million Maya still living in Mexico, Guatemala, Honduras, etc., almost exactly as they did hundreds, if not thousands of years ago. They plant rice, spices, cocoa, make impressive clothes and still follow the ancient calendar systems of their ancestors. They have also preserved their language and writing and always pass this knowledge on to their children.

I am sure that if the Spaniards had not landed in Vera Cruz (Yocatán) around 1511 and had not massacred the natives with great force and violence, the natives of Central America would never have had to take up arms and we would probably find a completely different world today.

But back to the oracle of the day. So the old Mayas knew the day seal of the child and the current wavespell in which the day sign is embedded. This was more than enough information for the shamans of that time to set the course for the future. And another hint, the Mayan system is anything but a caste system, as we know it from India, where the lowest casts (the untouchables) are even deeper than the animals and can be seen as a form of oppression.

With the Mayas it was about the maximum development of the individual and collective mind. The Mayans knew that everything is connected, yes, everyone is a part of the other. Their still today used greeting «In lak'ech a la KIN» means translated: **I am another yourself!** With this everything is actually already said, isn't it?

Thanks to the further development of the Maya knowledge (based on its mathematics, its calendar systems, its cosmology etc.) by Dr. José Argüelles, we have not only the birth°KIN and the wavespell as information available but much, much more!

The longer we deal with the topic time the more we realize that we have fallen into a bottomless barrel, respectively into a wormhole, which will not end and lead us into new worlds.

Based on a few simple additions, Dr. José Argüelles has additionally calculated an Analogue Partner (Support), an Antipodal Partner (Challenge) and an Occult Partner (Hidden Treasure), as well as a leader (in the same color as the Day°KIN), who additionally provides the birth sign with information from the higher levels (Intuition/Higher Self/Akasha).

These four signs make it possible to find out which people and which days can be more supportive and which more challenging.

When you start to calculate your environment (parents, siblings, friends, acquaintances, etc.) (their birth°KIN), you will experience some exciting surprises with great certainty and in the future you will know much better who (archetype) you are actually dealing with.

As a «white magician» I communicate quite differently than the following sign of the «blue eagle». While the magician can spin a whole story out of a seed (key skill), the archetype of the blue eagle wants it to be «short and crisp», to the point or «reduced to the max».

If you know this, you can communicate with each other much more attentively and connecting. The white magician doesn't go that far and the blue eagle is willing to hear a little story instead of a clear «yes» or «no». This creates connection, trust, closeness, friendships and much more, which could be summarized under the term «peace» or «love».

On the next double page you have on the right side five squares which build a cross. In the Center is your «birth KIN» and around you have the supporting powers. To calculate the birth KIN is quite easy, the four supporting seals are a bit more challenging. Due to limited space and time we decided to give you some websites, where you easily can calculate the whole «Dreamspell Oracle» based on your birthdate.

These websites give you even more informations about your KIN, about the oracle and finally the «wavespell» of your life.

As soon as you have calculated your oracle, I recommend to draw/paint it into the squares on the next page. That gives you a first visual impression of who you are. Afterwards you can read more information about all the symbols in the following pages where every sign is described in detail. Important to know is that we described all the 20 symbols from two different perspectives. The first (left column) explains the seal as a «person» who bears this symbol and the second description shows the energy of a specific day and what you could do on such a day.

And yes, there are lots of Maya apps, my favorite (iPhone) is: «13:20:Sync» for only $ 2.–. We are also in the process of creating our own «Zuvuya Surf App». If you have subscribed to our newsletter (highly recommended), you will be informed about everything new in time.

But now have fun calculating and decoding your and many other birthdays …

Use one of these websites to calculate your birth sign:

1. www.mayankin.com/daily-tzolkin
2. www.flow260.com (switch to english/button left under logo)
3. www.lawoftime.org/decode/

DEIN GEBURTSORAKEL | YOUR BIRTH ORACLE

Zeichenstunde

Nimm dir einen Moment Zeit und rechne dein Maya Geburtsorakel auf den folgenden Seiten aus oder lass es dir berechnen auf dieser Website:
> www.maya.at/Kin-Info/
   Kin-Info-Index.htm

Ausserdem erscheint demnächst unser eigenes «Zuvuya App» mit dem du deinen persönlichen Maya-Rechner stets dabei hast.

Male das Orakel anschliessend in die leeren Felder. Noch besser ist, wenn du dein Orakel zusätzlich auf ein grösseres Blatt Papier (A4/A3) malst und es gut sichtbar bei dir Zuhause aufhängst. So erinnerst du dich immer daran, welchen galaktischen Archetypen du repräsentierst und welches Potential in dir steckt.

Falls du jemandem ein magisches Geburtsorakel schenken möchtest, bieten wir dir hochwertige Kunstdrucke an auf unserer Projektwebsite unter:

Um tiefer in das Mysterium der Zeit einzutauchen empfehle ich dir mein Buch **«Einführung ins Zuvuyasurfen»**, welches ebenfalls in unserem Shop gedruckt oder als eBook erhältlich ist.

> www.shop.zuvuya-agenda.ch

drawing lesson

Take a moment and calculate your Maya birth oracle or have it calculated on these websites:

> www.mayankin.com/daily-tzolkin
> www.flow260.com (switch to
   english/button left under logo)
> www.lawoftime.org/decode

Then draw the oracle into the empty fields. It is even better if you paint your oracle on a larger sheet of paper (A4/A3) and hang it up at home. So you always remember which galactic archetypes you represent and which potential you have.

If you would like to give someone a magical birth oracle, we offer you high-quality art prints on our project website:

And if you want to dive deeper into the mystery of natural time we highly recommend you the Book of Mariela Maya: **«Practical Guide to the Tzolkin»** which you find in her shop.
> www.mayankin.com/learning/

> www.shop.zuvuya-agenda.ch

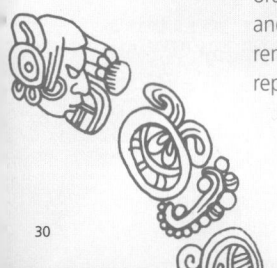

1 Geburtskin
2 Geburtswelle
3 Führungssiegel
4 Analoger Partner
5 Antipodaler Partner
6 Okkulter Partner

1 Birth°KIN
2 Birth wavespell
3 Guiding seal
4 Analog (supporting) seal
5 Antipodal (challenging) seal
6 Occult (hidden power) seal

ANLEITUNG

1. Dein Geburtskin

A Notiere die Jahreszahl deines Geburtsjahres (Tabelle A)
B Notiere die Monatszahl deines Geburtsmonats (Tabelle B)
C Notiere den genauen Tag deines Geburtsmonats
D Zähle die drei Zahlen zusammen. Ist die Zahl grösser als 260, ziehe so oft 260 ab, bis sie kleiner ist als 260.

Diese Nummer ist dein Geburts-KIN:

Beispiel:
Geboren am 16. Dezember 1986

A Jahreszahl, Tabelle A, 1986 **242**
B Monatszahl, Tabelle B, Dezember **74**
C Tag, 16 **16**
D 242 + 74 + 16 = **332**

Das Ergebnis ist grösser als 260
Deshalb: 332 − 260 = 72
Du bist KIN 72

Blättere auf die nächste Seite zum **Tzolkin**: Folge der Zahl 72 nach links, wo die 20 Siegel abgebildet sind. Dort findest du ein gelbes Zeichen mit einem grossen Zahn. Auf den nächsten Seiten erfährst du, dass dies das Zeichen des Gelben Menschen ist. Weiter siehst du beim Zeichen 72 einen Strich mit 2 Punkten. Nach der Schreibweise der Maya ist das der 7. Ton, auch «resonanter» Ton genannt. Zusammen ergibt das den «Gelben resonanten Menschen», KIN 72 – gratuliere, du kennst nun den vollständigen Namen deines Geburts-KIN!
Trage ihn hier ein.

Name deines Geburts-KIN

Für die weiteren Berechnungen (Geburtswelle, etc.) benötigst du auch die Siegelnummer und deinen Ton.

Siegel Nummer (1 bis 20)

Ton (1 bis 13)

2. Deine Geburtswelle

Wenn du dein Geburts-KIN ausgerechnet hast – in unserem Beispiel KIN 72 – kannst du nun dein Lebensthema herausfinden. Dazu brauchst du nur nachzuschauen, in welche 13er Welle (Wavespell) du hineingeboren wurdest. Wenn du zum Beispiel auf Position 7 bist (KIN 72), dann gehe rückwärts (im Tzolkin auf Seite 18) zum ersten Zeichen der Welle das nur einen Punkt aufweist! In unserem Fall kommst du zu KIN 66. Wenn du wieder in der linken Spalte nachschaust, befindet sich dort ein weisses Zeichen, der Weisse Weltenüberbrücker. Du brauchst nun lediglich nachzulesen, was dieses Zeichen bedeutet und schon hast du eine grobe Ahnung, worum es grundsätzlich in deinem Leben geht.

Anmerkung: Falls dein Zeichen sich auf der ersten Position der 13er Welle befindet, bedeutet das, dass dein Geburts-KIN auch dein Lebensthema ist. Dann bist du nicht nur der Repräsentant dieses galaktischen Archetypen, sondern dieser Archetyp gibt dir auch grad die Reiserichtung vor. Du bist sozusagen das Gefährt und gleichzeitig das Reiseziel!

Geburtswelle

Beispiel:
KIN 72, Gelber Resonanter Mensch (7. Ton)
KIN 66, Weltenüberbrücker-Welle (1. Ton)

Tabelle A | Table A

Jahrgang	Year of birth		Jahreszahl Year number
2020	1968	1916	172
2019	1967	1915	67
2018	1966	1914	222
2017	1965	1913	117
2016	1964	1912	12
2015	1963	1911	167
2014	1962	1910	62
2013	1961	1909	217
2012	1960	1908	112
2011	1959	1907	7
2010	1958	1906	162
2009	1957	1905	57
2008	1956	1904	212
2007	1955	1903	107
2006	1954	1902	2
2005	1953	1901	157
2004	1952	1900	52
2003	1951	1899	207
2002	1950	1898	102
2001	1949	1897	257
2000	1948	1896	152
1999	1947	1895	47
1998	1946	1894	202
1997	1945	1893	97
1996	1944	1892	252
1995	1943	1891	147
1994	1942	1890	42
1993	1941	1889	197
1992	1940	1888	92
1991	1939	1887	247
1990	1938	1886	142
1989	1937	1885	37
1988	1936	1884	192
1987	1935	1883	87
1986	1934	1882	242
1985	1933	1881	137
1984	1932	1880	32
1983	1931	1879	187
1982	1930	1878	82

Das komplette Maya*Orakel, basierend auf dem Dreamspell kannst du auf folgenden Seiten ausrechnen lassen:

calculate your full maya oracle on the Dreamspell) please visit one of these websites:

www.maya.at/Kin-Info/
Kin-Info-Index.htm
www.mayankin.com/daily-tzolkin/

Jahrgang	Year of birth			Jahreszahl Year number
1981	1929	1877		237
1980	1928	1876		132
1979	1927	1875		27
1978	1926	1874		182
1977	1925	1873		77
1976	1924	1872		232
1975	1923	1871		127
1974	1922	1870		22
1973	1921	1869		177
1972	1920	1868		72
1971	1919	1867		227
1970	1918	1866		122
1969	1917	1865		17
1968	1916	1864		172
1967	1915	1863		67
1966	1914	1862		222

Tabelle B | Table B

Monat	Month	Zahl	number
Januar	0
Februar	31
März	59
April	90
Mai	120
Juni	151
Juli	181
August	212
September	243
Oktober	13
November	44
Dezember	74

TUTORIAL

1. Your birth°KIN

A Note the year number of the your year of birth (Table A)
B Note the number of your month of birth (Table B)
C Note the day of your month of birth
D Add up the three numbers. If the number is greater than 260, subtract 260 until it is less than 260.

This number is your birth°KIN:

Example:
Born on 16th December 1986.

A Year, Table A, 1986   242
B Number of months, Table B,
      December   74
C Day, 16   16
D 242 + 74 + 16 = **332**

The result is larger than 260
Therefore: 332 - 260 = 72
You are KIN 72.

Flip to the next side (page 18): Find the number 72 (4th column) in the **Tzolkin**. Follow the row (of the number 72) to the left, where the 20 seals are depicted. There you will find a yellow sign with a large tooth. On the following pages you will learn that this is the seal of the «Yellow Human». Further you see a line with 2 dots at sign 72. According to the spelling of the Maya this is the 7th tone, also called «resonant» tone. Together this results in the «Yellow Resonant Human», KIN 72 – congratulations, you now know the full name of your birth°KIN!

Enter it here.
Name of your birth°KIN

For the further calculations (the full oracle) you also need the seal number and your tone. Every of the 20 seals has its unique place in the row from one to twenty. The «Yellow Human» for example, has the position 12.

Seal number (1 to 20)

Tone (1 to 13)

2. Your birth wave

If you have calculated your birth°KIN – in our example KIN 72 – you can now find out your life theme. All you have to do is look up which of the 13-days-wave (called «Wavespell» or «Trecenna») you were born into.

For example, if you are at the 7th position like KIN 72, go backwards/upwards (in the Tzolkin) to the first sign that has only one point. In our case you come to KIN 66. If you go to the left column in the same row, there is a white sign, the «White Worldbridger». All you have to do now is read what this sign means and you have a rough idea of what your life is all about.

Note: If your sign is on the first position of the wavespell, it means that your birth°KIN is also your life theme. Then you are not only the representative of this galactic archetype, but this archetype also gives you the travel direction. You are, so to speak, the vehicle and at the same time the destination!

**Birth wavespell
Example:**

KIN 72, Yellow Resonant Man
(7th tone) = Your Avatar
KIN 66, Worldbridger Wavespell
(1st tone) = Life theme

DAS TZOLKIN-RASTER

1	21	41	61	81	101	121	141	161	181	201	221	241
2	22	42	62	82	102	122	142	162	182	202	222	242
3	23	43	63	83	103	123	143	163	183	203	223	243
4	24	44	64	84	104	124	144	164	184	204	224	244
5	25	45	65	85	105	125	145	165	185	205	225	245
6	26	46	66	86	106	126	146	166	186	206	226	246
7	27	47	67	87	107	127	147	167	187	207	227	247
8	28	48	68	88	108	128	148	168	188	208	228	248
9	29	49	69	89	109	129	149	169	189	209	229	249
10	30	50	70	90	110	130	150	170	190	210	230	250
11	31	51	71	91	111	131	151	171	191	211	231	251
12	32	52	72	92	112	132	152	172	192	212	232	252
13	33	53	73	93	113	133	153	173	193	213	233	253
14	34	54	74	94	114	134	154	174	194	214	234	254
15	35	55	75	95	115	135	155	175	195	215	235	255
16	36	56	76	96	116	136	156	176	196	216	236	256
17	37	57	77	97	117	137	157	177	197	217	237	257
18	38	58	78	98	118	138	158	178	198	218	238	258
19	39	59	79	99	119	139	159	179	199	219	239	259
20	40	60	80	100	120	140	160	180	200	220	240	260

DER TZOLKIN

Die universelle Zeit°Schablone

Der wichtigste Kalender in ganz Mesoamerika war und ist es auch heute noch, der «Tzol'KIN» (Zähler der KIN). Nicht nur die Mayas nutzten ihn, auch die Olmeken, die Zapoteken, die Inkas, Azteken, etc. meistens jedoch unter einem anderen Namen.

Diese Schablone besteht aus 20 Reihen (für die 20 Siegels/Archetypen) und 13 Spalten (für die 13 Töne der Schöpfung). Zusammen multipliziert, ergibt das ein Teppich mit exakt 260 KIN's oder Feldern. Diese 260 Tage entsprechen exakt dem durchschnittlichen Schwangerschaftszyklus (9 Monate), was uns bereits aufzeigt, dass dieses Mass den irdischen Schöpfungsprozess bereits integriert hat.

Diese Zahlen tauchen auch überall in der Natur auf bis hin zur Musik, die ebenfalls mit Intervallen und Zyklen arbeitet, welche wir im Tzolkin entdecken können.

Der Tzolkin ist jedoch auch ein universelles Mass. Damit dies möglich ist, muss er fraktaler Natur sein. Das bedeutet nichts anderes, als dass sein Mass (260) auch in grösseren Massstäben anzutreffen ist. Eines der bekanntesten Beispiele dafür ist die Präzession, auch «Platonisches Jahr» genannt, welches rund 26'000 Jahre dauert (also das 100-fache des Tzolkins) und den «Wobbeleffekt» der Erde ausmacht.

Wenn man den Tzolkin in seiner linearen Form anschaut, erhält man den Eindruck von einem Computercode oder Programm, das links oben beginnt, nach unten fährt, dann in die zweite Spalte nach oben springt, bis es am Ende unten rechts angekommen ist. Anschliessend beginnt es wieder von vorne (oben links).

Der Tzolkin enthält noch weitere Geheimnisse, die zum Teil erforscht und entdeckt wurden. Aber noch immer ist dieser Schlüssel für viele ein Geheimnis voller Geheimnisse. So bilden zum Beispiel die dunkleren Felder den «Webstuhl der Maya» (engl. «Loom of Maya»), eine Art Struktur innerhalb des Tzolkins, der für mich persönlich aussieht wie ein Ausschnitt unserer DNS.

Wenn du dich länger und vertiefter mit dem Tzolkin und den anderen Kalendern auseinandersetzt, wirst du immer wieder gewisse Zahlen auftauchen sehen. Du wirst sie schliesslich nicht nur im Kalender entdecken, sondern sogar in deinem Lieblingsyoghurt.

Hier ein paar dieser sehr wichtigen Zahlen zum Starten:
1, 2, 3, 4, 5, 7, 13, 20, 26, 28, 52, 65, 91, 144, 260, 365, 520 ...

Halte einfach die Augen offen und lass dich überraschen.

THE TZOLKIN

The universal time°template

The most important and central calendar in Mesoamerica was and still is the «Tzol'KIN» (counter of the KIN). Not only the Mayas used it, but also the Olmecs, the Zapotecs, the Incas, the Aztecs, etc. mostly under a different name.

This template consists of 20 rows for the 20 seals/archetypes) and 13 columns (for the 13 tones of creation). When multiplied together, this results in a carpet with exactly 260 KIN's or squares. These 260 days correspond exactly to the average pregnancy cycle (9 months), which already shows us that this measure has already integrated the earthly creation process.

These numbers appear everywhere in nature up to the music, which also works with intervals and cycles, which we can discover in Tzolkin.

But the Tzolkin is also a universal measure. For this to be possible, it must be fractal in nature. This means nothing other than that his measure (260) can also be found in larger scales. One of the best known examples of this is the precession, also called the «Platonic Year», which lasts about 26,000 years (100 times that of Tzolkins) and which constitutes the «sweep effect» of the Earth.

If you look at the Tzolkin in its linear form, you get the impression of a computer code or program that starts at the top left, goes down, then jumps up into the second column until it reaches the bottom right. Then it starts again from the front (top left).

The Tzolkin contains more secrets, some of which have been researched and discovered. But for many this key is still a secret full of secrets. For example, the darker fields form the «Loom of Maya», a kind of structure within the Tzolkin, which looks like a section of our DNA to me personally.

As you get to know the Tzolkin and the other calendars in more detail, you'll see certain numbers appear again and again. You'll find them not only in the calendar, but even in your favorite yogurt.

Here are some of these very important numbers to start with:
1, 2, 3, 4, 5, 7, 13, 20, 26, 28, 52, 65, 91, 144, 260, 365, 520 ...

Just keep your eyes open and let yourself be surprised.

ZAHNRÄDER

Wenn wir vom linearen Zeitverständnis in ein zyklisches Zeitbewusstsein eintauchen möchten, ist es wichtig, sich immer wieder vor Augen zu halten, dass beispielsweise die schablonenhafte Darstellung des Tzolkins auf der linken Seite viel über seine verborgenen Geheimnisse preisgibt, jedoch nicht der radialen Dynamik der Zeit entspricht.

Viel treffender ist die Darstellung von zwei unterschiedlich grossen Zahnrädern, von denen das kleinere die 13 Töne und das grössere die 20 Siegel (Archetypen) beinhaltet.

Diese beiden Zahnräder sind so ineinander verzahnt, dass, wird an einem der beiden gedreht, das andere mitdreht.

Zu Beginn befinden sich die beiden Zahnräder in der Ausgangsposition, dort wo der Rote Drache mit dem ersten Ton verbunden ist. Dreht sich das Zahnrad der Töne auf die zweite Position, bewegt sich auch das «Siegelrad» weiter zum Weissen Wind.

So läuft das kleinere Rad bis zur dreizehnten Position, wo sich dann beim «Siegelrad« der Rote Himmelswanderer befindet. Damit geht die erste «13-er Welle» (die «Rote Drachenwelle») zu Ende.

Dreht sich das «Tonrad» weiter, gelangt es wieder zum ersten (magnetischen) Ton. Das grössere «Siegelrad» ist jedoch noch nicht am «Ende» angelangt (gibt es ja eigentlich gar nicht bei einem Rad!) und dreht sich weiter auf die Position des Weissen Magiers. Somit haben wir die Kombination von Ton Eins (magnetischer Ton) und dem Weissen Magier. Eine neue 13-er Welle beginnt (die «Weisse Magierwelle»).

Drehen wir nun weiter auf den zweiten (lunaren) Ton, erhalten wir den «Blauen lunaren Adler».

Das ganze Spiel geht weiter, bis wir beim «Siegelrad» schliesslich auch zum «letzten» (gibt es ebenfalls nicht auf einem Rad) Zeichen, der gelben Sonne gelangen. Das «Tonrad» befindet sich jetzt auf der Position Sieben, dem «resonanten» Ton. Wir haben also die Kombination (KIN) «Gelbe resonante Sonne». Jetzt hat sich auch das «Siegelrad» einmal um 360° gedreht.

Wenn wir jetzt das «Tonrad» weiterdrehen, gelangen wir zum achten (galaktischen) Ton, während das «Siegelrad» wieder zum roten Drachen weiterdreht und daher den «Roten galaktischen Drachen» ergibt.

So drehen diese beiden Räder weiter und weiter, bis alle 260 Möglichkeiten (Kombinationen) durchgespielt wurden und wir schliesslich wieder zum «roten magnetischen Drachen» gelangen, mit dem ein neuer Tzolkin-Durchlauf beginnt.

Der Tzolkin links ist also die grafische Darstellung aller 260 Kombinationen, wobei er in 13 Spalten und 20 Zeilen (für die 20 Zeichen von oben nach unten) eingeteilt ist.

Diese Darstellung ist zwar linear (von links oben nach unten, dann ein Sprung in die zweite Spalte nach oben und das ganze Spiel bis wir unten rechts ankommen. Dann «springt» der Tzolkin wieder zurück nach links oben, wobei wir jetzt ja wissen, dass es eigentlich keinen Sprung gibt, sondern nur zwei Räder, die endlos drehen und drehen und drehen … bis wir alle 260 Lektionen gelernt haben.

Nachdem wir nun den Tzolkin und seinen Aufbau (13/20) näher kennengelernt haben, stellen wir dir als nächstes die 20 Archetypen/Spielfiguren der Zeit im Detail vor. Denk daran, dass dies lediglich die Zusammenfassung der wichtigsten Eingeschaften ist. Je länger du dich mit den 20 Archetypen und den 13 Tönen beschäftigst, desto mehr wirst du entdecken und deine Wahrnehmung vertiefen und verfeinern können.

TOOTHED WHEELS

If we want to immerse ourselves from a linear understanding of time into a cyclic consciousness of time, it is important to keep in mind that for example, the stenciled depiction of Tzolkins on the left reveals much about his hidden secrets, but does not correspond to the radial dynamics of time.

Much more accurate is the representation of two gears of different sizes, the smaller one containing the 13 tones and the larger one the 20 seals (archetypes).

These two gears are interlocked in such a way that when one of them is rotated, the other one rotates as well.

At the beginning, the two gears are in the starting position, where the red dragon is connected to the first tone. When the gear wheel of the tones turns to

the second position, the «seal wheel» also moves further to the white wind.

Thus the smaller wheel runs up to the thirteenth position, where the Red Sky Walker is located at the «Sealing Wheel». With this the first «13'er wave» (the «Red Dragon Wave») comes to an end.

As the «Tonewheel» continues to rotate, it returns to the first (magnetic) sound. However, the larger «sealing wheel» has not yet reached the «end» (there is actually no such thing as a wheel!) and continues to rotate to the position of the white magician. Thus we have the combination of tone one (magnetic tone) and the white magician. A new 13'er wave (the «white magician wave») begins.

If we turn now further on the second (lunar) tone, we receive the «Blue lunar eagle».

The whole game continues until we finally reach the «last» sign of the yellow sun at the «Sealing Wheel». The «tone wheel» is now in position seven, the «resonant» tone. So we have the combination (KIN) «yellow resonant sun». Now the «sealing wheel» has also rotated 360° once.

If we now turn the «Tonewheel» further, we arrive at the eighth (galactic) sound, while the «Sealing Wheel» turns again to the red dragon and therefore results in the «Red Galactic Dragon».

So these two wheels turn on and on until all 260 possibilities (combinations) have been played through and we finally reach the «Red Magnetic Dragon» again, with which a new Tzolkin run begins.

The Tzolkin on the left is the graphic representation of all 260 combinations, whereby it is divided into 13 columns and 20 lines (for the 20 characters from top to bottom). This representation is indeed linear (from top left to bottom, then a jump into the second column upwards and the whole game until we arrive at the bottom right. Then the Tzolkin «jumps» back up to the left again, whereby we now know that there is actually no jump, but only two wheels that rotate and rotate and turn endlessly ... until we have learned all 260 lessons.

Now that we've got to know Tzolkin and his (cyclic) structure (13/20) better, we'll introduce you to the 20 archetypes/game figures of the time in detail. Remember, this is only a summary of the most important features. The longer you study the 20 archetypes and the 13 tones, the more you will discover and deepen and refine your perception.

Du siehst hier die zwei Räder des Tzolkin (13-er und 20-er Zyklus), die miteinander verzahnt sind und unseren 13 Monde Kalender damit täglich «füttern» (mit einer der 260 Kombinationen).

You see here the two wheels of the Tzolkin (13 cycle and 20 cylce), which are interlocked with each other and «feed» our 13 moon calendar daily with it (with one of the 260 combinations/KIN).

DIE 20 GALAKTISCHEN SPIELFIGUREN

Die Zeitpotentiale verstehen und optimal nutzen

In dieser Agenda haben wir die 20 Siegel (Archetypen der Zeit) zweimal aufgeschlüsselt und dargestellt.

Einerseits gibt es zu jedem der 20 Zeichen einen Erklärungstext, der zu deinem **Geburts°KIN** passt, also deinem Geburtspotential. Diese Texte zeigen dir auf, welche Licht- und Schattenseiten diese Siegel aufweisen und wie du dein **Geburtspotential** optimal nutzen kannst.

Ähnlich, und doch ein bisschen anders, gilt es, die jeweiligen Tagespotentiale zu lesen.

Jeder Tag weist eine **spezifische Tagesqualität** auf, und zwar eines der 260 möglichen KINs des Tzolkins.

Angenommen, wir haben heute das Zeichen der «Roten Schlange», dann findest du auf der Seite 38 ein paar Hinweise, wie du diesen Tag optimal gestalten oder nutzen kannst. Bei der Roten Schlange geht es um den physischen Körper, um Bewegung, Schwitzen, Spiralen und vieles mehr. Es sind ideale Tage für einen Saunagang, eine Yogasession oder um dich wie ein Derwisch im Kreis zu drehen. Oder du nimmst einen Stift und zeichnest auf einem Papier unzählige Spiralen, um dabei der Schlange auf die Schliche zu kommen.

Nach der Roten Schlange folgt immer der «Weisse Weltenüberbrücker». Dieses Zeichen erinnert uns an die eigene Vergänglichkeit, ans Sterben, an Loslassen und den Tod. Darüber hinaus weist der Weltenüberbrücker auch auf die Auferstehung hin, und die Möglichkeiten, die das Loslassen erlauben.

An diesen Weltenüberbrücker-Tagen empfiehlt es sich, z. B. ein paar Seiten im berühmten **«Tibetanischen Totenbuch»** zu lesen, sich seine eigene «Grabrede» zu schreiben oder auch, an unsere Ahnen zu denken und für sie eine Kerze anzuzünden, oder das Grab unserer Vorfahren zu besuchen. Ausserdem eignen sich diese Tage zum entrümpeln auf geistiger und physischer Ebene.

Wenn du solche «Handlungen» auf der konkreten Ebene oder auch im Geist (über den Tod nachdenken) machst, verbindest du dich mit dem **geistigen Feld des Archetypen**, der gerade am Wirken ist. Somit stellst du sozusagen eine Hotline oder Verbindung zu ihm her, und er wird dich dafür mit Erkenntnissen, Erlebnissen, Einsichten und hilfreichen Synchronisationen «belohnen».

Du bist dann «eingetuned» und wirst immer mehr diese feinen, subtilen Inputs aus dem aktiven, geistigen Feld hören oder spüren. Oder nochmals anders ausgedrückt: Dieser Vorgang hilft dir, deine Intuition zu verbessern, bis du irgendwann gar keine Zuvuya-Agenda mehr benötigst, da du alles von innen her spüren wirst.

Falls du noch einen Schritt weitergehen möchtest, kannst du dich an jedem Tag fragen, wie du **dein Geburtspotential** mit dem **Tagespotential** verbinden/verknüpfen kannst.

Als Weisser elektrischer Magier frage ich mich jeden Tag: Was macht ein Weisser Magier an einem «Schlangen Tag», an einem «Weltenüberbrücker Tag» oder an einem «Hand-Tag»? Jede spontane, noch so verrückte Antwort/Idee ist ein Hinweis, wie du diesen Tag auf eine besonders kreative Art und Weise gestalten und realisieren kannst.

Vergiss nicht, das Ganze weniger als Studium, sondern als **Spiel** zu betrachten, in welchem es kein Richtig oder Falsch gibt, sondern nur unendlich viele, **kreative Möglichkeiten**.

20 Bausteine des Lichts

Hier noch ein weiterer, lichtvoller Gedanke zu den 20 Siegeln. Dr. José Argüelles hat mal erwähnt, dass die 20 essentiellen Aminosäuren die Bausteine des Lebens, und die 20 Siegel die Bausteine des Lichts sind, aus dem wir alle bestehen.

THE 20 GALACTIC GAME CHARACTERS

Understanding the time potentials and using them optimally

In this agenda we have broken down and presented the 20 seals (archetypes of time) twice.

On the one hand there is an explanatory text for each of the 20 signs, which fits to your **birth°KIN**, i.e. your birth potential. These texts show you which light and shadow sides these seals have and how you can optimally use your **birth potential**.

Similarly, and yet a bit differently, it is important to read the respective daily potentials.

Each day has a **specific daily quality**, namely one of the 260 possible KINs of the Tzolkin.

Assuming we have the sign of the «Red Serpent» today, you will find a few hints on page 38 on how to make the most of this day. The Red Serpent is about the physical body, movement, sweating, spirals and much more. These are ideal days for a sauna session, a yoga session or to spin in a circle like a dervish. Or you can take a pencil and draw countless spirals on a piece of paper in order to find the snake.

After the Red Serpent always follows the «White Worldbridger». This sign reminds us of our own transience, of dying, of letting go and of death. In addition, the Worldbridger also points to the resurrection and the possibilities that allow letting go.

On these Worldbridger days it is advisable to read a few pages in the famous **«Tibetan Book of the Dead»**, for example, to write one's own «eulogy» or to think of our ancestors and light a candle for them, or to visit the grave of your ancestors. These days are also suitable for clearing out mental and physical problems.

If you do such «actions» on the concrete level or also in the spirit (thinking about death), you connect yourself with the **spiritual field of the archetype** that is working right now. In this way you establish a hotline or connection to it, so to speak, and it will «reward» you with insights, experiences and helpful synchronizations.

You will then be «tuned in» and will hear or feel more and more these fine, subtle inputs from the active, spiritual field. Or to put it another way: This process helps you to improve your intuition until you no longer need any Zuvuya agenda, because you will feel everything from the inside.

If you want to go one step further, you can ask yourself every day how you can connect **your birth potential** with the **daily potential**.

As a white electric wizard I ask myself every day: What does a white wizard do on a «serpent day», a «worldbridger day» or a «hand day»? Every spontaneous, crazy answer/idea is an indication of how you can design and realize this day in a particularly creative way.

Don't forget to regard the whole thing less as a study, but as a **game** in which there is no right or wrong but only infinite **creative possibilities.**

20 building blocks of light

Here's another bright thought about the 20 seals. Dr. José Argüelles once mentioned that the 20 essential amino acids are the building blocks of life, and the 20 seals are the building blocks of the light we all consist of.

**01
ROTER DRACHE
Red Dragon
IMIX**

Geburtssiegel

Nähren | Gebären | Sein Kraft des Beginnens Mutterprinzip | Feuer Sinneslust Freude Inspiration | Kooperation | grosse Gewässer (Ozeane) | andere Realitäten | Wahnsinn Verrücktheit | Mystik

Lichtweisheit
Urmutter, Quelle des Lebens, weibliches Schöpfungsprinzip, Urvertrauen, Sicherheit, Schutz, Fürsorge, Verständnis, leidenschaftlich, hellsichtig, Träumer, Visonäre

Schattenweisheit
Mangel an Urvertrauen, Existenzangst, Egoismus, sich selbst nicht gut versorgen können, Angst vor Neuem (Neues zu beginnen), lethargisch, Nervosität, Unsicherheit, Zweifel, Wahnsinn, Verrücktheit, exzentrisch, obsessiv

Potentiale/Berufe
Hebamme, Mutter, Betreuung, Kinderhort leiten, Koch, Ernährungsberaterin, Projekt Initiator, Visionär, Inspirator, Hypnosetherapeut

Tagesenergie

Die Kraft der Geburt
Vertrauen in die eigene Schöpferkraft

Der Rote Drache symbolisiert die Urmutter, die Einheit mit der Schöpfung, das universelle morphogenetische Feld, in welchem alles als Quantenpotential zur Verfügung steht und darauf wartet, realisiert zu werden. Daher kann man sich die Energie des Roten Drachen auch als energetisches Gitternetz vorstellen, welches alle Potentiale miteinander verbindet.

Guter Tag für ...
Vereinigung mit anderen, Zusammenarbeit, Synchronizität und Telepathie. Gehe mit jemandem Essen oder noch besser, lade ein paar Freunde ein, kocht gemeinsam ein Festmenu im Bewusstsein, dass das Prinzip der Urmutter immer genügend Essen und Trinken für alle bereit hält. Wir werden alle durch sie genährt, nicht nur physisch, sondern auch auf der feinstofflichen Ebene.

Birth seal

Nurturing | Giving Birth Being | The power of beginning | Mother principle | Fire | Pleasure Delight | Joy

Light Wisdom
Primordial mother, Source of life, female principle of creation, basic trust, receiving

Shadow Wisdom
Lack of basic trust, existential fear, egoism, not being able to take care for oneself, fear of the new, fear of starting something new, lethargic

Potentials/professions
Midwife, mother, caregiver, running a creche/day nursery, nutritionist, project starter/promoter

Day energy

Power of birth
Trust in ones ability to create

The Red Dragon symbolizes the primordial mother, die unity with creation, the universal morphogenetic field («the divine matrix») in which all the quantum possibilities are waiting to be seized. Therefore you can imagine the energy of the Red Dragon as an energetic web which connects all the potentials, quite similar to «Indra's Web».

A good day for ...
Connection and reunion with others, cooperation, synchronicity and telepathy. Go out for lunch/dinner with someone you love or even better, invite some friends and cook together a delicious banquet. Remember that the source always delivers food, drink, shelter in abundance for everyone. We are all nurtured by the source not only on a physical level, but as well on all the etheric planes and levels.

**02
WEISSER WIND
White Wind
IK**

Geburtssiegel

**Denken | Kommunizieren
Atem | Geist | Struktur
Verstand | Sprache
Ordnung**

Lichtweisheit
Urvater, männliches Schöpfungsprinzip, Aufmerksamkeit, Präsenz, Klarheit, Wahrheit, streng, fordernd, fördernd, unterstützend, impulsiv, stark, selbstsicher, anpassungsfähig, offener Geist, beweglich, flexibel

Schattenweisheit
Trennungsthemen, fehlendes Gottvertrauen, Inspirationslosigkeit, kühl und berechnend, introvertiert, Prinzipienreiter, abstrakt und lieblos

Potentiale / Berufe
Vater, Philosophie, Atemtherapeutin, Lehrer, Wissenschaftler, Forscher, Sprachgestaltung, gewaltfreie Kommunikation, Feng Shui, Mediator, Coaching

Tagesenergie

Die Kraft des Geistes
Erkenntnisse aus der feinstofflichen Welt

Der Weisse Wind steht für das Rauschen des Windes, das Plätschern des Wassers und natürlich für unsere menschliche Kommunikation: das Sprechen, Lesen, Schreiben, Singen, Musizieren. Er steht für den göttlichen Atem, auch Chi, Ki, Prana genannt, welcher alles Sein belebt und zugleich strukturiert.

Guter Tag für ...
Das Zimmer aufräumen, ein Projekt strukturieren, die Ferienreise planen, Ideen schmieden, sich von allem Möglichen inspirieren zu lassen und die Zukunft zu visualisieren. Ausserdem ideal für Atemübungen, Räucherungen, Musik hören, mit jemandem ein bisschen plaudern und bei einem Gespräch einfach mal nur zuhören.

Birth seal

**Thinking | Communication | Breath | Spirit
Structure | Intellect
Language | Order**

Light Wisdom
Forefather, male principle of creation, attention, presence, clarity, truth, strict, severe, challenging, supporting, assisting

Shadow Wisdom
themes of disconnection and separation, lack of trust in godfather, lack of inspiration, uncaring, coolish, calculating, introverted, pedant, dogmatist, abstract, loveless, affectionless

Potentials / professions
Father, philosophy, breath therapeut, teacher, scientist, explorer, working with languages, non violent communication, feng shui, mediator, coach

Day energy

Power of Spirit
Wisdom of the etheric realms

The White Wind stands for the soft sound of wind blowing through leaves, the gurgle of the water and of course the human communication: The talking, reading, writing, singing, toning, making music and even dancing and all the non-verbal expressions of our human being. The wind symbolizes the divine breath, Chi, Ki, Prana, Orgon, ether and so on which all sustain our lifes and even give structure to it.

A good day for ...
Cleaning up rooms, plan and structure a project, imagining your next holiday travels, let yourself be inspired by everything around you (radio, television, newspaper, magazine, nature, people, kids, etc.) and visualize your desired future. Beside of this it's a good day to do some work of breathing (e.g. Pranayama, holotropic breathing, etc.), smokings (e.g. cleaning rituals), listen to wonderful music, talking with somebody who tells you his story.

**03
BLAUE NACHT
Blue Night
AKBAL**

Geburtssiegel

**Kreativität | Träume
Intuition | Fülle
Reichtum | Wachstum
Unterbewusstsein
Vorstellungskraft
Phantasie | Illusionen
Potentiale | Leere
Dunkelheit | Nacht,
Dämmerung | Einsamkeit**

Lichtweisheit
Überfluss, Fülle, Geborgenheit und Sicherheit, geben und empfangen, Stille, innerer Reichtum, Trost, Mysterium, Nicht-Wissen, geschehen lassen, luzides Träumen

Schattenweisheit
Starke emotionale Schwankungen, Depressionen, Selbstverurteilung, Angst vor Veränderung, starke Ich-Bezogenheit, diffus und unklar, Müdigkeit, Antriebslosigkeit, Gefühl von Einsamkeit und Leere

Potentiale / Berufe
Psychologie, Psychotherapie, Spiritualität, kreative Berufe, Coaching, Monetäre Berufe (z.B. Treuhänder, Business Angels, etc.), Mystiker, Neo-Schamane, Künstler, Poet, Schriftsteller, Betreuer, Hauswart, Verwalter

Tagesenergie

Die Kraft der Kreativität
Verbindung zu Unterbewusstsein/Seele

Die Blaue Nacht lädt dich ein, dein kreatives Potential zu erkennen und es in die Welt zu bringen. Ausserdem erinnert sie uns damit gleichzeitig an die Fülle unseres Universums. So wie es Milliarden von Sternen und Galaxien gibt, gibt es auch genug für jeden einzelnen Menschen hier auf Erden. Und schliesslich ermöglicht uns die Blaue Nacht eine direkte Verbindung zu unserem Unbewussten, dem Raum der Seele.

Guter Tag für ...
Kreativen Ausdruck, ob zeichnen, malen, singen, musizieren, aktiviere deine kreative Ader, denn sonst versiegt sie und du wirst den Verlust dieser kreativen Quelle in deinem Leben spüren. Sei ausserdem dankbar für alles, was du bereits besitzt und erlebt hast. Denn Dankbarkeit ist einer der Schlüssel für mehr von dem, was du bereits hast.

Birth seal

**Creativity | Dreams
Intuition | Abundance
Richness | Wealth
Growth | Unconsciousness | Imagination
Fantasy | Illusions**

Light Wisdom
Copiousness, abundance, security, protection, giving and receiving, stillness, inner richness, consolation, mystery, not knowing, let it happen, lucid dreaming

Shadow Wisdom
Strong emotional fluctuations, depressions, self judging, fear of change, strong self-reliance, diffuse and unclear, fatigue, exhaustion, no impulsions, feelings of loneliness and emptiness

Potentials / professions
Psychologist, psychotherapy, spirituality, creative professions, coaching, financial affairs (e.g. trustee, fiduciary, etc.), mystic, neo-shaman

Day energy

Power of creativity
Connection to unconsciousness/soul

The Blue Night invites you to fully recognize your creative potential and to bring it into the world. Akbal reminds you as well to the infinite abundance of our universe. As we have trillions of stars and galaxies we have enough for everyone here on planet earth. And the Blue Night is as well the direct connection to our unconsciousness, the realm of our soul and the deep mystery of our planetary being.

A good day for ...
Creative expressions, no matter if drawing, painting, singing, making sound or music, just activate your creative veins and let creativity flow through you. If you don't use it, you gonna loose it and this can lead to sadness and depression. Then we are here to express Time as Art. Be grateful for everything you possess and what you have experienced so far in your life. Because gratitude is one of the main keys to attract more of what you already have or love.

**04
GELBER SAME
Yellow Seed
KAN**

Geburtssiegel

Säen | Erblühen | Zielen
Fokus | Geduld | Ausdauer | Möglichkeiten
Sexualität | Künstler
Poet | Schriftsteller
Betreuer | Hauwart
Verwalter

Lichtweisheit
Aufmerksamkeit, Zielgerichtetheit, Fruchtbarkeit, Wachstum, reifen, Wissen um den richtigen Zeitpunkt, ins Schwarze treffen, blindes (Gott-) Vertrauen, geduldig, Ruhepol

Schattenweisheit
Unkonzentriert, verstreut, lustlos, keine Ziele, Motivationsschwierigkeiten, zu früh/zu spät (unpünktlich), verzögern, Angst vor Wachstum und Fülle, Sicherheit statt Abenteuer, Ausdruckslosigkeit

Potentiale/Berufe
Coach, Potentialentfalter, Gärtner & Gartengestalter, Lehrer, Tantralehrer, Sexualtherapeutin, Heiler, Kräuterkundiger, Hebamme, Arzt

Tagesenergie

Die Kraft des richtigen Zeitpunktes
Erkennen des wahren Potentials

In jedem Samen steckt in holografischer Form der ganze Bauplan. Wenn wir uns geistig ausrichten, uns über längere Zeit auf ein spezifisches Ziel fokussieren, dann wird dieser geistige Samen seiner Verwirklichung entgegenwachsen. Erst wenn wir unsere Wünsche und Träume ganz genau kennen, können wir deren Realisation bewusst unterstützen.

Guter Tag für ...
Gartenarbeit, neue Projekte, Visualisierungen, Bogenschiessen, sich in Geduld üben, den Mondkalender studieren, etwas zu Ende bringen (gelbe Farbe), einen Baum pflanzen, Potentialentfaltung, Coaching, neue Möglichkeiten erwägen, Sexualität (Tantra), ein Kind zeugen.

Birth seal

Sowing | Flowering
Targeting | Focus
Patience | Perseverance
Possibilities | Sexuality
Fertility | Fractality

Light Wisdom
Attention, concentration, fertility, growth, ripening, knowledge of the right point in time and about cycles, hit the bull's eye, trust, blind trust in god, confidence, patient, center of peacefulness, sacred sexuality

Shadow Wisdom
Unfocused, scattered, apathetic, bored, spiritless, no goals, motivational difficulty, too early/late (not on time), fear of growing and abundance, overwhelmed, security instead of adventure, inexpressiveness

Potentials/professions
Coach, gardener, landscaping, teacher, tantra teacher, sexual therapeut, healer, herbalist, midwife, doctor

Day energy

Power of the exact point of time
Knowledge of true potential

In every seed lies the whole masterplan in holographic form. If we align ourself mentally for a longer time on a specific goal, the (etheric) seed will search for its fulfillment by itself. Only by knowing our deepest wishes and dreams can we support them consciously.

A good day for ...
Gardening, new projects, visualisations, archery, to deepen ones patience, study the moon cycles, to fulfill something, to plant a tree (or a flower), unfold some hidden potentials, coaching, to think about new possibilities in your life, sacred sexuality (tantra), create or give birth to a child

**05
ROTE SCHLANGE
Red Snake
CHICCHAN**

Geburtssiegel

Lebenskraft | Schöpferkraft | Sexualität Instinkt | Überleben kosmische Spirale

Lichtweisheit
Instinktiv handeln, Kundalini-Energie, Sexualität, Leidenschaft, Realismus, Realisation, Umsetzungskraft, Schlauheit, sensibel, medial, erdverbunden, kraftvoll, vital, lebendig

Schattenweisheit
Starre Gewohnheiten, Überbewertung körperlicher und sinnlicher Wünsche, Angst vor Intimität, Angst vor Wandlung, nicht loslassen können, verkrampft, krank sein, Jähzorn, Wutanfälle, unkontrolliertes Leben, unausgeglichen, Angst vor der Natur

Potentiale/Berufe
(Spitzen-)Sportler, Fitness-Coach, Yogalehrerin, Heiler, Masseur, intensive, körperliche Berufe, Künstler, Poet, Schriftsteller, Betreuer, Hauwart, Verwalter

Tagesenergie

Die Kraft der Spirale
Entdecke deine Lebenskraft

Die Rote Schlange symbolisiert die Lebenskraft, die spiralförmig alles durchdringt. Es ist wichtig, diese Schlangenkraft zu aktivieren, denn sie sorgt für ein langes, gesundes Leben und erinnert uns daran, immer wieder Altes loszulassen, indem sie sich häutet.

Guter Tag für …
Kundalini-Yoga, Atemübungen, Tanzen, Sauna und andere (schweisstreibende) Aktivitäten. Ebenfalls guter Tag für die Integration der Sexualität in den Alltag. Auch Zärtlichkeiten, Berührungen, Massagen sind ideal geeignet, um der eigenen Sexualität auf die Spur zu kommen. Arbeit im Garten oder mit Tieren

Birth seal

Life force | Power of Creation | Sexuality Instinct | Survival | Kundalini | Cosmic Spiral

Light Wisdom
Acting instinctively, kundalini energy, sexuality, passion, realism, realization, implementation power, cleverness, shrewdness, sensitive, mediumistic, earthy, powerful, vital, alive, spirited

Shadow Wisdom
Stubbornness, sticking to old habits, overrating physical and sensual wishes, fear of intimacy, fear of change and transformation, not able to let go (shedding), tight, anxious, become sick, hot temper, bursts of anger, uncontrolled life, unbalanced, fear of nature

Potentials / professions
Top athletic, fitness coach, yoga teacher, healer, masseur, physically intensive professions

Day energy

Power of universal Spiral
Discover your life force

The Red Serpent symbolizes the powerful life force, which permeates helicoidally (in the form of a spiral) everyone and everything. It is important to activate this kundalini power in order to have a long, healthy life. And Chicchan remembers us always to let go of the old again and again (shedding).

A good day for …
Kundalini Yoga, breath work, dancing, sauna (sweat lodge) and other sweat driving activities. A great day to read a book about tantra or explore sexuality in your life. As well a good day for tenderness, loving touches, massages and sensuality. Gardening or working with animals.

06
WEISSER WELTENÜBERBRÜCKER
White Worldbridger
CIMI

Geburtssiegel

Loslassen | Tod | Möglichkeiten | Ausgleichen Jenseits | Schamanismus | Ahnen | Rückverbindung

Lichtweisheit
Altes loslassen, Demut, sich hingeben, Sterblichkeit, Offenbarung, sterben, begleiten, unterstützen, sich Neuem öffnen können, kontaktfreudig, sich in andere versetzen können

Schattenweisheit
Opferhaltung, Kontrollzwang, Kampf und Widerstand, festhalten, klammern, Angst vor Tod/Sterben, Niedergeschlagenheit, Traurigkeit, Depression, Gefühl von Wertlosigkeit, fehlende Visionen, introvertiert, blockiert

Potentiale / Berufe
Sterbebegleitung, Geburtshelfer, Schamane, Geriatrie, Pflegeberufe, Medium, Traumatologe, Reinkarnationstherapeut, Reisebegleiter,

Tagesenergie

Die Kraft der Todes
Offenbarungen und Weisheit der Ahnen

Der Weisse Weltenüberbrücker ist der Schamane mit der Fähigkeit ins Reich des Todes hinabzusteigen und lebendiger als zuvor wieder zurückzukehren. Er erinnert uns daran, dass wir alle ausnahmslos auf den Schultern unserer Eltern und Ahnen stehen.

Guter Tag für ...
Sich der eigenen Vergänglichkeit bewusst zu werden und symbolisch zu sterben, einen Besuch auf dem Friedhof, das Lesen des «Tibetanischen Totenbuches», das Verfassen des eigenen Testaments, die fiktive Planung der eigenen Beerdigung, eine Kerze anzuzünden, an seine Eltern, Grosseltern zu denken und ihnen zu danken. Studium von Schamanismus, Ritualen (z.B. Rauhnächte) und Entwicklung von eigenen kraftvollen Zeremonien.

Birth seal

Letting go | Dying Death | Resurrection Possibilities | Equalize Hereafter | Shamanism Ancestors | Connection to the past

Light Wisdom
Letting go of the old, humility, surrender, mortality, revelation, dying, accompany, guide, afterlife, bardo, support, open up for the new, sociable, be able to put oneself in others

Shadow Wisdom
Victimisation, control obsession, fight and resistance, control, hold on, hanging on to, fear of death and dying, dejection, sadness, hopelessness, feeling of worthlessness, lack of visions, introverted, blocked

Potentials / professions
Terminal care, obstetrician, shaman, healer, geriatrics, care taker, nurser, master of ceremony

Day energy

Power of Death
Revelations and wisdom of the ancestors

The White Worldbridger is the shaman with the ability to travel in the realm of the dead and come back full of life even more. He reminds us that we all stand on the shoulders of our parents and ancestors and that we regularly should be grateful and remember them.

A good day for ...
To become aware of ones own temporality and mortality, to die symbolically, to visit the graveyard, to read the Tibetan «Book of the dead», writing ones own last will, to plan ones own fictive funeral, to light a candle, to remember ones own (grand) parents and to thank them, study of shamanism and how to implement that in ones life, to use or create powerful rituals and ceremonies.

**07
BLAUE HAND
Blue Hand
MANIK**

Geburtssiegel

**Heilen | Wissen
Handeln | Manifestieren
Umsetzung | Segnen
Pflegen | Begleiten**

Lichtweisheit
Tiefe Heilung, inneres Wissen, Vollendung, Tatkraft, massieren, tun, jemandem zur Hand gehen, unterstützen, leidenschaftlich, Begeisterung, Erfüllung in der Arbeit

Schattenweisheit
Zu viel reden/tun, gestresst sein, zappelig werden, mit den Händen Schaden anrichten, Konflikt zwischen Freiheit und Verantwortung, Energieblockaden, Unsinn machen

Potentiale/Berufe
Masseur, Hand auflegen, Heilerin, Bäcker, Handwerker, Maler, Künstlerin, Pflegeberufe, mit Menschen arbeiten, zusammenarbeiten, Coach, Künstler, Poet, Schriftsteller, Betreuer, Hauswart, Verwalter

Tagesenergie

Die Kraft der Umsetzung
Die Schöpferkraft der Hände

Fast alles, was wir mit unseren Händen greifen können, wurde auch durch Menschenhände geschaffen. Wir brauchen unsere Hände, um den Wecker zu stellen, auf der Tastatur herumzutippen, am Steuerrad (des Lebens) zu drehen, einen Kuchen zu backen, ein Loch zu graben, ein Buch zu halten, jemandem zuzuwinken und wir füllen mit ihnen unsere Steuererklärung aus.

Guter Tag für ...
Etwas (Neues) anpacken, anreissen, umsetzen, in Angriff nehmen, backen, kochen, basteln, zeichnen, malen, formen, etc. Oder wir nutzen unsere Hände, um jemandem eine Umarmung zu schenken, ihn liebevoll zu berühren, zu halten, zu massieren, zu heilen, zu segnen.

Birth seal

**Healing | Knowledge
Wisdom | Acting | Manifestation | Realizing
Blessing | Caring | Supporting | Guiding**

Light Wisdom
Deep healing, inner knowledge, completion, perfection, vigor, power, giving a massage, to do, to create, to assist, to give someone a hand, supporting, passionate, enthusiasm, exaltation, fulfillment through work, accomplishing things

Shadow Wisdom
Too much talking/acting, being stressed, wriggly, restless, to do harm with the hands, conflict between freedom and responsibility, energy blocks, doing nonsense, depleting ones energy

Potentials / professions
Professional masseur, laying hands, healer, baker, craftsman, painter, artist, care taker, working together with other people, coach

Day energy

Power of Manifestation
The vital energy of your hands

More or less everything which we can touch has been manufactured by human hands. We need our hands to put the alarm clock off, to create delicious food, to type on the keyboards, to steer the wheel (of our life), to dig a hole, to hold a book, to wave to someone and to fill out our tax return.

A good day for ...
To start something new, to realize a project, to bake a cake, to cook, to perform handicraft work, to draw, paint, form, etc. Or we use our hands to cuddle, cherish, touch, hold, massage, heal or bless someone.

08
GELBER STERN
Yellow Star
LAMAT

Geburtssiegel

**Schönheit | Anmut
Kunst | Balance
Harmonie | Ausgleich
Vollendung | Reife**

Lichtweisheit
Kunst & Kultur, Harmonie, soziale Aktivitäten, Sinn für Schönheit/Eleganz, Reifeprozesse, Perfektion, künstlerische Tätigkeiten, Qualitätskontrolle, immer das Beste anstrebend

Schattenweisheit
Selbstzweifel, unbestimmt, Lektionen der Disharmonie, das Gefühl, vom Göttlichen getrennt oder am falschen Platz zu sein, verurteilen, Dogmatismus, gefangen in Mustern, Trägheit, das Gefühl von Wertlosigkeit, nach dem Wertlosen greifen

Potentiale/Berufe
Kunst/Künstlerin, Kunsthandel, Feng Shui Beraterin, Raumgestalter, Coiffeur, Beauty, Pediküre, Styleberaterin

Tagesenergie

Die Kraft der Ästhetik
Die Harmonie in allem

Wenn Zeit tatsächlich eine Energie ist, die vor allem harmonische und rhythmische Eigenschaften aufweist, müsste ja alles, was durch die Zeit entsteht, ebenfalls harmonisch und ästhetisch sein. Ein Blick in die Natur zeigt, dass dem so ist. Und da wir ebenfalls ein Teil der Natur sind, ist auch unsere physische Erscheinung ein lebendiges Kunstwerk.

Guter Tag für ...
Einen Besuch im Museum, ein Gemälde länger zu betrachten, Musik zu hören oder zu machen, in einem Gedichtband zu lesen, selber zu zeichnen und zu malen, Feng Shui im eigenen Haus anzuwenden und loszulassen was nicht mehr wirklich nützlich und schön ist. Ästhetik und Proportionen zu studieren.

Birth seal

**Beauty | Grace | Art
Balance | Harmony
Equilibrium | Perfection
Maturity**

Light Wisdom
Art & culture, harmony, social activities, sense of beauty/elegance, maturing processes, perfection, artistic activities, quality control, always striving for the best

Shadow Wisdom
Self-doubt, indeterminate, lessons of disharmony, the feeling of being separated from the divine or being in the wrong place, condemning, dogmatism, trapped in patterns, laziness, the feeling of worthlessness, reaching for the worthless

Potentials/professions
art/artist, art trade, Feng Shui consultant, interior designer, hairdresser, beauty, pedicure, style consultant, landscape architect, graphic designer, photographer

Day energy

The Power of aesthetics
The harmony in everything

If time is indeed an energy that has above all harmonious and rhythmic characteristics, then everything that is created by time should also be harmonious and aesthetic. A look into nature shows that this is indeed the case. And since we are also part of nature, our physical appearance is also a living work of art.

A good day for ...
A visit to the museum to look at a painting, to listen to music or to make music, to read in a volume of poems, to draw and paint yourself, to apply Feng Shui in your own house and to let go of what is no longer really useful and beautiful. To study aesthetics and proportions. To take a walk in nature and to marvel about the creating force behind every flower, tree and butterfly. To hum, sound, sing or even play an instrument.

**09
ROTER MOND
Red Moon
MULUC**

Geburtssiegel

**Wasser | Reinigung
Blut | Flow | Lymphe
Identität | Seelenkraft
Blockadenbrecher**

Lichtweisheit
Reinigende Kraft, wahre Identität, authentische Gefühle, Aufmerksamkeit, gesundes Blutbild, Aktivität, in Bewegung sein, Fliessprinzip, tanzen, sich gehen lassen, loslassen

Schattenweisheit
Unredliche Gedanken und Gefühle, unbewusstes Handeln, Ego-Probleme, Selbstzerstörungstendenzen, sein Licht verstecken, Hindernis für andere, nutzlos herumstehen, Gefühl im Stau zu stehen, kraftverschleissende Tätigkeiten, Disharmonie erzeugen

Potentiale/Berufe
Psychotherapeutin, Psychologie, Beratung, Perkussion, Schwimmlehrerin, Reinigungsgeschäft, Tanzlehrer, Tanzen

Tagesenergie

Die Kraft der Emotionen
Alles fliesst!

Der Rote Mond steht primär für das Prinzip «Flow»: alles fliesst. Wie beim Mond geht es auch bei diesem Archetypen um alles, was mit Fliessen und Strömen zu tun hat. Vom Wasser in unserem Körper, in unseren Zellen, zwischen den Zellen, dem Blut, den Lymphen, der Rückenmarkflüssigkeit bis hin zu den Tränen, die fliessen.

Guter Tag für ...
Einen intensiven Hausputz, Auto waschen, Zimmer aufräumen, Pflanzen entstauben, ein Bad nehmen, sich reinigen und schön machen, sich entgiften, Feng Shui im eigenen Haus, ausgeliehene Dinge zurückbringen. Weiter alle Tätigkeiten, die einem rasch in einen «flow» Zustand hineinbringen, wie zum Beispiel Trommeln, Tanzen, Singen, Mantras rezitieren, etc.

Birth seal

**Water | Cleaning
Purification | Blood
Flow | Lymph | Identity
Soul power | Blockade
Breaker**

Light Wisdom
Cleansing power, true identity, authentic feelings, attention, healthy blood count, activity, being in motion, flow principle, dancing, letting go, surrender

Shadow Wisdom
Dishonest thoughts and feelings, unconscious acting, ego problems, self-destructive tendencies, hiding one's light, obstacle for others, standing around uselessly, feeling stuck in a traffic jam, power-wearing-out activities, creating disharmony

Potentials/professions
Psychotherapist, psychology, counseling, percussion, swimming instructor, cleaning business, dance instructor, dancing

Day energy

The Power of emotions
Everything flows!

The Red Moon primarily stands for the principle «flow»: everything flows. As with the moon, this archetype is also about everything that has to do with flows and streams. From the water in our body, in our cells, between the cells, the blood, the lymphs, the spinal cord fluid to the tears that flow.

A good day for ...
An intensive house cleaning, washing the car, cleaning the rooms, dusting the plants, taking a bath, cleaning yourself and making yourself beautiful, detoxifying yourself, Feng Shui in your own house, bringing back borrowed things. Furthermore, all activities that quickly bring you into a «flow» state, such as drumming, dancing, singing, reciting mantras, etc.

**10
WEISSER HUND
White Dog
OC**

Geburtssiegel

(Selbst) Liebe | Freundschaft | Loyalität | Herz Gefühle | Treue | Geduld

Lichtweisheit
Beziehungen, Gefühlstiefe, Verbundenheit, starke Loyalität, unterstützen, begleiten, führen (lassen), Freude am Leben, sich um etwas kümmern

Schattenweisheit
Einengende & kontrollierende Beziehungen, besitzergreifend, Neid, Egoismus, Dramen erzeugen, kompliziertes Leben, andere hintergehen und (Selbst-) Betrug, Aggressionen, sich zuviel zumuten, die Probleme anderer tragen, sich nicht abgrenzen können

Potentiale / Berufe
Kinderkrippe, Hundebetreuer, Paartherapeutin, Sexualtherapeut, Arbeit mit Menschen und Tieren

Tagesenergie

Die Kraft der Liebe
Liebe ist die stärkste Kraft

Der weisse Hund erinnert uns daran, dass ohne Liebe gar nichts läuft. Obwohl wir alle wissen, dass es die Schwerkraft/Gravitation gibt, kann kein Wissenschaftler erklären, warum sie da ist! Unter den spirituell Suchenden ist die Gravitation nichts anders als die bedingungslose Liebe, die möchte, dass alles wieder zusammenkommt und sich daher gegenseitig anzieht.

Guter Tag für …
Freundschaften pflegen, einen Freund besuchen, jemanden zum Tee einladen, mit dem Hund spazieren gehen, auf unbekannte Menschen zugehen, mit dem Nachbarn plaudern, mit dem Partner ins Kino/Essen gehen.

Birth seal

(Self) Love | Friendship Loyalty | Heart | Feelings | Fidelity | Patience Protection | Security

Light Wisdom
Relationships, friendships, depth of feeling, solidarity, strong loyalty, support, accompany, leading, guiding, joy of life, taking care of something, devotion

Shadow Wisdom
Constricting & controlling relationships, possessive, envy, selfishness, creating dramas, complicated life, undermining others, (self) deception, aggression, too much to put oneself through, bearing the problems of others, unable to distance oneself from others, to subdue oneself

Potentials / professions
Crèche, dog caregiver, couple therapist, sex therapist, work with people and animals, doctor, safeguard

Day energy

The Power of love
Love is the strongest force

The white dog reminds us that nothing works without love. Although we all know that gravity exists, no scientist can explain why it exists! Among spiritual seekers, gravity is nothing other than unconditional love, which wants everything to come back together and attract and support each other.

A good day for …
To cultivate friendships, to visit a friend, to invite someone for tea, to go for a walk with the dog, to approach unknown people, to chat with the neighbor, to go to the cinema/to eat with the partner, to help someone cross the street.

**11
BLAUER AFFE
Blue Monkey
CHUEN**

Geburtssiegel

**Spielen | Humor
Inneres Kind | Magie
Illusionen | Fröhlichkeit
Lebensfreude**

Lichtweisheit
Leichtigkeit, verspielte Magie, mit den Illusionen spielen, Kreativität, Lachen, erfinden, Schabernack, (ver-)zaubern, lustvoll, verspielte Form der Sexualität

Schattenweisheit
Fehlender Humor, unflexibel, zynisch und sarkastisch, emotionale Distanziertheit, Verschwiegenheit, Traurigkeit, zu grosse Ernsthaftigkeit, lebensmüde, lustlos

Potentiale/Berufe
Arbeit mit Kindern und Jugendlichen, Komiker, Geschichtenerzähler, Clown, Coach, Zauberer, Sexualtherapeutin, Lehrer

Tagesenergie

Die Kraft des Spiels
Ein bisschen mehr «Uga uga»

Der blaue Affe ist das innere, göttliche Kind. Dieses möchte spielen, lachen, kreativ sein, Feste feiern und ab und zu «den Affen tanzen lassen». In den ersten Lebensjahren lernen Kinder die Welt spielend und spielerisch kennen. Sie erforschen ohne Ängste und Tabus, loten ihre Grenzen aus und sorgen durchaus ab und zu für Chaos (und neue Ordnungen).

Guter Tag für ...
Ein Spiel mit Freunden, auf den Jahrmarkt gehen und auf vielen Bahnen Runden drehen, Kinder hüten und sich von ihrer Phantasie anstecken lassen, ein spontanes (Geburtstags-)Fest feiern, Brainstorming für unkonventionelle Ideen, einen neuen Witz erfinden und möglichst vielen weitererzählen, neue Spiele erfinden, Schabernack treiben, jemanden auf den Arm nehmen.

Birth seal

Play | Humor | Inner Child | Magic | Illusions | Happiness | Joie de vivre | Life Artist | Creativity | Unpredictability

Light Wisdom
Lightness, playful magic, playing with illusions, creativity, laughter, inventing, joking, enchant, lustful, playful form of sexuality, every form of creativity and artwork, unpredictable actions to enchant people

Shadow Wisdom
Lack of humor, inflexible, cynical and sarcastic, emotional distance, concealment, sadness, too much seriousness, weary of life, listless, feeling uninspired

Potentials / professions
Working with children and teenagers, comedians, storytellers, clowns, coaches, magicians, sex therapists, teachers, artists, street performers

Day energy

The Power of playing
A little bit more «Uga uga»

The blue monkey is the inner, divine child. He wants to play, laugh, be creative, celebrate parties and «let the monkey dance» from time to time. In the first years of life kids get to know the world in a playful way. They explore without fears and taboos, find out their limits and sometimes cause chaos (and new orders).

A good day for ...
A game with friends, going to the fair and doing rounds on many tracks, taking care of children and to let your imagination get infected by them celebrate a spontaneous (birthday) party, brainstorm for unconventional ideas, invent a new joke and pass it on to as many people as possible, invent new games, make fun of someone.

**12
GELBER MENSCH
Yellow Human
EB**

Geburtssiegel

**Freier Wille | Einfluss
Weisheit | Aufmerksamkeit | Dualität | Macht
Führung**

Lichtweisheit
Souveränität, Mitschöpferkraft, Meisterschaft, Polarität überwinden, Willensstärke, Führungsqualitäten, Individualität, überwinden von Karma, lösungsorientiert, absichtsvoll, Verantwortung übernehmen, mit beiden Beinen auf dem Boden stehen

Schattenweisheit
Gefangen im Werten und Verurteilen, Überbewertung des Verstandes, Machtgebahren, Emotionen unterdrücken, auf Negativität fokussiert sein, sich festbeissen, andere überfordern

Potentiale/Berufe
Influencer, Geschäftsführer, Politiker, Coach, Projektleiter

Tagesenergie

Die Kraft der Entscheidung
Wo ein Wille ist, ist ein Weg

Der Gelbe Mensch mit seinem vorstehenden Zahn ist das Symbol für unsere Willenskraft, für unsere Ausdauer, für den «Biss», welchen wir im Leben ab und zu benötigen, um eine Aufgabe zu vollenden. Der Gelbe Mensch erinnert uns daran, dass wir mit jeder Entscheidung, sei sie noch so klein, neue Welten erschaffen.

Guter Tag für ...
Bewusst Entscheidungen fällen, die Weichen für unser weiteres Leben stellen, eine Firma oder Familie gründen, ein Projekt initiieren, unsere Meinung ausdrücken, ein grösseres Problem lösen, Bündnisse eingehen, klare Anweisungen geben, Einfluss nehmen (auf Prozesse, Gemeinschaften, Politik, etc.). Yin/Yang (Polaritäten) zu studieren und im Alltag meisterhaft anzuwenden.

Birth seal

**Free will | Influence
Wisdom | Attention
Duality | Power
Leadership | Mastery
Sacred Path of Life
Protector**

Light Wisdom
Sovereignty, creative power, mastery (over polarity), overcoming duality, strength of will, leadership qualities, individuality, overcoming karma, solution-oriented, full of intentions, assuming responsibility, standing with both feet on the ground, focus, walk the talk, knowing the sacred path of life

Shadow Wisdom
Caught in values and condemnation, overestimation of the intellect, power behavior, suppressing emotions, being focused on negativity, biting oneself down, overtaxing others, dominate, controlling behavior

Potentials/professions
Influencer, Managing Director, Politician, Coach, Project Manager, (Mountain) Guide, Aikido Sensei, Teacher

Day energy

The Power of decision
Where there is a will, there is a way

The Yellow Human with his protruding tooth is the symbol for our willpower, for our perseverance, for the «bite» that we sometimes need in life to complete a task. The Yellow Human reminds us that with every decision, no matter how small, we create new worlds.

A good day for ...
Make conscious decisions, set the course for our future life, found a company or family, initiate a project, express your opinion, solve a bigger problem, form alliances, give clear instructions, influence (on processes, communities, politics, etc.). To study Yin/Yang (polarities) and apply them masterfully in everyday life.

**13
ROTER HIMMELSWANDERER
Red Skywalker
BEN**

Geburtssiegel

**Freiheit | Forschen
Ausdehnung | Raum
Grenzenlos | Universell**

Lichtweisheit
Möglichkeiten erkennen, Grenzen überschreiten, Entdecker, Freiheit, reisen, mit Traditionen brechen, herausfordern, Abenteuerlust, ausprobieren und forschen, überwinden

Schattenweisheit
Angst vor Unbekanntem, Engegefühl, unbeweglich, Wunsch nach Zurückgezogenheit, Einsamkeit, Burnout, asozial, verbittert, kleinlich, Vertrauen in sich verlieren, Hoffnungslosigkeit, Zukunftsängste, unsicher, sich an Bekanntes klammern

Potentiale / Berufe
Forscher, Reisebegleiter, Kunst- und Kulturvermittler, Mediator, Raumgestalter, Heilpraxisleiterin

Tagesenergie

Die Kraft der Freiheit
Das Erforschen des Raums

Der Rote Himmelswanderer möchte den Raum erforschen, Grenzen überschreiten und Neues kennenlernen. Er ist der Nomade unter den Archetypen, der immer bereit ist für ein weiteres Abenteuer. Seine Neugier ist unersättlich und jeder einzelne Moment birgt für ihn die Gelegenheit, sein Wissen zu erweitern und neue Erfahrungen zu machen.

Guter Tag für …
Einen ausgedehnten Spaziergang oder eine Wanderung durch neue Gebiete, eine Reise planen oder antreten, draussen übernachten, ein neues Restaurant ausprobieren, auf Unbekannte zugehen und ein Gespräch beginnen, Fremdsprachen lernen, sich mit anderen Kulturen beschäftigen.

Birth seal

**Freedom | Research
Expansion | Freedom
Exchange | Travel
Guidance | (Virtual) Space | Boundless | Global
Universal | Home**

Light Wisdom
Recognizing possibilities, crossing borders, discoverers, freedom, traveling, breaking with traditions, challenging, adventurous, trying out and researching, overcoming hurdles, stability, exchanging ideas, cultural exchange, remote viewing, dreamworlds

Shadow Wisdom
Fear of the unknown, tightness, immobility, desire for withdrawal, loneliness, burnout, asocial, bitter, petty, losing confidence in oneself, hopelessness, fear of the future, insecure, clinging to one's acquaintance, loosing oneself in virtual realities,

Potentials / professions
Researcher, travel companion, art and culture mediator, mediator, interior designer, scientist, flight attendant, pilot, bus or taxi driver, mountain guide

Day energy

The Power of freedom
Exploring space

The Red Skywalker wants to explore space, cross borders and get to know new things. He is the nomad among the archetypes who is always ready for another adventure. His curiosity is insatiable and every single moment gives him the opportunity to broaden his knowledge and experience.

A good day for …
Take a long walk or a hike through new areas, plan or start a journey, spend the night outside, try out a new restaurant, approach unknown people and start a conversation, learn foreign languages, deal with other cultures.

14
WEISSER MAGIER
White Wizard
IX

Geburtssiegel

Magie | Verzaubern
Zeitlosigkeit | Schamane
Geschichtenerzähler
Jaguar

Lichtweisheit
Schöpferische Kraft, Integrität, Brücke zu den Anderswelten, Herzwissen, Aufnahmefähigkeit, Lichtträger, intuitives Wissen und Handeln, Zauberer, Künstlerin, Lehrer

Schattenweisheit
Persönliche Macht und Kontrolle, egoistisches Handeln, Bestätigung im Aussen suchen, Sarkasmus, Wissen und Können missbrauchen, (sich selber) beschwindeln, komplexe und verwickelte Beziehungen, kopflastig, verschlossen, reizbar

Potentiale / Berufe
Lehrer, Künstler, Vermittler, Mediator, Coach, Psychologie, Heilerberufe, Stadt-Schamane, Change-Maker

Tagesenergie

Die Kraft der Magie
Avrah kh'davra (aramäisch)
I create as I speak

Der Weisse Magier ist der Brückenbauer (Antakarana), welcher Menschen, Kulturen, Völker, Kontinente, Welten und Dimensionen verbindet. Die Brücke ist eine Metapher für das Herz, respektive die Liebe. Denn seine Liebe zur Schöpfung ist es, die alles mit allem verbindet.

Guter Tag für ...
So gut wie alles! Denn wer in jedem einzelnen Augenblick die Magie der Schöpfung erkennen/erblicken kann, für den ist alles magisch! So einfach ist das. Für alle anderen gilt: Übung macht den Meister. Werde Harry Potter Jr., der Zauberlehrling. Mache heute eine Räucherung (Essenzen, Öle, Kräuter, etc.), lies ein Buch über Magie, schnitze dir einen Zauberstab/Stock, erstelle einen kleinen Steinkreis in deinem Garten, zeichne/male verschiedene magische Symbole (OM, Sri Yantra, Blume des Lebens, etc.).

Birth seal

Magic | Enchant
Timelessness | Shaman
Storyteller | Mediator
Mystic | Divination |
Spiritual Power
Intuition | Cosmic Artist

Light Wisdom
Creative power, integrity, bridge to other worlds, heart knowledge, receptivity, light carrier, intuitive knowledge and action, cosmic wisdom, magician, artist, teacher, guide, prayer and meditation, introspection and contemplation, clairvoyance, sense giver

Shadow Wisdom
Personal power and control, selfish action, seeking external confirmation, sarcasm, abusing knowledge and ability, deceiving, complex and intricate relationships, top-heavy, closed, irritable, manipulating, lying, prideful, being distracted by the outer world, superficial

Potentials / professions
Teacher, Artist, Mediator, Coach, Psychology, Healing professions, City Shaman, change maker, horse whisperer, peacemaker

Day energy

The Power of magic
Avrah kh'davra (Aramaic)
I create as I speak

The White Magician is the bridge builder (Antakarana) who connects people, cultures, peoples, continents, worlds and dimensions. The bridge is a metaphor for the heart, or rather love. Because it is his love for creation that connects everything with everything.

A good day for ...
Just about everything! Because whoever, in every single moment, combines the magic of creation, for him everything is magical! It is as simple as that. For all others, practice makes perfect. Become Harry Potter Jr., the sorcerer's apprentice. Do a smoking today (essences, oils, herbs, etc.), read a book about magic, carve a magic wand / stick, create a small stone circle in your garden, draw/paint different magic symbols (OM, Sri Yantra, flower of life, etc.).

**15
BLAUER ADLER
Blue Eagle
MEN**

Geburtssiegel

Macht | Vision Kollektiv | Erschaffen Verstand | Übersicht Fokus

Lichtweisheit
Eigenverantwortung, planetare Aufgabe, kollektiver Geist & Wissen, Vision, eindrückliche Taten, Engagement für das Kollektiv, selbstloser Dienst, Träume, Selbstbewusstsein

Schattenweisheit
Überheblichkeit, Helfersyndrom, Machtgehabe, Mangel an Hoffnung und eigener Meinung, Illusionen nachjagen, sich in etwas festkrallen, nicht loslassen können, nicht nein sagen können, ehrgeizig, realitätsflüchtig, Boden unter den Füssen verlieren

Potentiale/Berufe
Lektorin, Trendforscher, Visionär, Think-Thank Leiter, Geschäftsführer

Tagesenergie

Die Kraft der Vision
Ich sehe, also bin ich

Auf den Magier folgend erhebt sich die «Galaktische Entwicklungsgeschichte» in höchste Höhen mit dem Blauen Adler, dem König der Lüfte. Der Adler überblickt alles in seinem Zuständigkeitsrevier und darüber hinaus. Somit schaut er über seinen Horizont hinaus und übernimmt freiwillig eine grössere Verantwortung.

Guter Tag für …
An Blauen-Adler-Tagen haben wir die besten Voraussetzungen, mal wieder so richtig abzuheben. Heute sind Höhenflüge erlaubt, denn der Adler möchte, dass wir uns einen Überblick erschaffen, das Gelände erkunden, uns an die Träume erinnern, mit den Wolken sprechen, Visionen haben. Unternimm eine Wanderung auf einen Berg und geniesse die Aussicht, den Überblick und die Weitsicht. Mache das gleiche (im Geist) mit Alltagsproblemen oder Aufgaben.

Birth seal

Power | Vision | Collective | Community | Kingdom | Ethics | Create Mind | Intellect | Focus | Authority | Choice | Fly

Light Wisdom
Personal responsibility, planetary task, collective mind & knowledge, vision, impressive actions, commitment to the collective, selfless service, (lucid) dreams, self-consciousness, self-confidence, wealth, clarity and profound understanding, natural authority, influence, guiding and protecting, bringing good fortune

Shadow Wisdom
Arrogance, power behavior, lack of hope, chasing after illusions, to cling to something, not being able to let go, ambitious, volatile in reality, losing ground under your feet, fearful, impulsively, bad habits, being controlled or influenced, uncertain

Potentials/professions
Proofreader, trend researcher, visionary, Think-Thank, director, pilot, business strategist, medium, king or queen

Day energy

The Power of visionI
I see, so I am

Following the magician, the «Galactic History of Development» rises to the highest heights with the Blue Eagle, the King of the Air. The eagle overlooks everything in its area of responsibility and beyond. Thus he looks beyond his horizon and voluntarily assumes a greater responsibility.

A good day for …
On Blue Eagle days we have the best conditions to take off again. Today, high flights are allowed, because the eagle wants us to create an overview, to explore the terrain, to remember our dreams, to talk to the clouds, to have visions. Make a walk on a mountain and enjoy the view, the overview and the far view. Do the same (in your mind) with everyday tests or tasks.

16
GELBER KRIEGER
Yellow Warrior
CIB

Geburtssiegel

Angstlosigkeit | Intelligenz | Fragen | Reife | Bewusstsein | Mut | Führer

Lichtweisheit
Harmonie von Herz & Verstand, Integrationsfähigkeit, Selbstvergebung, Schutz, Führungsbewusstsein, intuitives Handeln, Unterrichten, mutig & selbstbewusst sein, Suvuyasurferin

Schattenweisheit
Mangelndes (Ur-)Vertrauen in inneres Wissen & Fähigkeiten, Überlebenskampf, Ängste, fehlendes Urteilsvermögen, Unentschlossenheit, Wankelmut, Naivität, unsicher sein

Potentiale / Berufe
Forstwart, Flüchtlingshelfer, Aktivist für eine bessere Welt, Journalist, Romanschreiber, Führungskraft, Politiker, Vorbild

Tagesenergie

Die Kraft der Wahrheit
«Nur die Wahrheit ist wahr» aus: «Ein Kurs in Wundern»

Zurück auf der Erde übernimmt der Gelbe Krieger das Zepter. Er ist der vollendete Mensch. Er ist ein Krieger des Lichtes, ausgerüstet mit dem Schwert der Wahrheit. Er kennt die Spielregeln und lebt nach ihnen. Mit seinem Schwert «Excalibur» beschützt er alles Lebendige und ist bereit, sein Leben dafür herzugeben, weil er weiss, dass seine Seele unsterblich ist.

Guter Tag für ...
Raus in die Natur, Bäume umarmen, unter einer Eiche meditieren, mit nackten Füssen auf Moos gehen. Die Berührung mit der Natur schenkt dem Krieger neue Energie. Die Tiere sind seine Freunde, er hat vor nichts Angst. Wo andere Probleme sehen, sieht er nur Lösungen. Doch er drängt sie keinem auf. Sitz in einem Café und strahle dein Licht in alle Richtungen. Falls du angesprochen wirst, bleibe wahrhaftig.

Birth seal

Fearlessness | Intelligence | Questions | Maturity | Consciousness | Courage | Guide Wisdom | Ancestors | Respect | Integrity | Compassion | Power | Joy

Light Wisdom
Harmony of heart & mind, integration ability, self-forgiveness, protection, leadership, intuitive and responsible acting, teaching, courageous & self-confident, connected with the ancestors and their wisdom, respectful, compassion and empathy, asks profound questions

Shadow Wisdom
Lack of trust in inner knowledge & abilities, struggle for survival, fears, lack of judgement, inconclusiveness, fickleness, naivety, uncertainty, envy and hate, disconnected, unconscious acting, holding a grudge, want to take revenge, sticking to the past, immovable

Potentials / professions
Forest warden, refugee helper, activist, journalist, leader, politician, judge, police officer, teacher

Day energy

The Power of truth
«Only the truth is true» from «A Course in Miracles»

Back on Earth, the Yellow Warrior takes the scepter. He is the perfect man. He is a warrior of light, equipped with the sword of truth. He knows the rules of the game and lives by them. With his sword «Excalibur» he protects all life and is willing to give his life for it, because he knows that his soul is immortal.

A good day for ...
Out into nature, hug trees, meditate under an oak tree, walk on moss with bare feet. The contact with nature gives the warrior new energy. The animals are his friends, he is not afraid of anything. Where others see problems, he only sees solutions. But he does not impose them on anyone. Sit in a café and shine your light in all directions. If you are addressed, remain truthful.

**17
ROTE ERDE
Red Earth
CABAN**

Geburtssiegel

Evolution | Synchronizität | Kollektiv | Navigation | Vernunft | Sozial

Lichtweisheit
Gegenwärtigkeit, Synchronizität, sich führen lassen, Urvertrauen, naturverbunden, aufgeschlossen, zentriert, die Träume im Leben umsetzen, intuitives Handeln

Schattenweisheit
Naturfern, fehlendes Urvertrauen, innere Stimme/Führung nicht hören, herumirren, vorschnelles Folgern, Zerstörungswut, nicht zentriert sein, sich in der Zukunft/Vergangenheit verlieren, von Träumen überwältigt sein, streitlustig

Potentiale/Berufe
Soziale Berufe, Lehrerin, Forstwart, Gärtner, Gartenpflege, Gruppenleiterin, Naturpädagoge, Waldkindergarten, Landart

Tagesenergie

Die Kraft der Synchronisation
Synchronizität ist eine Realität

Mutter Erde ist ein lebendiges Wesen, das alle seine Mitbewohner/innen kennt und liebt. Genau so wie wir wissen, wo wir uns kratzen müssen, wenn es uns zwickt, weiss «Terra Gaia» von jedem einzelnen Lebewesen, wo es sich zurzeit aufhält und wie es sich fühlt.

Guter Tag für ...
Begegnungen mit der Natur. Ob einfach nur draussen im Garten oder bei einem ausgedehnten Spaziergang im Stadtwald, Hauptsache wir hören die Vögel zwitschern und atmen frische Luft. Die Erde versorgt uns mit allem, was wir brauchen. Mach dir einen feinen, frischen Salat, ein Gemüse oder Früchte-Smoothie und leg dich einfach mal draussen auf den Rasen. Die Geräusche der Natur haben alle ein riesiges Oberton-Frequenz-Spektrum, welche heilsam für Psyche und Körper sind. Laufe barfuss herum.

Birth seal

Evolution | Synchronicity Inner Rhythms | Collective | Wisdom | Memory Navigation | Rationality Social | Patience | Guidance | Introspection

Light Wisdom
Presence, synchronicity, letting oneself be guided, basic trust, nature-loving, open-minded, centered, realizing dreams in life, intuitive action, eduction, counseling and advising, collective intelligence, circadian time, introspection and meditation, councils and gatherings, divine matrix, morphogenetic field

Shadow Wisdom
Far from nature, lack of basic trust, not listening to the inner voice/leadership, wandering around, hasty reasoning, destructive rage, not being centered, losing oneself in the future/past, overwhelmed by dreams, stagnant sentiments, unorganized

Potentials/professions
Social professions, teacher, forest warden, gardener, group leader, nature pedagogue, landscape art, group process facilitator

Day energy

The Power of synchronization
Synchronicity is the guiding force

Mother Earth is a living being that knows and loves all its fellow inhabitants. Exact just as we know where we have to scratch ourselves when it pinches us, «Terra Gaia» knows about every single creature where it is at the moment and how it feels.

A good day for ...
Encounters with nature. Whether simply outside in the garden or during a long walk in the forest, the main thing is that we hear the birds chirping and breathe fresh air. The earth provides us with everything we need. Make yourself a fine, fresh salad, a vegetable or fruit smoothie and simply lie outside on the lawn. The sounds of nature all have a huge overtone frequency spectrum, which is healing for the psyche and body. Run around barefoot.

**18
WEISSER SPIEGEL
White Mirror
ETZNAB**

Geburtssiegel

Klarheit | Selbsterkenntnis | Reflexion Ordnung | Struktur Raumlosigkeit

Lichtweisheit
Unterscheidungsfähigkeit, Weisheit, Wahrhaftigkeit, Klarheit, Struktur, geschickt, gesellig, Zeitlosigkeit, Selbstreflexion, kritisch, erkennend

Schattenweisheit
Illusionen, Selbstzweifel, übermässiges Kritisieren, Projektionen auf andere, unklar sein, sich verlieren in Details, unnötige Schärfe & Strenge im Alltag, unerledigte Arbeiten, Wahrnehmungslücken, innere und äussere Zwänge & Muster

Potentiale / Berufe
Coach, Entwicklungshelfer, Psychologie, Berufsberater, Planung, Feng Shui

Tagesenergie

Die Kraft der Reflektion
Spieglein, Spieglein an der Wand

Wer sich erkennen möchte, braucht nur tief in den Spiegel hineinzuschauen. Mit der Zeit wird dir die Tiefe des Spiegels bewusst und du erkennst, dass du endlos und ewig bist. «Erkenne dich selbst» lautete die Inschrift beim Orakel von Delphi. Der Weisse Spiegel zeigt dir unbestechlich, wer du bist, jederzeit und überall.

Guter Tag für ...
Auch wenn es keinen einzelnen Moment gibt, in welchem der Archetyp des Weissen Spiegels nicht aktiv ist, so sind die Reflexionen an diesen Tagen besonders klar, eindeutig, unübersehbar und immer hilfreich, manchmal schmerzhaft, jedoch nur für das sterbende EGO. Schaue bewusst einen Film und erkenne dich in allen Figuren oder besuche ein Café und verbinde dich im Geist mit allen anwesenden Gästen und sag zu dir: «Das (Der/Die) bin ich auch»!

Birth seal

Clarity | Self-Knowledge Reflection | Order Structure | Spacelessness | Truth | Healing Light | Resolution

Light Wisdom
Discrimination, wisdom, truthfulness, clarity, structure, skillful, sociable, self-reflection, endlessness, critical, discerning, polishing, purification, depth, reality, recognition, sharpness, Insight

Shadow Wisdom
Illusions, self-doubt, excessive criticism, projections on others, being unclear, losing oneself in details, unnecessary severity in everyday life, unfinished work, gaps in perception, inner and outer constraints & patterns, lack of clarity, self-deceiving, unethical, falsehood, deception, mental illness, mental suffering, lying, foggy, toxic thoughts and patterns

Potentials / professions
Coach, development worker, psychology, psychiatrist, professional consultant, planning, Feng Shui, healer, surgeon, diplomacy, politician, journalist, interviewer, hypnotist,

Day energy

The Power of reflection
Mirror, mirror on the wall

Whoever wants to recognize himself only has to look deep into the mirror. In time you will become aware of the depth of the mirror and you will realize that you are endless and eternal. «Know Yourself» was the inscription on the oracle of Delphi. The White Mirror shows you incorruptibly who you are, anytime and anywhere.

A good day for ...
Even if there is no single moment in which the archetype of the White Mirror is not active, the reflections on these days are particularly clear, unequivocal, unmistakable and always helpful, sometimes painful, but only for the dying EGO. Watch a film consciously and recognize yourself in all the characters or visit a café and connect yourself in spirit with all the guests present and say to yourself: «That's me, too!»

**19
BLAUER STURM
Blue Storm
CAUAC**

Geburtssiegel

Transformation | Katalysator | Energie | Kraft Beschleunigung

Lichtweisheit
Veränderung, Transformation, Befreiung von Identifikationen, (Selbst-)Erneuerung, auflösen, Wiedervereinigung, Ekstase der Freiheit, unbegrenzte Möglichkeiten

Schattenweisheit
Angst vor Veränderung & Unbekanntem, Rastlosigkeit, Realitätsflucht, Verlustangst, Machtmissbrauch, Gewaltanwendung, Zweifel, Unsicherheiten, Suchtverhalten, Desintegration, festhalten an Traditionen, Starrheit, Sturheit

Potentiale / Berufe
Heilerberufe, (Business-)Coach, Chemiker, Physiker, Putzinstitut, Ritualbegleiterin, tanzender Derwisch

Tagesenergie

Die Kraft der Transformation
Riders of the Storm

Der Blaue Sturm sorgt auf der zweitletzten Position dieser «Heldenreise» dafür, dass du ordentlich durchgekämmt vor deinen Schöpfer trittst. Falls dein Kleid noch ein paar Schmutzflecken von der vergangenen Reise aufweist, wird es jetzt porentief gewaschen.

Guter Tag für ...
Ob du heute deine Wäsche wäschst oder Seelenhygiene betreibst (heisses Bad, Massage, etc.), es gibt unzählige Arten, wie du deine aktuelle Realität in dein persönliches Paradies umwandeln kannst. Schreib ein paar ausgediente, hinderliche Muster von dir auf ein Papier und verbrenne es dann in einem Feuer. Oder geh intensiv tanzen und drück deine Stimmung durch Bewegung aus. Geh an einen Ort, wo man dich nicht hören kann und schreie alles was du transformieren möchtest, laut heraus.

Birth seal

Transformation | Catalyzer | Energy | Force Acceleration | Vortex Power | Rainstorm | Cell Regeneration | Female Energy | Destruction

Light Wisdom
Change, transformation, liberation from identifications, (self-)renewal, dissolution, reunification, ecstasy of freedom, unlimited possibilities, female energy, spiritual connection, community, life-giving waters, growth, purification, strength and power, midwives, mothers, female healers, sisterhood, well-being

Shadow Wisdom
fear of change & unknown, restlessness, escape from reality, fear of loss, abuse of power, use of violence, doubts, uncertainties, addictive behavior, disintegration, adherence to traditions, rigidity, stubbornness, overpower, overwhelming, floods, destruction

Potentials / professions
Healing professions, coach, chemist, physicist, cleaning institute, ritual companion, dancing dervish

Day energy

The Power of transformation
Riders of the storm

On the second last position of this «Hero's Journey», the Blue Storm ensures that you step in front of your creator, properly combed. If your dress still has a few dirt stains from the past journey, it will now be washed pore-deep.

A good day for ...
Whether you do your laundry today or do soul hygiene (hot bath, massage, etc.), there are countless ways in which you can transform your current reality into your personal paradise. Write a few worn out, obstructive patterns of yourself on a piece of paper and burn it in a fire. Or go dancing intensively and express your mood through movement. Go to a place where one can't hear you and scream out loud everything you want to transform.

**20
GELBE SONNE
Yellow Sun
AHAU**

Geburtssiegel

Bedingungslose Liebe
Feuer | Licht | Leben
Erleuchtung

Lichtweisheit
Ganzheitliche Wahrnehmung, Christusbewusstsein, Erleuchtung, Aufstieg, Vollendung, Mitgefühl, Freude am Leben, Frieden, Kraft des Herzens, Einheit, Verbindung

Schattenweisheit
Begrenzte Liebe durch Kopflastigkeit, unrealistische Erwartungen, Überidentifikation, Intoleranz gegenüber Schwachen, Bevormundung, einengen, kontrollieren, Gefühl fehlerhaft & unvollkommen zu sein, Traurigkeit, Lustlosigkeit, lebensverneinend

Potentiale / Berufe
Sängerin, Schauspielerin, Kinderbetreuer, Ritualbegleiterin, Pfarrer

Tagesenergie

Die Kraft des Erwachens
«Wer nach aussen schaut, träumt. Wer nach innen schaut, erwacht»
C.G. Jung

«Nach Regen folgt Sonnenschein». So simpel diese Volksweisheit ist, so klar zeigt sie auf eine versteckte Wahrheit hin: Alles wiederholt sich zyklisch. Nach Regen folgt Sonne, folgt Regen, folgt Sonne, folgt Regen

Guter Tag für ...
Den Sonnengruss (Surya Namaskar/Yoga) zu praktizieren. Das Leben geniessen, dir einen schönen Tag machen, dir etwas gönnen und dich verwöhnen. Du hast ein weiteres Etappenziel erreicht und darfst dich jetzt einfach unter der Sonne auftanken. Geniesse ihre wärmenden Strahlen, es ist pure Energie. Organisere ein kleines Fest mit guten Freunden und macht ein Feuer im Garten um das Licht im Innen und Aussen zu mehren.

Birth seal

Unconditional Love
Fire | Solar Flares | Light | Life | Courage Heroism | Inspiration Enlightenment

Light Wisdom
Holistic perception, Christ consciousness, enlightenment, ascension, illumination, perfection, compassion, joy of life, leadership, intuitive power, peace, power of heart, unity, connection to everything, gratitude, oneness, universal wisdom, akashic, universal matrix, quantum field, ancestors, knowledge of the past, source of light,

Shadow Wisdom
Limited love through top-heaviness, unrealistic expectations, over-identification, intolerance of the weak, paternalism, control, constrictions, feeling to be flawed & incomplete, sadness, listlessness, life-negating, loosing, emotional and mental struggles, to much ambition, envy, lies, ungrateful, doubtful

Potentials / professions
Singer, actress, child carer, ritual attendant, pastor, guide, teacher, guru

Day energy

The Power of awakening
«He who looks out, dreams. He who looks inside awakens»
C.G. Jung

«After rain follows sunshine». As simple as this folk wisdom is, so clearly it points to a hidden truth: Everything repeats itself cyclically. After rain follows sun, follows rain, follows sun, follows rain ...

A good day for ...
To practice the sun salutation (Surya Namaskar/ Yoga). Enjoy life, have a nice day, treat yourself to something and spoil yourself. You have reached another stage goal and now you can just relax to recharge your batteries in the sun. Enjoy their warmth – the rays, it is pure energy. Organize a small party with good friends and make a fire in the garden to increase the light inside and outside.

13 TÖNE DER SCHÖPFUNG

Die 13'er Welle kann man sich entweder wie eine Sinuswelle vorstellen, die ihren Höhepunkt auf der 7. Position hat (Wellenbauch) oder eher wie eine Meereswelle, die auf der 10. Position ihren Höhepunkt erreicht. Je nach dem passt die eine 0p0oder andere Form besser für dich. Erinnere dich daran, dass die 7. (resonante) Position viel Synchronisation, Resonanz und Empathie (harmonisches Mitschwingen) ermöglicht, während die 10. (planetare) Position das Ergebnis der Welle sichtbar macht. Und ja, letztlich bilden die Wellen eine pulsierende, ewige Spirale. Je länger du surfst, desto harmonischer werden sie.

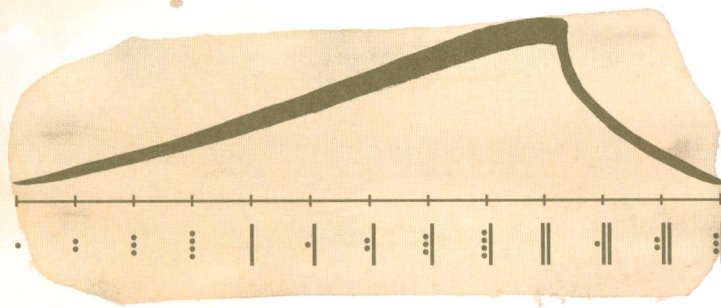

MAGNETISCHER TON HUN

Zweck | Einheit | Absicht

Mit der Eins beginnt alles. Dieser Ton trägt die Kraft für einen Neustart in sich und definiert die Absicht der Welle: Was ist mein Ziel, mein Vorhaben, meine Aufgabe?

LUNARER TON KA

Dualität | Stabilität
Herausforderung

Die Zwei fordert heraus und spannt den Bogen für eine maximale Herausforderung. Denn schliesslich wollen wir über uns hinauswachsen!

ELEKTRISCHER TON OX

Aktivieren | Dienen
Dynamik

Mit der Drei gehts erst richtig los. Die Kraft der Drei ist der Dynamo der Welle. Hier siehst du, wie du das Ganze in Bewegung bringen und anderen dienen kannst!

SELBSTEXISTIERENDER TON KAN

Definieren | Messen | Form

Die Vier ist die formgebende Zahl in jeder Welle. Sie zeigt das Ausmass und die Machbarkeit des Vorhabens auf. Nutze die Klarheit dieser Position für den nächsten Schritt!

OBERTON TON HO

Ermächtigen | Befehlen
Strahlen

Die Fünf ist eine Schlüsselposition innerhalb der 13 Töne. Hier erhält die Welle einen weiteren Energieschub Richtung Manifestation! Die Fünf gilt auch als weibliche Zahl (Pentagramm).

RHYTHMISCHER TON UAK

Organisieren | Balancieren
Gleichgewicht

Mit der Sechs haben wir die Möglichkeit, das Begonnene auszubalancieren und ins Gleichgewicht zu bringen, damit das Ergebnis stimmt. Gleichgewicht ist angesagt.

RESONANTER TON **UK**

**Einstimmen | Inspiration
Kanalisieren**

Die Sieben ist die Mitte der Welle – auf beiden Seiten sechs Positionen. Wer auf dieser Position seine Mitte hält, empfängt weitere Informationen – wie ein eingestimmter (Radio-)Empfänger.

GALAKTISCHER TON **UAXAK**

**Harmonisieren | Modellieren
Integration**

Auf der Position Acht wird unser Vorhaben nochmals geprüft. Sind wir wirklich im Einklang mit unserer Absicht? Dann volle Kraft voraus! Zündung ist angesagt.

SOLARER TON **BOLON**

**Pulsieren | Realisation
Intention**

Eine Position vor dem Ergebnis wird nun definitiv gezündet. Mobilisiere deine Reserven und dehne dich grenzenlos aus wie die Strahlen einer Sonne!

PLANETARER TON **LAHUN**

**Perfektion | Produktion
Verwirklichung**

Es ist soweit! Egal, was bisher gelaufen ist, heute wird das Ergebnis sichtbar. Jetzt kann geerntet und gefeiert werden! Gratulation.

SPEKTRALER TON **HUN LAHUN**

**Auflösen | Befreiung
Integration**

Die Show ist vorbei, nun muss aufgeräumt werden. Auch die Integration des Erlebten ist angesagt! Was hat die Welle mir gebracht? Wo gibt es Verbesserungsmöglichkeiten?

KRISTALLENER TON **KA LAHUN**

**Kooperation | Hingabe
Ausdehnung**

Halt Rückschau: Verbinde dich mit anderen am runden Tisch. Lass die letzten 12 Schritte Revue passieren und tausche dich aus! Denn die Erkenntnisse bringen dich schliesslich weiter.

KOSMISCHER TON **OX LAHUN**

**Transzendieren
Loslassen | Überdauern**

Die Dreizehn möchte, dass du alles loslässt, damit du zum «Magischen Flug» ansetzen kannst und auf der nächsten Welle sogleich weiter surfst. Geniesse dieses Getragen werden – den «Flow».

Legende
1. Dreamspell Name
2. Maya Name
3. Die drei wichtigsten Schlüsselwörter zum Ton
4. Erklärungstext zum Ton

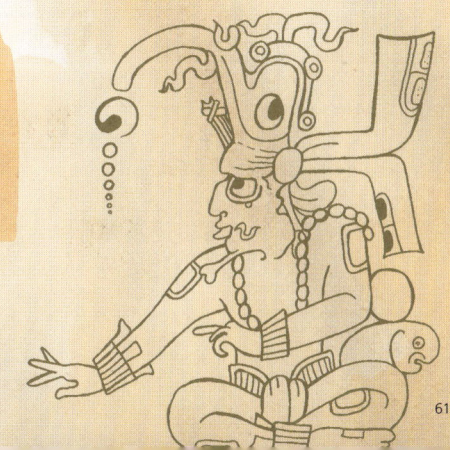

13 TONES OF CREATION

The 13'er wave can be imagined either like a sine wave, which has its climax on the 7th position (wave belly) or rather like a sea wave, which reaches its climax on the 10th position. You can choose which image best suits for you. Remember that the 7th (resonant) position allows much synchronization, resonance and empathy (harmonious resonance), while the 10th (planetary) position makes the result of the wave visible.

And yes, finally the waves form a pulsating, eternal spiral. The longer you surf, the more harmonious they become.

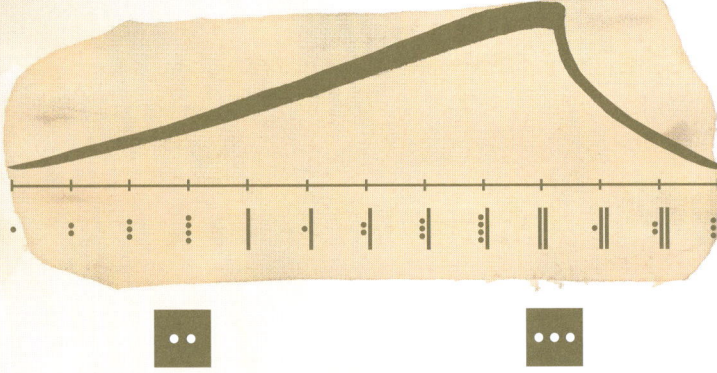

MAGNETIC TONE HUN

Purpose | Unity | Purpose

It all starts with One. This tone carries the power for a new start and defines the intention of the wave: What is my goal, my intention, my task? What do I want to achieve with this wavespell?

LUNAR TONE KA

Duality | Stability | Challenge

The Two challenges and stretches the bow for a maximum challenge. After all, we want to grow beyond ourselves! Ask yourself, what could be the difficulties, where will I be challenged with the wavespell theme?

ELECTRIC TONE OX

Activate | Serve | Dynamics

The Three's only just getting started. The power of the three is the dynamo of the wavespell. Here you can see how you can get the whole thing moving and serve others! But the three is also very volatile (wild) and can also be very challenging. The question about the third tone is: What do my actions look like in this wavespell

SELF-EXISTING TONE KAN

Define | Measure | Form

The Four is the shaping number in each wavespell. It shows the extent and feasibility of the project. Use the clarity of this position for the next step! Think about how you can bring the wavespell theme into a stable structure.

OVERTONE TONE HO

Authorize | Order | Radiance

The Five is a key position within the 13 tones. Here the wavespell receives another energy boost towards manifestation! As the wavespell now gains speed (intensity), the question could be on the fifth day (position): What resources do I need and how can I use them?

RHYTHMIC TONE UAK

Organize | Balance | Equality

With the Six we have the possibilit to balance and bring into equilibri um what has begun, so that the re sult is right! Balance is the order c the day. This day is a good day t prepare for the next steps and to as yourself what the best course shoul be for the next few days, regardles of whether you are planning a pro ject or as example a birthday party.

RESONANT SOUND UK

Attune | Inspiration | Channeling

The Seven is the center of the shaft – on both sides six positions. If you hold your center in this position, you will receive more information – like a tuned (radio) receiver. On this day it is worthwhile to meditate a little and go to «reception». Ask yourself today how you can resonate with the wavespell theme, your project or life at all! Because the Seven offers the possibility to synchronize us optimally with the cosmic rays (e.g. solar winds).

PLANETARY TONE LAHUN

Perfection | Production Realization

It's time! No matter what has been done so far, today the result is visible. Similar to a creative order (e.g. flyer design), the print data has now arrived at the print shop or the office printer and is printed out. Whether a birthday card, a report or a graphic, whether black and white or in color, the tenth day is all about the realization. Look at it and ask yourself if there is anything you can improve.

GALACTIC TONE UAXAK

Harmonize | Model | Integrity

In position eight, our project will be reviewed once again. Are we really in line with our intentions (e.g. wavespell theme)? Check whether your feelings, thoughts and actions are optimally aligned. If yes, then full power ahead!

SPECTRAL TONE HUN LAHUN

Dissolve | Liberation | Integration

The show's over, now it's time to clean up. We let go of the result to make room for a new project. The Spectral Day is therefore ideal for asking what needs to be let go so that the result/project can either continue to grow or be transformed into a new, expanded, larger form.

COSMIC TONE OX LAHUN

Transcend | Let go | Endure

The Thirteen wants you to let go of everything so that you can get ready for the «Magic Flight» and continue surfing on the next wavespell immediately. Therefore I recommend to enjoy this day, to relax and to celebrate what has been achieved, preferably with friends and Zuvuya surfers. Enjoy being carried – the «flow» and receive the gifts, insights and experiences of the past 13 days.

SOLAR TONE BOLON

Pulse | Realize | Intention

A position before the result is now definitely ignited. Mobilize your reserves and expand boundlessly like the rays of a sun! If necessary, take time again for rest and introspection, so that everything runs optimally on the following day. If your feeling tells you that you are ready for the big show, light the rocket.

CRYSTAL TONE KA LAHUN

Cooperation | Devotion Expansion

The Crystal Day is very suitable for a review. If several people were involved (e.g. project, play, etc.) organize a round table. Everyone now has the opportunity to express themselves, praise, criticise or bring in new ideas. The crystal frequency ensures crystal-clear communication and that the essence of the wavespell can be revealed. Suitable questions for the twelfth position could be: What can we (from each other) learn and share?

Caption
1. Dreamspell name
2. Maya name
3. The three most important keywords
4. Details for the tone

WELLENTEXTE

Nachdem du jetzt die 20 Siegel und die 13 Töne im Detail kennengelernt hast, kann es losgehen. Auf den Agendaseiten findest du täglich das Tages°KIN aus dem Dreamspell und dem Longcount. Falls du neu einsteigst, empfehle ich dir, dich zu Beginn hauptsächlich auf den Dreamspell zu fokusieren. Wenn du jedoch nach 2–3 Wochen das Gefühl hast, dass überhaupt nichts synchron und passend ist, wechsle zum Longcount. Letztlich ist es egal, denn alle Zeitspuren führen früher oder später ins «ewige Jetzt».

Gehe am besten so vor, dass du am Morgen nach dem Aufstehen kurz in die Agenda reinschaust, das Tages°KIN anschaust, seinen Namen liest und dazu noch die jeweils drei wichtigsten Schlüsselwörter zum jeweiligen Archetypen und Ton. Dann hast du bereits einen bunten Cocktail an Informationen für deinen Tag: Das Zeichen, der Ton, der vollständige Name, die Farbe und insgesamt sechs Schlüsselwörter. Das ganze dauert keine Minute und dein Bewusstsein ist bereits «imprägniert» und es liegt an dir, WAS du jetzt mit diesen Informationen machst. Halte einfach die Augen offen nach Menschen, Situationen, Produkten, Farben, Zeitschriften, etc. die etwas mit dem Tages°KIN zu tun haben. Damit synchronisierst du dich bereits mit der Tagesenergie.

Meine persönliche Empfehlung ist ausserdem, das Zeichen tagsüber immer mal wieder zu zeichnen. Entweder auf ein Post-IT im Büro, auf eine Serviette im Restaurant oder ein Papier wenn du zu Hause bist. Dadurch tauchst du noch schneller ins Zuvuya°Surfen ein.

Für den absoluten Flow benötigst du jetzt nur noch ein bisschen zusätzliches Wissen über die 13'er Wellen (Wavespells), die ununterbrochen ablaufen und nicht nur auf dein Leben, sondern auf alles Leben in unserem Universum einwirken.

Immer, wenn du im Agendateil ein Zeichen mit einem Punkt (= Magnetischer Ton) siehst, beginnt eine neue 13'er Welle. Such dann einfach den passenden Wellentext (im externen Booklet), damit du optimal auf die nächsten 13 Tage vorbereitet bist. Zuerst gibt es jeweils die drei wichtigsten Themen in Stichworten, anschliessend folgt der ausführliche Beschrieb.

Ausserdem empfehle ich dir meine Wellenvideos auf unserem Youtube und Vimeo Kanal.

> www.vimeo.com/zuvuya
> youtube.com > u.r.s. jOsé zuber

WAVESPELLS

Now that you have gotten to know the 20 seals and the 13 tones in detail, you are ready to flow. On the agenda pages you will find the daily°KIN from the Dreamspell and the Longcount. If you are a «newbie», I recommend that you focus mainly on the Dreamspell at the beginning. However, if you feel after 2–3 weeks that nothing is synchronous and fitting at all, switch to the longcount. In the end it doesn't matter, because all time tracks sooner or later lead to the «eternal now».

The best thing to do is to take a quick look at the agenda in the morning after getting up, look at the day's°KIN, read its name and the three most important keywords for each archetype and tone. Then you already have a colourful cocktail of information for your day: the sign, the tone, the full name, the colour and a total of six keywords. The whole thing doesn't take a minute and your consciousness is already «impregnated» (inspired) and it's up to you WHAT you're doing with this information now. Just keep your eyes open for people, situations, products, colors, magazines etc. that have something to do with the day°KIN. With this you already synchronize yourself with the daily energy.

My personal recommendation is also to draw the sign every now and then during the day. Either on a Post-IT in the office, on a napkin in a restaurant or on paper when you are a home. This will immerse you even faster in Zuvuya°Surfing.

For the ultimate flow you now only need a little additional knowledge about the wavespells, which run uninterruptedly and affect not only your life, but all life in our universe.

Due to the fact, that our english booklet is not born yet, we strongly recommand you either the book «Practical Guide to the Tzolkin» from Mariela Maya and her website with powerful informations:
> bridgingworlds.net/practical-guide-to-the-tzolkin.html

Or visit this website (german/english) which delivers as well in a visual very creative way (The 20 symbol look totally different – but coOol!) a the necessary informations about the actual wavespell:

> www.flow260.com/wave.html

Whenever you see a sign with a do (= magnetic tone) in the agenda fil part, a new wave begins. In order to know what the theme of this specifi wave is all about, just read the deta informations of the first seal with just ONE POINT (1st position). Fo example, if the first symbol of the wave is the «Yellow Human» thi wavespell is all about: focus, deter mination, walk your talk, influence knowing, wisdom and mastery (abou polarity!).

Early Bird

GUTSCHEIN

Liebe Zeit*Reisende Freunde

Wie im vergangenen Jahr verzichten wir inzwischen auf ein Crowdfunding und dank grosszügiger Unterstützung von Zuvuya*SurferInnen (zinslose Darlehen/Geldschenkungen/etc.) und zahlreichen Vorbestellungen (Early Bird/Subskriptionspreis) konnten wir auch die vierte Auflage realisieren, welche du jetzt in deinen Händen hältst.

Für die Agenda 2022 werden wir wieder den gleichen Weg gehen und euch ab Frühling 2021 (In der Agenda sind Hinweise enthalten :-) !) die nächste Agenda zum «Early Bird» Preis anbieten und wenn du beim Bestellprozess noch das Zauberwort **«surfanotherwave2022»** eingibst (digitaler Gutscheincode), erhältst du zusätzlich zur gedruckten Version noch die digitale Ausgabe der «Zuvuya Agenda 2022» dazu (Wert CHF 20.–), welche du nach Belieben nutzen und weiterverschenken darfst.

Ps.: Wenn du die digitale Version 2021 (PDF) nicht bis Ende dieses Jahres 2020 erhalten hast, schreibe uns bitte und wir werden dir den Link manuell zusenden!

•••

Dear Time*Traveler Friends

Like last year, we now do without crowdfunding and thanks to the generous support of Zuvuya*SurferInnen (interest-free loans/money gifts/etc.) and numerous pre-orders (early bird/subscription price) we were able to create the fourth edition, which you now hold in your very hands.

For the Agenda 2022 we will go the same way again and offer you the next Agenda at the «Early Bird» price starting in spring 2021 (the Agenda contains visual hints :-) !) and if you enter the magic word **«surfanotherwave2022»** (digital voucher code) during the ordering process, you will receive the digital edition of the «Zuvuya Agenda 2022» (value CHF 20.–) in addition to the printed version, which you may use and give away as a gift.

Ps.: If you don't get the digital Version 2021 (PDF) till the end of this year 2020, please write us and we will send you the link manually!

» support@zuvuya-agenda.ch

13 MONDE KALENDER

Tiefer tauchen und höher springen im Jahreszyklus

Falls du die Einleitung gelesen has[t] und inzwischen bereits einige Ze[it] mit unserer «Zuvuya Agenda» u[nter]wegs bist, möchtest du vielleich[t] tiefer ins Wunderland eintauchen[.] Dazu benötigst du einfach ein biss[-]chen mehr Details, welche dir nich[t] nur aufzeigen, wie fein strukturier[t] alles aufgebaut ist, sondern dic[h]

1. MAGNETISCHER MOND

1	2	3	4	5	6	7
26/7	27/7	28/7	29/7	30/7	31/7	1/8
8	9	10	11	12	13	14
2/8	3/8	4/8	5/8	6/8	7/8	8/8
15	16	17	18	19	20	21
9/8	10/8	11/8	12/8	13/8	14/8	15/8
22	23	24	25	26	27	28
16/8	17/8	18/8	19/8	20/8	21/8	22/8

2. LUNARER MOND

1	2	3	4	5	6	7
23/8	24/8	25/8	26/8	27/8	28/8	29/8
8	9	10	11	12	13	14
30/8	31/8	1/9	2/9	3/9	4/9	5/9
15	16	17	18	19	20	21
6/9	7/9	8/9	9/9	10/9	11/9	12/9
22	23	24	25	26	27	28
13/9	14/9	15/9	16/9	17/9	18/9	19/9

3. ELEKTRISCHER MOND

1	2	3	4	5	6	7
20/9	21/9	22/9	23/9	24/9	25/9	26/9
8	9	10	11	12	13	14
27/9	28/9	29/9	30/9	1/10	2/10	3/10
15	16	17	18	19	20	21
4/10	5/10	6/10	7/10	8/10	9/10	10/10
22	23	24	25	26	27	28
11/10	12/10	13/10	14/10	15/10	16/10	17/10

4. SELBSTEXISTIERENDER MOND

1	2	3	4	5	6	7
18/10	19/10	20/10	21/10	22/10	23/10	24/10
8	9	10	11	12	13	14
25/10	26/10	27/10	28/10	29/10	30/10	31/10
15	16	17	18	19	20	21
1/11	2/11	3/11	4/11	5/11	6/11	7/11
22	23	24	25	26	27	28
8/11	9/11	10/11	11/11	12/11	13/11	14/11

25. JULI
GRÜNER TAG
Tag ausserhalb der Zeit

5. OBERTON MOND

1	2	3	4	5	6	7
15/11	16/11	17/11	18/11	19/11	20/11	21/11
8	9	10	11	12	13	14
22/11	23/11	24/11	25/11	26/11	27/11	28/11
15	16	17	18	19	20	21
29/11	30/11	1/12	2/12	3/12	4/12	5/12
22	23	24	25	26	27	28
6/12	7/12	8/12	9/12	10/12	11/12	12/12

6. RHYTHMISCHER MOND

1	2	3	4	5	6	7
13/12	14/12	15/12	16/12	17/12	18/12	19/12
8	9	10	11	12	13	14
20/12	21/12	22/12	23/12	24/12	25/12	26/12
15	16	17	18	19	20	21
27/12	28/12	29/12	30/12	31/12	1/1	2/1
22	23	24	25	26	27	28
3/1	4/1	5/1	6/1	7/1	8/1	9/1

7. RESONANTER MOND

1	2	3	4	5	6	7
10/1	11/1	12/1	13/1	14/1	15/1	16/1
8	9	10	11	12	13	14
17/1	18/1	19/1	20/1	21/1	22/1	23/1
15	16	17	18	19	20	21
24/1	25/1	26/1	27/1	28/1	29/1	30/1
22	23	24	25	26	27	28
31/1	1/2	2/2	3/2	4/2	5/2	6/2

auch unterstützen, deine kostbare Lebenszeit ebenfalls mit ein paar magischen Momenten auszuschmücken. Erinnere dich, die Zeitformel «**Zeit ist Kunst**» bedeutet für uns alle, dass unser ganzes Leben ein riesiges Kunstwerk ist. Wir sind der Künstler, der Pinsel, die Farbe und auch die Leinwand. Und, was viele leider nur allzu oft «vergessen», wir sind auch der Betrachter unseres Bildes, das wir in jedem einzelnen Moment gestalten, ob bewusst oder unbewusst. Wer führt die Hand? Wer wählt die Farbe? Und das Sujet … ?

Du alleine bist es! Und diese Tatsache löst in vielen Menschen unbewusst eine grosse Angst aus. Denn wenn das, was wir täglich erleben, uns nicht gefällt, fällt es uns meistens leichter, den Job, die Chefin, die Kinder, den Partner, den Regen, den Terroristen, die Regierung und sogar unser Lieblingsyoghurt verantwortlich zu machen.

Solange wir damit jedoch nicht aufhören und die Verantwortung wieder voll und ganz zu uns selbst zurücknehmen, wird sich das Leben nicht gross ändern, weil wir uns so dem Spielball des Lebens ausgeliefert fühlen.

Darum heisst unser Motto **«Raus aus dem Hamsterrad – Hinein ins Leben».** Und damit meinen wir nicht nur das berufliche Hamsterrad, sondern auch die inneren Muster, Gewohnheiten, Ticks, etc., denen wir scheinbar ausgeliefert sind. Unsere Agenda unterstützt dich daher dabei, Licht ins Dunkle zu bringen und dein inneres und äusseres Leben in Einklang mit deinem Seelenauftrag zu bringen.

Der einzige Weg aus dem Hamsterrad ist, entweder langsamer zu gehen, bis das Rad anhält und du entspannt raustreten kannst, oder, wenn du mutig bist, einfach zu springen. Und du wirst überrascht sein, was auf dich wartet. Du bist zurück in deinem Leben, wo du der Superstar, die Heldin bist. Du wirst zu einem Zuvuya Surfer, der seine Wellen selber wählt.

Unsere «Zuvuya Agenda» startet zur Zeit noch mit dem gregorianischen Jahresbeginn am 1. Januar. Dies ist ein Kompromiss, den wir eingehen, da uns bewusst ist, dass wir alle noch völlig mit diesem unnatürlichen Jahresrhythmus verstrickt sind.

Der natürliche und harmonische **«13 Monde Zyklus/Kalender»** (nach Dr. José Argüelles) startet jeweils am 26. Juli und dauert bis zum 25. Juli des folgenden Jahres. Das bedeutet, dass unsere Zuvuya Agenda vom 1. Januar bis 25. Juli jeweils den Abschluss des aktuellen 13 Monde Kalenders umfasst und mit dem 26. Juli bis 31. Dezember jeweils die ersten rund sechs Monde des neuen 13 Monde Jahres.

3. KOSMISCHER MOND

1	2	3	4	5	6	7
27/6	28/6	29/6	30/6	1/7	2/7	3/7
8	9	10	11	12	13	14
4/7	5/7	6/7	7/7	8/7	9/7	10/7
15	16	17	18	19	20	21
11/7	12/7	13/7	14/7	15/7	16/7	17/7
22	23	24	25	26	27	28
18/7	19/7	20/7	21/7	22/7	23/7	24/7

12. KRISTALLENER MOND

1	2	3	4	5	6	7
30/5	31/5	1/6	2/6	3/6	4/6	5/6
8	9	10	11	12	13	14
6/6	7/6	8/6	9/6	10/6	11/6	12/6
15	16	17	18	19	20	21
13/6	14/6	15/6	16/6	17/6	18/6	19/6
22	23	24	25	26	27	28
20/6	21/6	22/6	23/6	24/6	25/6	26/6

11. SPEKTRALER MOND

1	2	3	4	5	6	7
2/5	3/5	4/5	5/5	6/5	7/5	8/5
8	9	10	11	12	13	14
9/5	10/5	11/5	12/5	13/5	14/5	15/5
15	16	17	18	19	20	21
16/5	17/5	18/5	19/5	20/5	21/5	22/5
22	23	24	25	26	27	28
23/5	24/5	25/5	26/5	27/5	28/5	29/5

10. PLANETARER MOND

1	2	3	4	5	6	7
4/4	5/4	6/4	7/4	8/4	9/4	10/4
8	9	10	11	12	13	14
11/4	12/4	13/4	14/4	15/4	16/4	17/4
15	16	17	18	19	20	21
18/4	19/4	20/4	21/4	22/4	23/4	24/4
22	23	24	25	26	27	28
25/4	26/4	27/4	28/4	29/4	30/4	1/5

GALAKTISCHER MOND

1	2	3	4	5	6	7
7/2	8/2	9/2	10/2	11/2	12/2	13/2
8	9	10	11	12	13	14
14/2	15/2	16/2	17/2	18/2	19/2	20/2
15	16	17	18	19	20	21
21/2	22/2	23/2	24/2	25/2	26/2	27/2
22	23	24	25	26	27	28
28/2	1/3	2/3	3/3	4/3	5/3	6/3

9. SOLARER MOND

1	2	3	4	5	6	7
7/3	8/3	9/3	10/3	11/3	12/3	13/3
8	9	10	11	12	13	14
14/3	15/3	16/3	17/3	18/3	19/3	20/3
15	16	17	18	19	20	21
21/3	22/3	23/3	24/3	25/3	26/3	27/3
22	23	24	25	26	27	28
28/3	29/3	30/3	31/3	1/4	2/4	3/4

Eine **Eigenschaft der Zeit** ist, dass sie **«fraktal»** (selbstähnlich) strukturiert ist. Das bedeutet, dass in jedem einzelnen Augenblick bereits eine zukünftige Zeitspanne enthalten ist.

Oder nochmals anders ausgedrückt: alles, was du an einem einzelnen Tag erlebst, wird sich irgendwann (zyklisch) in der Zukunft wiederholen, jedoch in einem grösseren Zeitrahmen.

Natürlich bedeutet das nicht, dass du alles nochmals ganz genau gleich erleben wirst, sondern dass Themen oder auch Begegnungen mit Menschen auf die Zukunft einwirken und man inzwischen sogar berechnen kann, wann du mit einer «Wiederholung» rechnen darfst.

Damit du das **fraktale Prinzip** der Zeit bereits üben und kennenlernen kannst, empfehlen wir dir, den 13 Monde Kalender ebenfalls immer mal wieder im Auge zu behalten. Dein **persönlicher 13 Monde Zyklus** beginnt jeweils mit deinem Geburtstag. Und genau so hat auch die Erde als lebendiges Wesen/Bewusstsein ihren persönlichen «Geburtstag», welcher von Dr. José Argüelles auf den 26. Juli festgesetzt wurde. An diesem Tag bilden der hellste Stern Sirius, unsere Sonne und die Erde eine Linie. Für den inzwischen verstorbenen Mayaforscher ist das so etwas wie eine **«Nullstunde»** für die Erde in Relation mit unserem Universum.

Wenn du in der Agenda den 26. Juli nachschlägst, wirst du eines der folgenden vier Zeichen vorfinden: roter Mond, weisser Magier, blauer Sturm oder den gelben Samen. Diese vier Zeichen bilden zusammen die **«Gateway Familie»**, die aus je einem Zeichen der vier Farben (rot/weiss/blau/gelb) besteht. Es gibt noch vier weitere Familien, die jedoch beim 13 Monde Kalender nicht im Vordergrund stehen. Falls du darüber mehr erfahren möchtest, empfehle ich dir meinen Videokanal unter:
> www.vimeo.com/zuvuya

Das erste Zeichen am Anfang des neuen 13 Monde Zyklus (26. Juli) prägt grundsätzlich das ganze Jahr. In diesem ersten Tag ist fraktal/holographisch bereits das komplette Jahr enthalten. Das bedeutet, dass es wirklich sehr, sehr wichtig ist, diesen ersten Tag möglichst bewusst zu gestalten. Und selbst wenn er von zahlreichen «unerwünschten» Erlebnissen geprägt gewesen sein sollte, dann weisst du jetzt bereits schon, auf was du dich so alles gefasst machen musst.

Die 13 Monde kann man auf zahlreiche Arten darstellen oder gruppieren. Eine der wichtigsten Formen ist diejenige auf der Doppelseite 50/51. Die 13 Monde ergeben so etwas wie einen kleinen Wirbel, der im Gegenuhrzeigersinn läuft.

Bei jeder 13'er Welle bilden die erste, fünfte, neunte und letzte, dreizehnte Position das energetische Skelett. Du hast sicher schon rausgefunden, dass bei der 13 Tage Welle diese vier Positionen (1/5/9/13) stets die gleiche Farbe haben. Oder anders ausgedrückt: Die Farbe des ersten Zeichens wiederholt sich auf der fünften, neunten und dreizehnten Position und gibt der Welle zusätzlich eine farbliche Qualität.

Beim 13 Monde Zyklus besteht jedoch jede der 13 Positionen nicht nur aus einem Tag, sondern aus 28 Tagen. Das führt mathematisch dazu, dass sich die Farbe des ersten Zeichens zum Jahresbeginn (26. Juli 2019 = Weisser Magier 26. Juli 2020 = Blauer Sturm) ebenfalls wiederholt, und zwar jeweils zum Beginn eines neuen Mondes. Das ist auf der Darstellung auf der vorderen Seite jedoch nicht sichtbar, weil wir hier nur das Gerüst OHNE die Maya Zeichen abgebildet haben. Wir werden zukünftig auch einen reinen 13 Monde Wandkalender herstellen, wo du das auf den ersten Blick sehen kannst. Das bedeutet nun, dass auch jeder einzelne Mond (à 28 Tage) ein kleiner Zyklus eingebettet im grossen (13 Monde) Zyklus ist. Das ist das Prinzip der Fraktalität. Und immer das erste Zeichen jedes einzelnen Mondes gibt dem jeweiligen Mond ebenfalls eine Prägung. So hat der zweite Mond, der am 23. August 2020 beginnt, das Zeichen «Blaue selbstexistierende Hand», welche für die folgenden 28 Tage die Richtung vorgibt. Der dritte Mond, der immer am 20. September 2020 beginnt, hat als erstes Zeichen den «Blauen Rhythmischen Adler».

Zusammengefasst bedeutet das folgendes: Das ganze 13 Monde Jahr vom 26. Juli 2019 bis 24. Juli 2020 steht unter der Herrschaft des «Weissen Magnetischen Magiers». Das ganze Jahr ist also eine Einladung an alle Menschen, gemeinsam mit der Erde die Kraft der Magie zurück ins Leben zu holen, mit welcher alles wie von alleine läuft. Jeder Mond hat jedoch noch zusätzlich eine eigene Qualität, welche das Jahresprogramm verfeinert. Das nächste 13 Monde Jahr beginnt am 26. Juli 2020 mit dem «Blauen Lunaren Sturm». Starke Transformationskräfte werden in diesem neuen Zyklus auf die Erde einwirken.

Das alles lässt sich auch auf deinen individuellen 13 Monde Zyklus übertragen, welcher dir Jahr für Jahr die Möglichkeit gibt, bewusst mit den Zeitthemen zu surfen, anstatt von ihnen überrollt zu werden. Falls dich dieses Thema interessiert, empfehle ich dir meine Video°Seite, wo du Videos zu diesem Thema findest. Ausserdem biete ich **individuelle Jahresreadings** an (schreib mir einfach auf urs@zuvuya-agenda.ch) oder lade dir das aufschlussreiche PDF auf der Website von Kössner runter:

> www.maya.at/Literatur/download Persoenlicher_13-Monde-Kalender.pdf

(bitte vergiss den freiwilligen Energieausgleich von ca. 3–5 CHF/Euro nicht)

Abschliessend für alle fortgeschrittenen SurferInnen noch folgendes: Da der 13 Monde Zyklus im 2019 mit dem weissen Magier auf der ersten Position (magnetischer Ton) beginnt, bedeutet das, dass wir einen grösseren weissen Zyklus à 13 Jahren beginnen. Dieser WEISSE Zyklus sorgt dafür, dass die Frequenzen der Wahrheit, Klarheit, Ehrlichkeit, Transparenz, des Lichts, der Unterscheidungsfähigkeit, der Läuterung, Reinigung und Klärung und viele mehr im kristallinen Herzen der Erde verankert werden. Diese Schwingungen sorgen dafür, dass es zunehmend schwieriger wird, «schmutzige Spiele» zu spielen, Ereignisse und Dinge zu verstecken oder zu vertuschen, Menschen zu manipulieren oder schlichtweg nicht wahrhaftig zu sein. Es wird also spannend werden, wohin uns die Erde in den nächsten 13 Jahren führen wird.

In diesem Sinne ein weiteres Mal In lak'ech a la Kin!

PS: Alle vier Wochen, wenn ein neuer Mond (nicht Monat!) beginnt, haben wir eine Doppelseite eingeschoben, welche dir die wichtigsten Infos und Qualitäten zum jeweiligen Mond vermittelt. Diese gelten für den globalen 13 Monde Kalender (Start 26. Juli) und deinen persönlichen 13 Monde Kalender, der mit einem jeweiligen Geburtstag beginnt. Von deinem Geburtstag ausgehend kannst du jeweils 28 Tage abzählen (vier Wochen weiterblättern) und dann beginnt der nächste 2./3. ... etc.) Mond. Zur Kontrolle gilt: Die Farbe des Zeichens an deinem Geburtstag (Rot/Weiss/Blau/Gelb) bestimmt auch das erste Zeichen deiner 13 Monde. Hast du ein weisses Zeichen an deinem Geburtstag, beginnen alle deine 13 Monde in diesem Jahr ebenfalls mit einem weissen Zeichen.

13 MOON CALENDAR

Dive deeper in the rabbit hole

If you have read the introduction and have already spent some time with our «Zuvuya Agenda», you may want to delve deeper into Wonderland. You just need a little more details which will not only show you how finely structured everything is, but will also help you to decorate your precious lifetime with a few magical moments. Remember, the time formula **«time is art»** means for all of us that our whole life is a huge work of art. We are the artist, the brush, the paint and also the canvas. And, what many unfortunately all too often «forget», we are also the viewer of our picture, which we create in every single moment, whether consciously or unconsciously. Who is leading the hand? Who chooses the color? And the subject?

You alone are it! And this fact unconsciously triggers a great fear in many people. Because if we don't like what we experience every day, it's usually easier for us to blame the job, the boss, the children, the partner, the rain, the terrorist, the government and even our favourite yoghurt.

But as long as we don't stop and take responsibility back to ourselves, life won't change much because we feel at the mercy of life.

That's why our motto is **«Get out of the hamsterwheel – into your life»**. And by this we mean not only the professional hamster wheel, but also the inner patterns, habits, ticks, etc. to which we seem to be at the mercy of. Our agenda therefore supports you in bringing light into the dark and bringing your inner and outer life into harmony with your soul mission.

The only way out of the hamster wheel is to either walk slower until the wheel stops and you can step out relaxed or, if you are brave, just jump. And you'll be surprised what's waiting for you. You are back in your life where you are the superstar, the heroine. You become a Zuvuya surfer who chooses his own waves.

Our «Zuvuya Agenda» starts with the gregorian beginning of the year on January 1st. This is a compromise that we make because we are aware that we are all still completely entangled with this unnatural annual rhythm.

The natural and harmonious **«13 Moon Cycle/Calendar»** (according to Dr. José Argüelles) starts on July 26th and lasts until July 25th of the following year. This means that our Zuvuya agenda from January 1 too July 25 includes the closing of the current 13 moons calendar and from July 26 until December 31 the first six moons of the new 13 moons year.

One characteristic of time is that it is structured **«fractally»** (self-similarly). This means that every single moment already contains a future time span.

Or to put it another way: everything you experience on a single day will repeat itself sometime (cyclically) in the future, but in a larger time frame.

Of course, this does not mean that you will experience everything exactly the same again, but that topics or encounters with people will have an effect on the future and you can even calculate when you can expect a «repetition».

So that you can already practice and get to know **the fractal principle** of time, we recommend that you also keep an eye on the 13 Moon Calendar from time to time. Your **personal 13 Moon cycle** starts with your birthday. And exactly the same the earth as a living being/consciousness has its personal «birthday», which was set by Dr. José Argüelles on July 26th. On this day the brightest star Sirius, our sun and the earth form a line. For the Maya researcher, who died in the meantime, this is something like a **«zero hour»** for the Earth in relation to our universe.

If you look up July 26th in the agenda, you will find one of the following four signs: red moon, white magician, blue storm or the yellow seed. These four signs together form the **«Gateway Family»**, which consists of one sign each of the four colours (red/white/blue/yellow). There are four more families, but they are not in the foreground of the 13 Moon Calendar. If you would like to learn more about them, I recommend my video channel at:

> www.vimeo.com /zuvuya

The first sign at the beginning of the new 13 Moon cycle (July 26th) basically marks the whole year. This first day already contains the complete year fractal/holographically. This means that it is really very, very important to make this first day as conscious as possible. And even if it should have been marked by numerous «unwanted» experiences, then you already know what you have to be prepared for.

The 13 moons can be represented or grouped in numerous ways. One of the most important forms is the one on the pages 50/51. The 13 moons result in something like a small vortex running counterclockwise.

With every 13'er wave the first, fifth, ninth and last, thirteenth position form the energetic skeleton. You have probably already found out that these four positions (1/5/9/13) always have the same color for the 13-day wave. Or to put it another way: the color of the first sign repeats on the fifth, ninth and thirteenth position and gives the wave an additional color quality.

In the 13 moon cycle, however, each of the 13 positions does not consist of only one day, but of 28 days. This leads mathematically to the fact that the color of the first sign at the beginning of the year (26 July 2019 = White Magician/26 July 2020 = Blue Storm) also repeats itself mathematically, in each case at the beginning of a new moon. However, this is not visible on the front page, because here we have only shown the scaffold WITHOUT the Mayan signs. In the future we will also produce a pure 13 Moons wall calendar, where you can see it at first sight.

This means now that every single moon (every 28 days) is also a small cycle embedded in the big (13 moons) cycle. This is the principle of fractality. And always the first sign of each individual moon also gives the respective moon an imprint. So the second moon, which begins on August 23, 2020, has the sign «Blue self-existing hand», which gives the direction for the following 28 days. The third moon, which always begins on September 20, 2020, has the «Blue Rhythmic Eagle» as its first sign.

In summary, this means the following: The whole 13 moons year from July 26, 2019 to July 24, 2020 is under the rule of the «White Magician». So the whole year is an invitation to all people, together with the earth, to bring back to life the power of magic, with which everything runs by itself. Each moon, however, has its own additional quality, which refines the annual program. The next 13 moons year begins on 26 July 2020 with the «Blue Lunar Storm». Strong transformation forces will affect the earth in this new cycle.

All this can also be transferred to your individual 13 Moon cycle, which year after year gives you the opportunity to surf consciously with the time themes instead of being overwhelmed by them. If you are interested in this topic, I recommend my Video°Page, where you can find videos on this topic. I also offer **indi-vidual readings** (just write me or urs@zuvuya-agenda.ch) or book an online course. I recommend the online course from Jacob Wyatt (Red Dragon).

> www.course.newtimecourse.com/welcome

And on the Law of Time Website you find as well other great documents like this one:

> www.lawoftime.org/13-moon-self-study-pilot-program/

Finally the following for all advanced surfers: Since the 13 moon cycle starts in 2019 with the white magician on the first position (magnetic sound), this means that we start a bigger white cycle of 13 years. This WHITE cycle ensures that the frequencies of Truth, Clarity, Honesty, Transparency, Light, Discrimination, Purification, Purification and Clarification and many more are anchored in the crystalline heart of the Earth. These vibrations make it increasingly difficult to play «dirty games», hide or cover up events and things, manipulate people, or simply be untruthful. So it will be exciting to see where the earth will lead us in the next 13 years.

In lak'ech

There is even a 13 Moon Calendar worldwide initiative! Check it out and support it!

> www.13months28days.info

PS: Every four weeks, when a new moon (not month!) starts, we have inserted a double moon page, which gives you the most important information and qualities about the next moon. These are valid for the global 13 Moon Calendar (start: 26. July) and your personal 13 Moon Calendar, which starts with your birthday. Starting from your birthday you can count 28 days each (turn four pages/weeks) and then the next (2./3. ... 12./13.) moon starts. As a check: The color of the sign on your birthday (red/white/blue/yellow) also determines the first sign of your 13 moons. If you have a white sign on your birthday, all your 13 moons in this year will also start with a white sign.

Xocolatl

Cacaorezept

Zutaten

2.5-3 DL (Vanille) Sojamilch
Ca. 25 G (Bio) Rohkost Cacao
1 EL Brauner Zucker
1 EL (Bio) Kokosöl
1/2 TL gemahlene Vanille
1 Prise (Meer)salz
1-2 Prisen Pfeffer
1 TL gemahlener Zimt
1/2 TL Chilli (nach Bedarf

Alles zusammen auf kleiner Flamme zum Schmelzen bringen. Und mit dem Schwingbesen schaumig rühren und servieren. Falls vorhanden Cacao in Porzellan/Steingut servieren.

XOCOLATL ALS GÖTTERGETRÄNK

Eine Bohne erobert die Welt

Als ich damals mit dem Schamanen «Temilotzin» in Mexico City unterwegs war, nahm er Flyer, die auf der Strasse verteilt wurden, stets dankend an. Die meisten schaute er gar nicht an und warf sie später weg. Als ich ihn darauf ansprach, meinte er nur, dass er damit die Arbeit der «Flyer Verteiler» würdige und ihnen zudem ein Erfolgserlebnis schenke. (Und ein Schamane kann allenfalls auch noch einen Segen im Geist zurückgeben.)

Dieser Gedanke hat mich seit damals nicht mehr losgelassen. Und wenn ich in einer neuen Umgebung (Stadt/Region) bin, nehme ich immer mal wieder ein paar Flyer mit und gucke sie mir dann zuhause genauer an, bevor die meisten dann im Altpapier landen.

Einer schaffte es vor und 2 bis 3 Jahren in meine Sammlung, weil er mich auch visuell sehr ansprach. Es war ein Flyer, der auf eine Cacao-Zeremonie in Zürich aufmerksam machte. Auf der Rückseite erfuhr ich, dass die beiden abgebildeten Frauen aus Berlin stammen und überall in Europa mit dem Cacao unterwegs sind.

Weiter erfuhr ich, dass sie nur den besten Cacao verwendeten, nämlich Rohkost Cacao (bio+fair). Das beeindruckte mich sehr, weil damit klar war, dass die beiden wussten, dass im rohen Cacao wertvolle Enzyme stecken, die bei Hitze über ca. 42 bis 45 °C zerstört werden. Werden diese jedoch im inaktiven Zustand (bei ca. 39 °C) mit einem warmen Cacao vom Körper aufgenommen, spüren selbst ziemlich unsensible Menschen eine relativ unmittelbare Wirkung.

Die Liste positiver Wirkungen auf Körper und Seele ist lang. Daher gehört diese warme Bohne auch zu den «Superfoods», wo sie entweder gemahlen oder granuliert oder in Platten angeboten wird. Wichtig ist einfach, dass der Cacao nicht über 42 °C erhitzt wird. Bei einigen bio+fair Marken/Produkten ist dies noch nicht gewährleistet, weil diese Erkenntnisse noch relativ jung sind und die Cacaobohne nach wie vor erforscht wird.

Aber der Name «Theobroma», «Göttergetränk» weist ja bereits in die Richtung.

Was auch immer du dir unter einem Göttergetränk vorstellst, für mich gehört der heisse (und ab und zu kalte) Cacao definitiv dazu, und zwar nach eigenem Rezept, welches ich mit meiner Partnerin und Cacaoqueen Andrea entwickelt habe, über eine Zeitspanne von rund zwei Jahren.

In diesen beiden Jahren war ein heisser Cacao oftmals **Medizin** für uns und unsere Partnerschaft. Zudem war er oftmals Inspiration für jegliche Formen von Kreativität und Kunst. Und schliesslich ist er natürlich, wie viele andere Substanzen von Mutter Erde, auch noch ein «Aphrodisiakum», welches zu sinnlichen, magischen Momenten der Zweisamkeit einlädt.

Damit auch du, lieber Freund, wo auch immer und wann auch immer du gerade bist, einen Cacao machen möchtest, drucken wir dir auf der anderen Seite unser nicht mehr so geheimes «Xocolatl» Cacao Rezept ab. Was die Zutaten angeht: Ich empfehle Pflanzenmilch, weil sie ebenfalls ein Produkt der Natur ist und ansonsten gilt: Je besser die Zutaten, desto besser das Ergebnis.

Oder mit den Worten von **Oskar Wilde**, dem unser Cacao mit Sicherheit geschmeckt hätte: «Ich habe einen ganz einfachen Geschmack. Ich wähle für mich nur das Beste!»

In diesem Sinne: wohl bekomms und beachte, das Rezept steht unter «Common Licence»!

PS: Der Cacao hat im Entwicklungsprozess dieser magischen Zuvuya Agenda wie bei den klassischen Maya eine wichtige Rolle gespielt. Die Farben sind durchweg von ihm inspiriert und ich übertreibe wohl nicht, wenn während den vergangenen Monaten literweise Cacao getrunken wurde. Zur Inspiration und manchmal auch als Medizin.

Einen der hochwertigsten rohkost Cacao (fairtrade) erhältst du bei unserem Projektpartner auf:
> www.cacaobliss.ch

oder auch in unserem Shop:
> www.shop.zuvuya-agenda.ch

WO FINDE ICH WAS?

Kalenderwoche

1. Dreamspell (nach Dr. José Argüelles)
2. Longcount (traditionelle Zählung der Mayas)
3. Tages-Siegel
4. KIN Nummer (1–260 des Tzolkin)
5. Ton
6. Tages-Siegel,-Nummer und Ton (Longcount)
7. Tag des aktuellen Mondes (1–28)

6/21 ☾ Aktueller Tag des Mondes

Aktueller Mond des 13 Monde Zyklus

8. Nationale und Keltische Feiertage
9. Astronomische Mondphase
10. Schreib hier deine Synchronizitäten auf und wofür du dankbar bist.
11. Portaltage
12. Together to One (siehe Seite 78)

Monde

13. Aktueller Mond
14. Wochentag des Mondes
15. Gregorianische Kalenderdaten
16. Information über den aktuellen Mond
17. Farbe des Wochenrhythmus (rot/weiss/blau/gelb)

MONDE

KALENDERWOCHE

Tag | Day

15 Montag / Monday 9/9

Blauer Kosmischer Affe: Magie, Spielen, Illusion
Ton: Durchhalten, Transzendieren, Präsenz

Blue Cosmic Monkey: Magic, Play, Illusion
Tone: Endure, Transcend, Presence

Longcount: Weisser Resonanter Weltenüberbrücker | White Resonant Worldbridger

12–21

07:00
08:00
09:00
10:00
11:00
12:00
13:00

20 Samstag / Saturday 9/14

Gelber Oberton Krieger: Intelligenz, Fragen, Angstlosigkeit
Ton: Ermächtigen, Befehlen, Strahlkraft

Yellow Overtone Warrior: Intelligence, Question, Fearlessness
Tone: Empowerment, Order, Radiance

Longcount: Blauer Kristallener Affe | Blue Crystal Monkey

Imbolc | Mondfest

08:00
12:00
14:00
16:00
18:00

März – KW 11

Info über beiden Zeitspuren Dreamspell und Longcount

In der Zuvuya Agenda findest du oben zwei «Zeitspuren». Die erste ist der sogenannte «Dreamspell», der von Dr. José Argüelles (1939–2011) basierend auf der Maya Mythologie entwickelt wurde. Die zweite Spur, der sogenannte «Long Count» (lange Zählung) hat einen anderen Startpunkt (3114 v. Chr.) und wurde von den «Tageshütern» (Mayapriester) bis in die heutige Zeit weitergeführt.

Wir betrachten den Dreamspell eher als «Rollenspiel», welcher dir deinen «Avatar» (Rolle/Spielfigur) im täglichen Leben aufzeigt. Falls du tiefer eintauchen möchtest (kollektives Unterbewusstsein/Archetyp/Seelenspur) ist der Longcount das Richtige für dich. Oder, du benutzt beide Spuren, je nachdem wo du dich im Leben befindest oder was du gerade benötigst. Du kannst dabei nichts falsch machen, jede Spur führt dich früher oder später in die magische «Zeitlosigkeit» (Hier und Jetzt/ewige Präsenz). Viel Spass.

PS: Beim Longcount steht jeweils nur der Name des Tages°KINs. Einfach bei den Erklärungen der «13 Töne der Schöpfung» und den «20 Archetypen der Zeit» nachschlagen für die Bedeutung.

WHERE DO I FIND WHAT?

Calendar week

1. Dreamspell
   (by Dr. José Argüelles)
2. Longcount (traditional Mayan Count)
3. Daily Seal (Dreamspell)
4. KIN number (1–260 of the Tzolkin)
5. Tone
6. Daily Seal, number und tone (Longcount)
7. Day of the actual moon (1–28)

6/21 ☽ Actual day of the moon
Actual moon of the 13 moon cycle

8. National and celctic holidays
9. Astronomical moon phase
10. Write down your synchronicities here and what you're thankful for.
11. Portal days
12. Together to One (page 80)

Moons

13. Actual moon
14. Weekday of the moon
15. Gregorianic calendar date
16. Informations about the actual moon
17. Color of the weekly rhythms (red/white/blue/yellow)

MOONS

CALENDAR WEEK

Tag | Day

15 Montag / Monday 9/9

Dreamspell

Blauer Kosmischer Affe: Magie, Spielen, Illusion
Ton: Durchhalten, Transzendieren, Präsenz

Blue Cosmic Monkey: Magic, Play, Illusion
Tone: Endure, Transcend, Presence

Longcount

Weisser Resonanter Weltenüberbrücker | White Resonant Worldbridger

07:00
08:00
09:00
10:00
11:00
12:00
13:00

12–21

20 Samstag / Saturday 9/14

Gelber Oberton Krieger: Intelligenz, Fragen, Angstlosigkeit
Ton: Ermächtigen, Befehlen, Strahlkraft

Yellow Overtone Warrior: Intelligence, Question, Fearlessness
Tone: Empowerment, Order, Radiance

Blauer Kristallener Affe
Blue Crystal Monkey

Imbolc | Mondfest

08:00
12:00
14:00
16:00
18:00

März KW 11

Information about the two time-tracks Dreamspell and Longcount

In the Zuvuya Agenda you will find two «time tracks» above. The first is the so-called «Dreamspell», developed by Dr. José Argüelles (1939–2011) based on Mayan mythology. The second trace, the so-called «Long Count», has a different starting point (3114 B.C.) and was continued by the «Day Keepers» (Mayan priests) until today.

We see the Dreamspell more as a role-playing game, which shows you your avatar in daily life. If you want to dive deeper (collective subconscious/archetypes/soulpath) the Longcount is the right thing for you. Or, you use both tracks, depending on where you are in life or what you need right now. You can't do anything wrong, every timeline sooner or later leads you into the magical «timelessness» (Here and Now/Eternal Presence). Have fun!

PS: With the Longcount only the name of the day°KINs stands in each case. If you need more information about the Longcount seal, just have a look at the detailed descriptions.

KOMM! JETZT IST UNSERE ZEIT DES WIRKENS

Wissenschaftler sagen uns, dass sich in den nächsten 10 Jahren entscheiden wird, wie unser Planet in die Zukunft geht. Bis 2030 müsste die Menschheit fähig sein, Lösungen für die komplexen Probleme unserer Zeit zu finden. Entscheidungsträger in Wirtschaft, Wissenschaft und Politik, Menschen in Institutionen und Organisationen reden vom Klimawandel, von der Energiewende, vom Welthunger, von der ungerechten Verteilung von Ressourcen, von ungeheurem Reichtum und unvorstellbarer Armut, von leidvollen Kriegen und folgenden Flüchtlingsströmen, von Artensterben, der zerstörerischen Wirkung von Plastik- und Chemieabfällen... Die Liste wird immer länger, wer mag's noch hören!?

Allerdings geht es um unsere Zukunft, um die Zukunft unserer Kinder und Kindes-Kinder, um die uns umgebende Natur, ganz allgemein um die Lebensqualität auf diesem Planeten. Wir sind jetzt aufgerufen zu handeln, zu wirken, uns einzusetzen und uns die Zukunft zu erschaffen, die wir wünschen. Bloss wie? Es ist leichter als Du denkst. Lass mich erklären.

Mein Name ist Susanne Triner. Seit Kindheit wollte ich wissen, weshalb wir Menschen zerstören, was wir vorher aufgebaut haben. Seit 1987 befasse ich mich mit den Möglichkeiten des Bewusstseinswandels, der Quantenphysik und der Arbeit mit Feldern. 2003 habe ich die Organisation Together to One gegründet, seit 2005 Miteinander-Methoden in konkreten Projekten, unter manchmal äusserst schwierigen Voraussetzungen erprobt und erfolgreich umgesetzt.

Vor zwei Jahren durfte ich an dieser Stelle das «Internet des Menschen» vorstellen. Die Rückmeldungen derjenigen Menschen, die es anwenden sind überwältigend positiv.

Akten & Fakten zum InnerNet dem Internet des Menschen (Rahmen, Farbwechsel)
- Du wirkst frei von Technik, Software & Updates
- Du hast jederzeit & überall gratis Zugang zum Together to One Feld
- Der Zugangs-Code ist weltweit der gleiche: 12–21
- Das Feld ist zum Wohl Aller programmiert
- Du wirkst über alle Grenzen, Sprachen, Kulturen & Religionen hinweg auf Deine ganz persönliche Art und Weise
- Du hast alles, was Du brauchst um mitzumachen

So wirkst Du mit Deiner Energie
Beim Zähneputzen, Schuhe anziehen, auf den Bus warten, vor dem Einschlafen oder nach dem Aufwachen sagst Du 12–21 (Eins, Zwei- Zwei, Eins) Damit bist Du verbunden. Es braucht ein wenig Übung. Sei einfach offen, für die Veränderungen in Deinem Leben. Du wirst die Verbindung nicht mehr missen wollen und Dich fragen, was und wie Du mehr tun kannst. Dann fängst Du richtig an, mitzumachen. Du schaust Dich in Deinem Leben um und verbindest Situationen, Menschen, Projekte, Ideen mit dem Together to One Feld. Damit ziehst Du die bestmögliche Version aus dem Feld an. Es scheint fast zu einfach, um wahr zu sein, aber es ist so.

Togetherness in Action – Wir wirken gemeinsam zum Wohl Aller

Vom 12. – 21. Tag des Monats bündeln wir unsere Kräfte. Wir bearbeiten ein gerade aktuelles Thema oder ein komplexes Problem. Unsere gebündelte Energie, unsere

Liebe zum Leben wird Berge versetzen und Lösungen aufzeigen. Alles was Du zum Mitmachen brauchst, ist die Bereitschaft, Dich einzugeben wie Du bist. Damit leistest Du Deinen Beitrag zur besten Version unserer gemeinsamen Zukunft.

Wie informierst Du Dich?
Die Zuvaya Agenda sagt Dir, wann die «Togetherness in Action» Tage beginnen. Du findest die Angabe oben beim Tages-Zeichen.
(Beispiel 12–21/7 bedeutet der 7. Tag unseres monatlichen Wirkens)

Unsere drei Ebenen des Miteinanders
InLine = in der Meditation, Kontemplation, künstlerischem Ausdruck
onLine = in Foren, sozialen Medien
(geh auf www.together21.org um mehr zu wissen)
inPerson = bei persönlichen Treffen
(geh auf www.together21.org für Daten)

Die Monatsthemen
Wir bestimmen gemeinsam, welche komplexen Probleme wir bearbeiten wollen. Anfang des neuen Monats findest Du die Auswahl unter www.together21.org. Hier kannst Du wählen, was für Dich wichtig wäre. Um den 10. Tag herum, wird entschieden. Ab dem 12. Tag wirken wir für das ausgewählte Thema.

Eine Anleitung dazu findest Du im Download Bereich unter StarterKit.

Am 21. Tag des Monats ist übrigens Together to One Freue-Tag. Wir feiern das Grosse Miteinander und freuen uns an den Entwicklungen unseres Experimentes.

Zukunft? Wer bestimmt? Rahmen Farbe
Weder komplexe Algorithmen, noch findige Smart Groups oder Thinktanks sollten uns die Aufgabe abnehmen unsere Zukunft zu bewirken. Was also ist zu tun?

Alle machen mit! Vom 12. – 21. Tag des Monats bearbeiten wir die komplexen Probleme unserer Zeit und bewirken die Zukunft zum Wohl Aller. Wir wirken mit dem InnerNet auf dem Together to One Feld, einem Feld ausserhalb von Raum und Zeit, programmiert zum Wohl Aller.

Nicht Macht! Nicht Ohnmacht! Macht mit!
Togetherness in Aciton – www.together21.org

Together to One –
Zukunft zum Mitmachen

Susanne Triner,
Gelber Lunarer Same

NOW IS THE TIME OF ACTION

Scientist proclaim the next 10 years to be crucial for planet earth, if mankind should fail to find solutions for the many complex problems we face today. Decision-makers in business, science and politics, in worldwide institutions and organizations point to global climate change, the needed energy transition, worldwide poverty and malnutrition. They can't name solutions to the unfair resource distribution, the growing gap between the rich and the poor, the unneeded wars causing too much suffering and a ever growing stream of refugees traveling the world. We are not talking about extinction of species, the destructive effect of plastic and chemical waste ... The list is getting longer and longer... who is still willing to listen?

Nevertheless, the topic is our common future, the future of our children and children's children. We talk about the quality of life in general, for us and our surroundings. It is time that we commit ourselves to co-create the future we desire. Just how? It is easier than you think. Let me explain.

My name is Susanne Triner. I always wanted to know why human beings are able to bring suffering to their beloved ones, and why humanity would destroy what they built up before. Since 1987 I have been studying the options of a shift in consciousness for humanity when implementing healing methods, the knowledge of quantum physics and the fascination of morphological fields. In 2003 the organization Together to One was founded with the aim to proof the benefit of working together in co-operative teams. Since 2005 we successfully implemented the Together to One method in concrete projects under challenging circumstances.

In the agenda 2018 we first announced the «InnerNet» – the Internet for human beings in addition to the internet of things. The feedback was quite positive.

Some facts about the InnerNet our co-creative field
- no technology, no software, no updates are needed in order to work
- the access to the new Together to One (Conscious) Field is free, everywhere and anytime
- 12–21 is the one global access code
- the Together to One conscious field is programmed for the Benefit of All
- we co-create across all borders, languages, cultures & religions
- You have everything you need to participate

This is how easily you give your impact to our common future
Just say 12–21 (one, two – two, one) when brushing your teeth, waiting for a bus, before going to sleep or before starting your day. That's the way, you connect to the field. Also, it connects you with the best version of your day, your situation, your project or your plans. Just stay tuned to it and observe while your body-mind-soul gets adjusted.
After some experience you may want to commit yourself further and participate in co-creational events. That's when you join Togetherness in Action.

Togetherness in Action – We co-create the Benefit of All

From the 12th to the 21st day of the month we bundle our talents, skills, our love for life and our energies to co-create solutions for the complex problems we, humanity is actually facing. Through this connection our contribute to the best version of our common future.

The Zuvaya Agenda co-operates with us
The agenda gives you notice when the Togetherness in Action starts. You may go to the Together to One website to find out about our actual monthly topic.

Our three levels of co-creation
(for more information please visit www.together21.org)
InLine = in meditation, contemplation, artistic expression
online = in forums, in social media and WhatsApp chatgroups
inPerson = at group gatherings, public events

The monthly topics
You may vote for the topic of the month between day 1 and 10 on the web-site. That's how you put your weight on a topic to be chosen. On the evening of the 10th, we decide and publish the «winner». Togetherness in Action starts on the 12th and ends on the 21st.

Furthermore you may find three Bbooklets in the download section of the Together to One website. More explanation, more information on how to use 12–21 the multi-dimensional field in own individual life, at work, in projects or in global actions is offered.

On the 21st day of the month is Together to One Celebration day. Check online for more information.

Together to One –
a future to participate

Who decides about our common future?
Would you want complex algorithms, smart groups or think tanks to define our common future? Should not we, all of us participate when important decisions are being taken?

Let's empower one another. Join for co-creation
Togetherness in Action – www.together21.org

Susanne Triner,
Gelber Lunarer Same

JAHRESÜBERSICHT 2021 | YEAR OVERVIEW 2021

JANUAR

	M	D	M	D	F	S	S
53	28	29	30	31	1	2	3
1	4	5	6	7	8	9	10
2	11	12	13	14	15	16	17
3	18	19	20	21	22	23	24
4	25	26	27	28	29	30	31

FEBRUAR

	M	D	M	D	F	S	S
5	1	2	3	4	5	6	7
6	8	9	10	11	12	13	14
7	15	16	17	18	19	20	21
8	22	23	24	25	26	27	28

MÄRZ

	M	D	M	D	F	S	S
9	1	2	3	4	5	6	7
10	8	9	10	11	12	13	14
11	15	16	17	18	19	20	21
12	22	23	24	25	26	27	28
13	29	30	31				

APRIL

	M	D	M	D	F	S	S
13				1	2	3	4
14	5	6	7	8	9	10	11
15	12	13	14	15	16	17	18
16	19	20	21	22	23	24	25
17	26	27	28	29	30		

MAI

	M	D	M	D	F	S	S
17						1	2
18	3	4	5	6	7	8	9
19	10	11	12	13	14	15	16
20	17	18	19	20	21	22	23
21	24	25	26	27	28	29	30

JUNI

	M	D	M	D	F	S	S
22		1	2	3	4	5	6
23	7	8	9	10	11	12	13
24	14	15	16	17	18	19	20
25	21	22	23	24	25	26	27
26	28	29	30				

JULI

	M	D	M	D	F	S	S
26				1	2	3	4
27	5	6	7	8	9	10	11
28	12	13	14	15	16	17	18
29	19	20	21	22	23	24	25
30	26	27	28	29	30	31	

AUGUST

	M	D	M	D	F	S	S
30							1
31	2	3	4	5	6	7	8
32	9	10	11	12	13	14	15
33	16	17	18	19	20	21	22
34	23	24	25	26	27	28	29
35	30	31					

SEPTEMBER

	M	D	M	D	F	S	S
35			1	2	3	4	5
36	6	7	8	9	10	11	12
37	13	14	15	16	17	18	19
38	20	21	22	23	24	25	26
39	27	28	29	30			

OKTOBER

	M	D	M	D	F	S	S
39					1	2	3
40	4	5	6	7	8	9	10
41	11	12	13	14	15	16	17
42	18	19	20	21	22	23	24
43	25	26	27	28	29	30	31

NOVEMBER

	M	D	M	D	F	S	S
44	1	2	3	4	5	6	7
45	8	9	10	11	12	13	14
46	15	16	17	18	19	20	21
47	22	23	24	25	26	27	28
48	29	30					

DEZEMBER

	M	D	M	D	F	S	S
48			1	2	3	4	5
49	6	7	8	9	10	11	12
50	13	14	15	16	17	18	19
51	20	21	22	23	24	25	26
52	27	28	29	30	31		

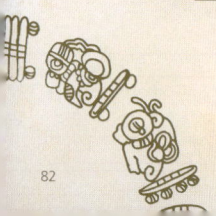

JAHRESÜBERSICHT 2022 | YEAR OVERVIEW 2022

JANUAR

	M	D	M	D	F	S	S
52						1	2
1	3	4	5	6	7	8	9
2	10	11	12	13	14	15	16
3	17	18	19	20	21	22	23
4	24	25	26	27	28	29	30
5	31						

FEBRUAR

	M	D	M	D	F	S	S
5		1	2	3	4	5	6
6	7	8	9	10	11	12	13
7	14	15	16	17	18	19	20
8	21	22	23	24	25	26	27
9	28						

MÄRZ

	M	D	M	D	F	S	S
9		1	2	3	4	5	6
10	7	8	9	10	11	12	13
11	14	15	16	17	18	19	20
12	21	22	23	24	25	26	27
13	28	29	30	31			

APRIL

	M	D	M	D	F	S	S
13					1	2	3
14	4	5	6	7	8	9	10
15	11	12	13	14	15	16	17
16	18	19	20	21	22	23	24
17	25	26	27	28	29	30	

MAI

	M	D	M	D	F	S	S
17							1
18	2	3	4	5	6	7	8
19	9	10	11	12	13	14	15
20	16	17	18	19	20	21	22
21	23	24	25	26	27	28	29
22	30	31					

JUNI

	M	D	M	D	F	S	S
22			1	2	3	4	5
23	6	7	8	9	10	11	12
24	13	14	15	16	17	18	19
25	20	21	22	23	24	25	26
26	27	28	29	30			

JULI

	M	D	M	D	F	S	S
26					1	2	3
27	4	5	6	7	8	9	10
28	11	12	13	14	15	16	17
29	18	19	20	21	22	23	24
30	25	26	27	28	29	30	31

AUGUST

	M	D	M	D	F	S	S
31	1	2	3	4	5	6	7
32	8	9	10	11	12	13	14
33	15	16	17	18	19	20	21
34	22	23	24	25	26	27	28
35	29	30	31				

SEPTEMBER

	M	D	M	D	F	S	S
35				1	2	3	4
36	5	6	7	8	9	10	11
37	12	13	14	15	16	17	18
38	19	20	21	22	23	24	25
39	26	27	28	29	30		

OKTOBER

	M	D	M	D	F	S	S
39						1	2
40	3	4	5	6	7	8	9
41	10	11	12	13	14	15	16
42	17	18	19	20	21	22	23
43	24	25	26	27	28	29	30
44	31						

NOVEMBER

	M	D	M	D	F	S	S
44		1	2	3	4	5	6
45	7	8	9	10	11	12	13
46	14	15	16	17	18	19	20
47	21	22	23	24	25	26	27
48	28	29	30				

DEZEMBER

	M	D	M	D	F	S	S
48				1	2	3	4
49	5	6	7	8	9	10	11
50	12	13	14	15	16	17	18
51	19	20	21	22	23	24	25
52	26	27	28	29	30	31	

JAHRESPLANER 2021 | YEAR PLANNER 2021

Januar	Februar	März	April	Mai	Juni
Fr 1 Neujahr	Mo 1 Imbolc, Mondfest	Mo 1	Do 1	Sa 1 Tag der Arbeit, Beltaine, Mondfest	Di 1
Sa 2	Di 2	Di 2	Fr 2 Karfreitag	So 2	Mi 2
So 3	Mi 3	Mi 3	Sa 3	Mo 3	Do 3 Fronleichnam
Mo 4	Do 4	Do 4	So 4	Di 4	Fr 4
Di 5	Fr 5	Fr 5	Mo 5 Ostermontag	Mi 5	Sa 5
Mi 6 Heilige drei Könige	Sa 6	Sa 6	Di 6	Do 6	So 6 Vatertag
Do 7	So 7	So 7	Mi 7	Fr 7	Mo 7
Fr 8	Mo 8	Mo 8	Do 8	Sa 8	Di 8
Sa 9	Di 9	Di 9	Fr 9	So 9 Muttertag	Mi 9
So 10	Mi 10	Mi 10	Sa 10	Mo 10	Do 10
Mo 11	Do 11	Do 11	So 11	Di 11	Fr 11
Di 12	Fr 12	Fr 12	Mo 12	Mi 12	Sa 12
Mi 13	Sa 13	Sa 13	Di 13	Do 13 Auffahrt	So 13
Do 14	So 14 Valentinstag	So 14	Mi 14	Fr 14	Mo 14
Fr 15	Mo 15	Mo 15	Do 15	Sa 15	Di 15
Sa 16	Di 16	Di 16	Fr 16	So 16	Mi 16
So 17	Mi 17	Mi 17	Sa 17	Mo 17	Do 17
Mo 18	Do 18	Do 18	So 18	Di 18	Fr 18
Di 19	Fr 19	Fr 19	Mo 19	Mi 19	Sa 19
Mi 20	Sa 20	Sa 20	Di 20	Do 20	So 20
Do 21	So 21	So 21	Mi 21	Fr 21	Mo 21 Sommersonnenwende, Sonnenfest
Fr 22	Mo 22	Mo 22	Do 22	Sa 22	Di 22
Sa 23	Di 23	Di 23	Fr 23	So 23	Mi 23
So 24	Mi 24	Mi 24	Sa 24	Mo 24 Pfingstmontag	Do 24
Mo 25	Do 25	Do 25	So 25	Di 25	Fr 25
Di 26	Fr 26	Fr 26	Mo 26	Mi 26	Sa 26
Mi 27	Sa 27	Sa 27	Di 27	Do 27	So 27
Do 28	So 28	So 28 Frühlingsäquinox Sonnenfest	Mi 28	Fr 28	Mo 28
Fr 29		Mo 29	Do 29	Sa 29	Do 29
Sa 30		Di 30	Fr 30	So 30	Fr 30
So 31		Mi 31		Mo 31	

Juli	August	September	Oktober	November	Dezember
Do 1	So 1 Bundesfeier, Lughnasadh, Mondfest	Mi 1	Fr 1	Mo 1 Allerheiligen, Samhain, Mondfest	Mi 1
Fr 2	Mo 2	Do 2	Sa 2	Di 2	Do 2
Sa 3	Di 3	Fr 3	So 3	Mi 3	Fr 3
So 4	Mi 4	Sa 4	Mo 4	Do 4	Sa 4
Mo 5	Do 5	So 5	Di 5	Fr 5	So 5 2. Advent
Di 6	Fr 6	Mo 6	Mi 6	Sa 6	Mo 6
Mi 7	Sa 7	Di 7	Do 7	So 7	Di 7
Do 8	So 8	Mi 8	Fr 8	Mo 8	Mi 8
Fr 9	Mo 9	Do 9	Sa 9	Di 9	Do 9
Sa 10	Di 10	Fr 10	So 10	Mi 10	Fr 10
So 11	Mi 11	Sa 11	Mo 11	Do 11	Sa 11
Mo 12	Do 12	So 12	Di 12	Fr 12	So 12 3. Advent
Di 13	Fr 13	Mo 13	Mi 13	Sa 13	Mo 13
Mi 14	Sa 14	Di 14	Do 14	So 14	Di 14
Do 15	So 15 Mariä Himmelfahrt	Mi 15	Fr 15	Mo 15	Mi 15
Fr 16	Mo 16	Do 16	Sa 16	Di 16	Do 16
Sa 17	Di 17	Fr 17	So 17	Mi 17	Fr 17
So 18	Mi 18	Sa 18	Mo 18	Do 18	Sa 18
Mo 19	Do 19	So 19	Di 19	Fr 19	So 19 4. Advent
Di 20	Fr 20	Mo 20	Mi 20	Sa 20	Mo 20
Mi 21	Sa 21	Di 21	Do 21	So 21	Di 21 Wintersonnenwende, Sonnenfest
Do 22	So 22	Mi 22	Fr 22	Mo 22	Mi 22 4. Advent
Fr 23	Mo 23	Do 23 Herbstäquinox Sonnenfest	Sa 23	Di 23	Do 23
Sa 24	Di 24	Fr 24	So 24	Mi 24	Fr 24
So 25 Grüner Tag	Mi 25	Sa 25	Mo 25	Do 25	Sa 25 Weihnachten
Mo 26 13 Monde Kalender «Neujahr»	Do 26	So 26	Di 26	Fr 26	So 26
Di 27	Fr 27	Mo 27	Mi 27	Sa 27	Mo 27
Mi 28	Sa 28	Di 28	Do 28	So 28 1. Advent	Di 28
Do 29	So 29	Mi 29	Fr 29	Mo 29	Mi 29
Fr 30	Mo 30	Do 30	Sa 30	Di 30	Do 30
Sa 31	Di 31		So 31 Ende der Sommerzeit		Fr 31 Silvester

JAHRESPLANER 2022 | YEAR PLANNER 2022

Januar	Februar	März	April	Mai	Juni
Sa 1 Neujahr	Di 1 Imbolc, Mondfest	Di 1	Fr 1	So 1 Tag der Arbeit, Beltaine, Mondfest	Mi 1
So 2	Mi 2	Mi 2	Sa 2	Mo 2	Do 2
Mo 3	Do 3	Do 3	So 3	Di 3	Fr 3
Di 4	Fr 4	Fr 4	Mo 4	Mi 4	Sa 4
Mi 5	Sa 5	Sa 5	Di 5	Do 5	So 5 Vatertag
Do 6 Heilige drei Könige	So 6	So 6	Mi 6	Fr 6	Mo 6 Pfingstmontag
Fr 7	Mo 7	Mo 7	Do 7	Sa 7	Di 7
Sa 8	Di 8	Di 8	Fr 8	So 8 Muttertag	Mi 8
So 9	Mi 9	Mi 9	Sa 9	Mo 9	Do 9
Mo 10	Do 10	Do 10	So 10	Di 10	Fr 10
Di 11	Fr 11	Fr 11	Mo 11	Mi 11	Sa 11
Mi 12	Sa 12	Sa 12	Di 12	Do 12	So 12
Do 13	So 13	So 13	Mi 13	Fr 13	Mo 13
Fr 14	Mo 14 Valentinstag	Mo 14	Do 14	Sa 14	Di 14
Sa 15	Di 15	Di 15	Fr 15 Karfreitag	So 15	Mi 15
So 16	Mi 16	Mi 16	Sa 16	Mo 16	Do 16 Fronleichnam
Mo 17	Do 17	Do 17	So 17	Di 17	Fr 17
Di 18	Fr 18	Fr 18	Mo 18 Ostermontag	Mi 18	Sa 18
Mi 19	Sa 19	Sa 19	Di 19	Do 19	So 19
Do 20	So 20	So 20	Mi 20	Fr 20	Mo 20
Fr 21	Mo 21	Mo 21	Do 21	Sa 21	Di 21 Sommersonnenwende, Sonnenfest
Sa 22	Di 22	Di 22	Fr 22	So 22	Mi 22
So 23	Mi 23	Mi 23	Sa 23	Mo 23	Do 23
Mo 24	Do 24	Do 24	So 24	Di 24	Fr 24
Di 25	Fr 25	Fr 25	Mo 25	Mi 25	Sa 25
Mi 26	Sa 26	Sa 26	Di 26	Do 26 Auffahrt	So 26
Do 27	So 27	So 27 Beginn der Sommerzeit	Mi 27	Fr 27	Mo 27
Fr 28	Mo 28	Mo 28 Frühlingsäquinox Sonnenfest	Do 28	Sa 28	Di 28
Sa 29		Di 29	Fr 29	So 29	Mi 29
So 30		Mi 30	Sa 30	Mo 30	Do 30
Mo 31		Do 31		Di 31	

Juli	August	September	Oktober	November	Dezember
1	Mo 1 Bundesfeier, Lughnasadh, Mondfest	Do 1	Sa 1	Di 1 Allerheiligen, Samhain, Mondfest	Do 1
2 Mariä Himmelfahrt	Di 2	Fr 2	So 2	Mi 2	Fr 2
3	Mi 3	Sa 3	Mo 3	Do 3	Sa 3
4	Do 4	So 4	Di 4	Fr 4	So 4 2. Advent
5	Fr 5	Mo 5	Mi 5	Sa 5	Mo 5
6	Sa 6	Di 6	Do 6	So 6	Di 6
7	So 7	Mi 7	Fr 7	Mo 7	Mi 7
8	Mo 8	Do 8	Sa 8	Di 8	Do 8
9	Di 9	Fr 9	So 9	Mi 9	Fr 9
10	Mi 10	Sa 10	Mo 10	Do 10	Sa 10
11	Do 11	So 11	Di 11	Fr 11	So 11 3. Advent
12	Fr 12	Mo 12	Mi 12	Sa 12	Mo 12
13	Sa 13	Di 13	Do 13	So 13	Di 13
14	So 14	Mi 14	Fr 14	Mo 14	Mi 14
15	Mo 15	Do 15	Sa 15	Di 15	Do 15
16	Di 16	Fr 16	So 16	Mi 16	Fr 16
17	Mi 17	Sa 17	Mo 17	Do 17	Sa 17
18	Do 18	So 18	Di 18	Fr 18	So 18 4. Advent
19	Fr 19	Mo 19	Mi 19	Sa 19	Mo 19
20	Sa 20	Di 20	Do 20	So 20	Di 20
21	So 21	Mi 21	Fr 21	Mo 21	Mi 21 Wintersonnenwende, Sonnenfest
22	Mo 22	Do 22	Sa 22	Di 22	Do 22
23	Di 23	Fr 23 Herbstäquinox Sonnenfest	So 23	Mi 23	Fr 23
24	Mi 24	Sa 24	Mo 24	Do 24	Sa 24
25 Grüner Tag	Do 25	So 25	Di 25	Fr 25	So 25 Weihnachten
26 13 Monde Kalender «Neujahr»	Fr 26	Mo 26	Mi 26	Sa 26	Mo 26
27	Sa 27	Di 27	Do 27	So 27 1. Advent	Di 27
28	So 28	Mi 28	Fr 28	Mo 28	Mi 28
29	Mo 29	Do 29	Sa 29	Di 29	Do 29
30	Di 30	Fr 30	So 30 Ende der Sommerzeit	Mi 30	Fr 30
31	Mi 31		Mo 31 Halloween		Sa 31 Silvester

28 Montag / Monday 6/16

Weisser Magnetischer Magier: Zeitlosigkeit, Verzaubern, Empfänglichkeit
Ton: Vereinheitlichen, Anziehen, Bestimmung

White Magnetic Wizard: Timelessness, Enchant, Receptivity
Tone: Unify, Attract, Purpose

 Roter Galaktischer Mond
Red Galactic Moon

07:00
08:00
09:00
10:00
11:00
12:00
13:00
14:00
15:00
16:00
17:00
18:00
19:00
20:00
21:00

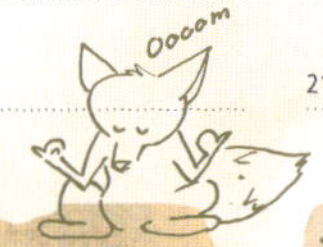

29 Dienstag / Tuesday 6/17

Blauer Lunarer Adler: Vision, Erschaffen, Geist
Ton: Polarisieren, Stabilisieren, Herausforderung

Blue Lunar Eagle: Vision, Create, Mind
Tone: Polarize, Stabilize, Challenge

 Weisser Solarer Hund
White Solar Dog

07:00
08:00
09:00
10:00
11:00
12:00
13:00
14:00
15:00
16:00
17:00
18:00
19:00
20:00
21:00

30 Mittwoch / Wednesday 6/18

Gelber Elektrischer Krieger: Intelligenz, Fragen, Angstlosigkeit
Ton: Aktivieren, Binden, Dienen

Yellow Electric Warrior: Intelligence, Question, Fearlessness
Tone: Activate, Bond, Service

 Blauer Planetarer Affe
Blue Planetary Monkey

07:00
08:00
09:00
10:00
11:00
12:00
13:00
14:00
15:00
16:00
17:00
18:00
19:00
20:00
21:00

31 Donnerstag / Thursday 6/19

 **Rote Selbstexistierende Erde:** Führung, Entwickeln, Synchronisation
Ton: Definieren, Messen, Form

Red Selfexisting Earth: Navigation, Evolve, Synchronicity
Tone: Define, Measure, Form

 | Gelber Spektraler Mensch / Yellow Spectral Human

Silvester

| 07:00 |
| 08:00 |
| 09:00 |
| 10:00 |
| 11:00 |
| 12:00 |
| 13:00 |
| 14:00 |
| 15:00 |
| 16:00 |
| 17:00 |
| 18:00 |
| 19:00 |
| 20:00 |
| 21:00 |

1 Freitag / Friday 6/20

 **Weisser Oberton Spiegel:** Endlosigkeit, Reflektieren, Ordnung
Ton: Ermächtigen, Befehlen, Strahlkraft

White Overtone Mirror: Endlessness, Reflect, Order
Tone: Empowerment, Order, Radiance

 | 233 Roter Kristallener Himmelswanderer | Red Crystal Skywalker

Neujahr

| 07:00 |
| 08:00 |
| 09:00 |
| 10:00 |
| 11:00 |
| 12:00 |
| 13:00 |
| 14:00 |
| 15:00 |
| 16:00 |
| 17:00 |
| 18:00 |
| 19:00 |
| 20:00 |
| 21:00 |

2 Samstag / Saturday 6/21

 **Blauer Rhythmischer Sturm:** Selbsterneuerung, Katalysieren, Energie
Ton: Organisieren, Balancieren, Gleichheit

Blue Rhythmic Storm: Self-generation, Catalyze, Energy
Tone: Organize, Balance, Equality

  | 234 Weisser Kosmischer Magier / White Cosmic Wizard

| 08:00 |
| 10:00 |
| 12:00 |
| 14:00 |
| 16:00 |
| 18:00 |

3 Sonntag / Sunday 6/22

 **Gelbe Resonante Sonne:** Universelles Feuer, Erleuchten, Leben
Ton: Kanalisieren, Inspirieren, Einstimmung

Yellow Resonant Sun: Universal Fire, Enlighten, Life
Tone: Channel, Inspire, Attunement

 | 235 Blauer Magnetischer Adler / Blue Magnetic Eagle

Januar KW 53

Acolotl

7. Resonanter Mond | Resonant Moon

1 10/1	2 11/1	3 12/1	4 13/1	5 14/1	6 15/1	7 16/1
8 17/1	9 18/1	10 19/1	11 20/1	12 21/1	13 22/1	14 23/1
15 24/1	16 25/1	17 26/1	18 27/1	19 28/1	20 29/1	21 30/1
22 31/1	23 1/2	24 2/2	25 3/2	26 4/2	27 5/2	28 6/2

Nimm die Zügel selbst in die Hand!

Zwischendurch lohnt es sich, die Zeitungen zu lesen, damit wir ein bisschen mitplaudern können im Kontakt mit den «anderen»! Aber eigentlich reicht es, wenn wir unsere Mitte halten. Das bedeutet, zentriert zu sein – und was zentriert ist, schwingt resonant mit allem! Wenn du resonant bist mit allem, was dich umgibt, gibt es keine Fragen mehr, nur noch Antworten! Die 28 Tage des Resonanten Mondes bilden die Mitte des 13 Monde Zyklus (und natürlich auch die Mitte deines individuellen 13 Monde Jahres: Halbzeit!) Es ist die Brücke von der ersten Halbzeit zur zweiten … Es ist die Pause, wenn du so willst – der Trainer hat dir ein paar wichtige Beobachtungen und Informationen mitzuteilen! Und ja, bis hierhin hat die Zeitdynamik die Zügel in den Händen gehalten, welche für die zweite Halbzeit dir übergeben werden. Oder nochmals anders ausgedrückt: mit dem 6. Mond sind wir in einen Kreisverkehr hineingefahren und im 7. Mond bestimmst du selber, welche Ausfahrt (Richtung) du nehmen möchtest. Falls du bisher aufmerksam warst, wirst du mit Sicherheit eine gute Entscheidung treffen.

Take the reins into your own hands!

In the meanwhile it is worth reading the newspapers, so that we can chat a little in contact with the «others»! But actually it is enough if we keep our middle. That means to be centered – and what is centered resonates with everything! If you are resonant with everything that surrounds you, there are no more questions, only answers! The 28 days of the resonant moon form the middle of the 13 moon cycle (and of course the middle of your individual 13 moon year: halftime!) It is the bridge from the first halftime to the second … It is the break, if you like – the trainer has some important observations and information to share with you! And yes, so far the time dynamics have held the reins in their hands, which will be handed over to you for the second half. Or to put it another way: with the 6th moon we entered a roundabout and in the 7th moon you decide yourself which exit (direction) you want to take. If you have been attentive so far, you will certainly make a good decision.

Tag | Day — Dreampspell — Long-count

4 Montag / Monday 6/23

Roter Galaktischer Drache:
Geburt, Nähren, Sein
Ton: Harmonisieren, Modellieren, Integrität

Red Galactic Dragon:
Birth, Nurture, Being
Tone: Harmony, Model, Integrity

21

236 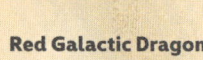 : Gelber Lunarer Krieger / Yellow Lunar Warrior

5 Dienstag / Tuesday 6/24

Weisser Solarer Wind:
Geist, Kommunikation, Atem
Ton: Pulsieren, Erkennen, Absicht

White Solar Wind:
Spirit, Communication, Breath
Tone: Pulse, Realize, Intention

22

237  : Rote Elektrische Erde / Red Electric Earth

6 Mittwoch / Wednesday 6/25

Blaue Planetare Nacht:
Fülle, Träumen, Intuition
Ton: Perfektionieren, Produzieren, Manifestation

Blue Planetary Night:
Abundance, Dream, Intuition
Tone: Perfect, Produce, Manifestation

23

238 : Weisser Selbstexistierender Spiegel | White Selfexisting Mirror

Heilige Drei Könige

Zeit	Montag	Dienstag	Mittwoch
07:00			
08:00			
09:00			
10:00			
11:00			
12:00			
13:00			
14:00			
15:00			
16:00			
17:00			
18:00			
19:00			
20:00			
21:00			

7 Donnerstag / Thursday 6/26

Gelber Spektraler Same: Erblühen, Zielen, Achtsamkeit
Ton: Auflösen, Loslassen, Befreiung

Yellow Spectral Seed: Flowering, Target, Awareness
Tone: Dissolve, Release, Liberation

 Blauer Oberton Sturm / Blue Overtone Storm

| 7:00 |
| 8:00 |
| 9:00 |
| 10:00 |
| 11:00 |
| 12:00 |
| 13:00 |
| 14:00 |
| 15:00 |
| 16:00 |
| 17:00 |
| 18:00 |
| 19:00 |
| 20:00 |
| 21:00 |

8 Freitag / Friday 6/27

Rote Kristallene Schlange: Lebenkraft, Überleben, Instinkt
Ton: Hingabe, Verteilen, Zusammenarbeit

Red Crystal Serpent: Life Force, Survive, Instinct
Tone: Dedicate, Universalize, Cooperation

 Gelbe Rhythmische Sonne / Yellow Rhythmic Sun

| 07:00 |
| 08:00 |
| 09:00 |
| 10:00 |
| 11:00 |
| 12:00 |
| 13:00 |
| 14:00 |
| 15:00 |
| 16:00 |
| 17:00 |
| 18:00 |
| 19:00 |
| 20:00 |
| 21:00 |

Important: For your optimal surfing through the year > Subscribe our Newsletter!

9 Samstag / Saturday 6/28

Weisser Kosmischer Weltenüberbrücker: Tod, Ausgleichen, Möglichkeiten
Ton: Durchhalten, Transzendieren, Präsenz

White Cosmic Worldbridger: Death, Equalize, Opportunity
Tone: Endure, Transcend, Presence

 Roter Resonanter Drache / Red Resonant Dragon

| 14:00 |
| 16:00 |
| 18:00 |

10 Sonntag / Sunday 7/1

Blaue Magnetische Hand: Vollendung, Wissen, Heilung
Ton: Vereinheitlichen, Anziehen, Bestimmung

Blue Magnetic Hand: Accomplishment, Know, Healing
Tone: Unify, Attract, Purpose

 Weisser Galaktischer Wind / White Galactic Wind

Januar KW 1

	11 Montag / Monday 7/2	**12** Dienstag / Tuesday 7/3	**13** Mittwoch / Wednesday 7/4
Dreamspell	 28 **Gelber Lunarer Stern:** Ästhetik, Verschönern, Kunst **Ton:** Polarisieren, Stabilisieren, Herausforderung 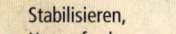 **Yellow Lunar Star:** Elegance, Beautify, Art **Tone:** Polarize, Stabilize, Challenge	29 **Roter Elektrischer Mond:** Universelles Wasser, Reinigen, Flow **Ton:** Aktivieren, Binden, Dienen **Red Electric Moon:** Universal Water, Purify, Flow **Tone:** Activate, Bond, Service	 30 **Weisser Selbstexistierender Hund:** Herz, Lieben, Loyalität **Ton:** Definieren, Messen, Form **White Selfexisting Dog:** Heart, Love, Loyality **Tone:** Define, Measure, Form
Long-count	243 Blaue Solarer Nacht / Blue Solar Night	244 Gelber Planetarer Same / Yellow Planetary Seed	245 Rote Spektrale Schlange / Red Spectral Serpent

		12–21		12–2.
07:00	07:00		07:00	
08:00	08:00		08:00	
09:00	09:00		09:00	
10:00	10:00		10:00	
11:00	11:00		11:00	
12:00	12:00		12:00	
13:00	13:00		13:00	
14:00	14:00		14:00	
15:00	15:00		15:00	
16:00	16:00		16:00	
17:00	17:00		17:00	
18:00	18:00		18:00	
19:00	19:00		19:00	
20:00	20:00		20:00	
21:00	21:00		21:00	

14 Donnerstag / Thursday — 7/5

Blauer Oberton Affe: Magie, Spielen, Illusion
Ton: Ermächtigen, Befehlen, Strahlkraft

Blue Overtone Monkey: Magic, Play, Illusion
Tone: Empowerment, Order, Radiance

 Weisser Kristallener Weltenüberbrücker | White Crystal Worldbridger

12–21

07:00
08:00
09:00
10:00
11:00
12:00
13:00
14:00
15:00
16:00
17:00
18:00
19:00
20:00
21:00

15 Freitag / Friday — 7/6

Gelber Rhythmischer Mensch: Freier Wille, Beeinflussen, Weisheit
Ton: Organisieren, Balancieren, Gleichheit

Yellow Rhythmic Human: Free Will, Influence, Wisdom
Tone: Organize, Balance, Equality

 Blaue Kosmische Hand / Blue Cosmic Hand

12–21

07:00
08:00
09:00
10:00
11:00
12:00
13:00
14:00
15:00
16:00
17:00
18:00
19:00
20:00
21:00

16 Samstag / Saturday — 7/7

Roter Resonanter Himmelswanderer: Raum, Erforschen, Wachsamkeit
Ton: Kanalisieren, Inspirieren, Einstimmung

Red Resonant Skywalker: Space, Explore, Wakefullness
Tone: Channel, Inspire, Attunement

 Gelber Magnetischer Stern / Yellow Magnetic Star

12–21

08:00
10:00
12:00
14:00
16:00
18:00

17 Sonntag / Sunday — 7/8

Weisser Galaktischer Magier: Zeitlosigkeit, Verzaubern, Empfänglichkeit
Ton: Harmonisieren, Modellieren, Integrität

White Galactic Wizard: Timelessness, Enchant, Receptivity
Tone: Harmony, Model, Integrity

 Roter Lunarer Mond / Red Lunar Moon

12–21

Januar KW 2

Tag | Day	Montag / Monday **18** 7/9	Dienstag / Tuesday **19** 7/10	Mittwoch / Wednesday **20** 7/11

Dreamspell

18 Montag / Monday — 7/9

Blauer Solarer Adler: Vision, Erschaffen, Geist
Ton: Pulsieren, Erkennen, Absicht

Blue Solar Eagle: Vision, Create, Mind
Tone: Pulse, Realize, Intention

19 Dienstag / Tuesday — 7/10

Gelber Planetarer Krieger: Intelligenz, Fragen, Angstlosigkeit
Ton: Perfektionieren, Produzieren, Manifestation

Yellow Planetary Warrior: Intelligence, Question, Fearlessness
Tone: Perfect, Produce, Manifestation

20 Mittwoch / Wednesday — 7/11

Rote Spektrale Erde: Führung, Entwickeln, Synchronisation
Ton: Auflösen, Loslassen, Befreiung

Red Spectral Earth: Navigation, Evolve, Synchronicity
Tone: Dissolve, Release, Liberation

Long-count

250 — Weisser Elektrischer Hund / White Electric Dog
251 — Blauer Selbstexistierender Affe / Blue Selfexisting Monkey
252 — Gelber Oberton Mensch / Yellow Overtone Human

For cozy nights: Raw Cacao (bio + fair) in our shop!

12–21

18 Mon	19 Tue	20 Wed
09:00	07:00	07:00
10:00	08:00	08:00
11:00	09:00	09:00
12:00	10:00	10:00
13:00	11:00	11:00
14:00	12:00	12:00
15:00	13:00	13:00
16:00	14:00	14:00
17:00	15:00	15:00
18:00	16:00	16:00
19:00	17:00	17:00
20:00	18:00	18:00
21:00	19:00	19:00
	20:00	20:00
	21:00	21:00

21 Donnerstag / Thursday 7/12

Weisser Kristallener Spiegel: Endlosigkeit, Reflektieren, Ordnung
Ton: Hingabe, Verteilen, Zusammenarbeit

White Crystal Mirror: Endlessness, Reflect, Order
Tone: Dedicate, Universalize, Cooperation

Roter Rhythmischer Himmelswanderer | Red Rhythmic Skywalker

12–21

22 Freitag / Friday 7/13

Blauer Kosmischer Sturm: Selbsterneuerung, Katalysieren, Energie
Ton: Durchhalten, Transzendieren, Präsenz

Blue Cosmic Storm: Self-generation, Catalyze, Energy
Tone: Endure, Transcend, Presence

Weisser Resonanter Magier / White Resonant Wizard

07:00
08:00
09:00
10:00
11:00
12:00
13:00
14:00
15:00
16:00
17:00
18:00
19:00
20:00
21:00

23 Samstag / Saturday 7/14

Gelbe Magnetische Sonne: Universelles Feuer, Erleuchten, Leben
Ton: Vereinheitlichen, Anziehen, Bestimmung

Yellow Magnetic Sun: Universal Fire, Enlighten, Life
Tone: Unify, Attract, Purpose

Blauer Galaktischer Adler / Blue Galactic Eagle

08:00
10:00
12:00
14:00
16:00
18:00

24 Sonntag / Sunday 7/15

Roter Lunarer Drache: Geburt, Nähren, Sein
Ton: Polarisieren, Stabilisieren, Herausforderung

Red Lunar Dragon: Birth, Nurture, Being
Tone: Polarize, Stabilize, Challenge

Gelber Solarer Krieger / Yellow Solar Warrior

Januar KW 3

Tag | Day

25 Montag / Monday 7/16

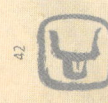

Weisser Elektrischer Wind: Geist, Kommunikation, Atem
Ton: Aktivieren, Binden, Dienen
....

White Electric Wind:
Spirit, Communication, Breath
Tone: Activate, Bond, Service

26 Dienstag / Tuesday 7/17

Blaue Selbstexistieren-de Nacht: Fülle, Träumen, Intuition
Ton: Definieren, Messen, Form
....

Blue Selfexisting Night:
Abundance, Dream, Intuition
Tone: Define, Measure, Form

27 Mittwoch / Wednesday 7/18

Gelber Oberton Same: Erblühen, Zielen, Achtsamke
Ton: Ermächtigen, Befehler Strahlkraft
—

Yellow Overtone Seed:
Flowering, Target, Awareness
Tone: Empowerment, Order, Radiance

Long-count

 257 ‖ Rote Planetare Erde / Red Planetary Earth

 258 ‖ Weisser Spektraler Spiegel / White Spectral Mirror

 259 ‖ Blauer Kristallener Sturm / Blue Crystal Storm

07:00	07:00	07:00
08:00	08:00	08:00
09:00	09:00	09:00
10:00	10:00	10:00
11:00	11:00	11:00
12:00	12:00	12:00
13:00	13:00	13:00
14:00	14:00	14:00
15:00	15:00	15:00
16:00	16:00	16:00
17:00	17:00	17:00
18:00	18:00	18:00
19:00	19:00	19:00
20:00	20:00	20:00
21:00	21:00	21:00

28 Donnerstag / Thursday 7/19

Rote Rhythmische Schlange: Lebenkraft, Überleben, Instinkt
Ton: Organisieren, Balancieren, Gleichheit

Red Rhythmic Serpent: Life Force, Survive, Instinct
Tone: Organize, Balance, Equality

29 Freitag / Friday 7/20

Weisser Resonanter Weltenüberbrücker: Tod, Ausgleichen, Möglichkeiten
Ton: Kanalisieren, Inspirieren, Einstimmung

White Resonant Worldbridger: Death, Equalize, Opportunity
Tone: Channel, Inspire, Attunement

30 Samstag / Saturday 7/21

Blaue Galaktische Hand: Vollendung, Wissen, Heilung
Ton: Harmonisieren, Modellieren, Integrität

Blue Galactic Hand: Accomplishment, Know, Healing
Tone: Harmony, Model, Integrity

 Gelbe Kosmische Sonne / Yellow Cosmic Sun

 Roter Magnetischer Drache / Red Magnetic Dragon

 Weisser Lunarer Wind / White Lunar Wind

Time	Time	Time
:00	07:00	08:00
:00	08:00	10:00
:00	09:00	12:00
:00	10:00	14:00
:00	11:00	16:00
:00	12:00	18:00
:00	13:00	
:00	14:00	
:00	15:00	
:00	16:00	
:00	17:00	
:00	18:00	
:00	19:00	
:00	20:00	
:00	21:00	

31 Sonntag / Sunday 7/22

Gelber Solarer Stern: Ästhetik, Verschönern, Kunst
Ton: Pulsieren, Erkennen, Absicht

Yellow Solar Star: Elegance, Beautify, Art
Tone: Pulse, Realize, Intention

Blaue Elektrische Nacht / Blue Electric Night

Januar KW 4

Jaguar

8. Galaktischer Mond | Galactic Moon

1	2	3	4	5	6	7
7/2	8/2	9/2	10/2	11/2	12/2	13/2
8	9	10	11	12	13	14
14/2	15/2	16/2	17/2	18/2	19/2	20/2
15	16	17	18	19	20	21
21/2	22/2	23/2	24/2	25/2	26/2	27/2
22	23	24	25	26	27	28
28/2	1/3	2/3	3/3	4/3	5/3	6/3

Ist du schon bereit für den grossen Auftritt?

Die liegende Acht symbolisiert die Endlosschlaufe und Unendlichkeit! Das gleiche Symbol, aber zwei unterschiedliche Sichtweisen – du entscheidest! Eine weitere (Endlos-)Schlaufe oder Weiterentwicklung in Richtung Ewigkeit? Der Galaktische Mond ist die erste wichtige Prüfung, ähnlich einer Hauptprobe! Hier darf noch einiges schief gehen, aber wir sollten diese 28 Tage nutzen, um eine möglichst gute Figur zu machen, denn hier offenbart sich eigentlich bereits ein erstes Ergebnis! Der achte Mond ist die Schwelle, bevor es zur Zündung geht. Wenn du bisher deine Hausaufgaben gemacht hast, dann brauchst du überhaupt keine Angst zu haben – es wird gut gehen! Eine weitere gute Nachricht: Sogar wenn du deine Vorbereitungszeit nicht optimal genutzt haben solltest, gibt es keinen Grund zum Verzweifeln, denn es gibt noch unzählige Möglichkeiten, die Sterne zu erreichen. Wichtig ist einfach, im 8. Mond erreichen wir einen ersten Verdichtungshöhepunkt. Dieser Mond ist nicht geeignet um Ferien zu machen, sondern bedeutet meistens intensive Arbeit.

·····························

Are you ready for the big show?

The lying figure eight symbolizes the endless loop and infinity! The same symbol, but two different points of view – you decide! Another (endless) loop or further development towards eternity? The Galactic Moon is the first important test, similar to a dress rehearsal! There are still some things that can go wrong here, but we should use these 28 days to make as good a figure as possible, because here actually already a first result reveals itself! The eighth moon is the threshold, before it goes to the ignition. If you have done your homework so far, then you don't have to be afraid at all – it will go well! Another good news: Even if you haven't used your preparation time optimally, there's no reason to despair, because there are still countless ways to reach the stars. The important thing is simply that in the 8th moon we reach a first peak of densification. This moon is not suitable for holidays, but mostly means intensive work.

Tag | Day

Dreamspell

1 Montag / Monday 7/23

 49

Roter Planetarer Mond:
Universelles Wasser, Reinigen, Flow
Ton: Perfektionieren, Produzieren, Manifestation

Red Planetary Moon:
Universal Water, Purify, Flow
Tone: Perfect, Produce, Manifestation

2 Dienstag / Tuesday 7/24

50

Weisser Spektraler Hund: Herz, Lieben, Loyalität
Ton: Auflösen, Loslassen, Befreiung

White Spectral Dog:
Heart, Love, Loyalty
Tone: Dissolve, Release, Liberation

3 Mittwoch / Wednesday 7/25

 51

Blauer Kristallener Affe: Magie, Spielen, Illusion
Ton: Hingabe, Verteilen, Zusammenarbeit

Blue Crystal Monkey:
Magic, Play, Illusion
Tone: Dedicate, Universalize, Cooperation

Long-count

 4 | Gelber Selbstexistierender Same | Yellow Selfexisting Seed

 5 | Rote Oberton Schlange / Red Overtone Serpent

 6 | Weisser Rhythmischer Weltenüberbrücker | White Rhythmic Worldbridger

Imbolc | Mondfest

07:00	07:00	07:00
08:00	08:00	08:00
09:00	09:00	09:00
10:00	10:00	10:00
11:00	11:00	11:00
12:00	12:00	12:00
13:00	13:00	13:00
14:00	14:00	14:00
15:00	15:00	15:00
16:00	16:00	16:00
17:00	17:00	17:00
18:00	18:00	18:00
19:00	19:00	19:00
20:00	20:00	20:00
21:00	21:00	21:00

4 Donnerstag / Thursday 7/26

Gelber Kosmischer Mensch: Freier Wille, Beeinflussen, Weisheit
Ton: Durchhalten, Transzendieren, Präsenz

Yellow Cosmic Human: Free Will, Influence, Wisdom
Tone: Endure, Transcend, Presence

 Blaue Resonante Hand / Blue Resonant Hand

- 07:00
- 08:00
- 09:00
- 10:00
- 11:00
- 12:00
- 13:00
- 14:00
- 15:00
- 16:00
- 17:00
- 18:00
- 19:00
- 20:00
- 21:00

5 Freitag / Friday 7/27

Roter Magnetischer Himmelswanderer: Raum, Erforschen, Wachsamkeit
Ton: Vereinheitlichen, Anziehen, Bestimmung

Red Magnetic Skywalker: Space, Explore, Wakefullness
Tone: Unify, Attract, Purpose

 Gelber Galaktischer Stern / Yellow Galactic Star

- 07:00
- 08:00
- 09:00
- 10:00
- 11:00
- 12:00
- 13:00
- 14:00
- 15:00
- 16:00
- 17:00
- 18:00
- 19:00
- 20:00
- 21:00

6 Samstag / Saturday 7/28

Weisser Lunarer Magier: Zeitlosigkeit, Verzaubern, Empfänglichkeit
Ton: Polarisieren, Stabilisieren, Herausforderung

White Lunar Wizard: Timelessness, Enchant, Receptivity
Tone: Polarize, Stabilize, Challenge

 Roter Solarer Mond / Red Solar Moon

- 08:00
- 10:00
- 12:00
- 14:00
- 16:00
- 18:00

7 Sonntag / Sunday 8/1

Blauer Elektrischer Adler: Vision, Erschaffen, Geist
Ton: Aktivieren, Binden, Dienen

Blue Electric Eagle: Vision, Create, Mind
Tone: Activate, Bond, Service

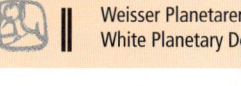 **Weisser Planetarer Hund / White Planetary Dog**

Februar KW 5

8 Montag / Monday 8/2

 Gelber Selbstexistie- render Krieger: Intelligenz, Fragen, Angstlosigkeit
Ton: Definieren, Messen, Form

Yellow Selfexisting Warrior: Intelligence, Question, Fearlessness
Tone: Define, Measure, Form

 Blauer Spektraler Affe
Blue Spectral Monkey

07:00
08:00
09:00
10:00
11:00
12:00
13:00
14:00
15:00
16:00
17:00
18:00
19:00
20:00
21:00

9 Dienstag / Tuesday 8/3

Rote Oberton Erde: Führung, Entwickeln, Synchronisation
Ton: Ermächtigen, Befehlen, Strahlkraft

Red Overtone Earth: Navigation, Evolve, Synchronicity
Tone: Empowerment, Order, Radiance

 Gelber Kristallener Mensch
Yellow Crystal Human

07:00
08:00
09:00
10:00
11:00
12:00
13:00
14:00
15:00
16:00
17:00
18:00
19:00
20:00
21:00

10 Mittwoch / Wednesday   8/4

Weisser Rhythmischer Spiegel: Endlosigkeit, Reflektieren, Ordnung
Ton: Organisieren, Balancieren, Gleichheit

White Rhythmic Mirror: Endlessness, Reflect, Order
Tone: Organize, Balance, Equality

 Roter Kosmischer Himmelswanderer | Red Cosmic Skywalker

07:00
08:00
09:00
10:00
11:00
12:00
13:00
14:00
15:00
16:00
17:00
18:00
19:00
20:00
21:00

11 Donnerstag / Thursday 8/5

Blauer Resonanter Sturm: Selbsterneuerung, Katalysieren, Energie
Ton: Kanalisieren, Inspirieren, Einstimmung

Blue Resonant Storm:
Self-generation, Catalyze, Energy
Tone: Channel, Inspire, Attunement

 Weisser Magnetischer Magier
White Magnetic Wizard

| 07:00 |
| 08:00 |
| 09:00 |
| 10:00 |
| 11:00 |
| 12:00 |
| 13:00 |
| 14:00 |
| 15:00 |
| 16:00 |
| 17:00 |
| 18:00 |
| 19:00 |
| 20:00 |
| 21:00 |

12 Freitag / Friday 8/6

Gelbe Galaktische Sonne: Universelles Feuer, Erleuchten, Leben
Ton: Harmonisieren, Modellieren, Integrität

Yellow Galactic Sun:
Universal Fire, Enlighten, Life
Tone: Harmony, Model, Integrity

 Blauer Lunarer Adler
Blue Lunar Eagle

12–21

| 07:00 |
| 08:00 |
| 09:00 |
| 10:00 |
| 11:00 |
| 12:00 |
| 13:00 |
| 14:00 |
| 15:00 |
| 16:00 |
| 17:00 |
| 18:00 |
| 19:00 |
| 20:00 |
| 21:00 |

Neu am Zuvuyasurfen? Crash Kurs in unserem Shop!

13 Samstag / Saturday 8/7

Roter Solarer Drache: Geburt, Nähren, Sein
Ton: Pulsieren, Erkennen, Absicht

Red Solar Dragon:
Birth, Nurture, Being
Tone: Pulse, Realize, Intention

 Gelber Elektrischer Krieger
Yellow Electric Warrior

12–21

| 08:00 |
| 10:00 |
| 12:00 |
| 14:00 |
| 16:00 |
| 18:00 |

14 Sonntag / Sunday 8/8

Weisser Planetarer Wind: Geist, Kommunikation, Atem
Ton: Perfektionieren, Produzieren, Manifestation

White Planetary Wind:
Spirit, Communication, Breath
Tone: Perfect, Produce, Manifestation

Rote Selbstexistierende Erde
Red Selfexisting Earth

Valentinstag

12–21

Februar KW 6

15 Montag / Monday 8/9

Blaue Spektrale Nacht: Fülle, Träumen, Intuition
Ton: Auflösen, Loslassen, Befreiung

Blue Spectral Night: Abundance, Dream, Intuition
Tone: Dissolve, Release, Liberation

 Weisser Oberton Spiegel / White Overtone Mirror

12-21

07:00
08:00
09:00
10:00
11:00
12:00
13:00
14:00
15:00
16:00
17:00
18:00
19:00
20:00
21:00

16 Dienstag / Tuesday 8/10

Gelber Kristallener Same: Erblühen, Zielen, Achtsamkeit
Ton: Hingabe, Verteilen, Zusammenarbeit

Yellow Crystal Seed: Flowering, Target, Awareness
Tone: Dedicate, Universalize, Cooperation

 Blauer Rhythmischer Sturm / Blue Rhythmic Storm

12-21

07:00
08:00
09:00
10:00
11:00
12:00
13:00
14:00
15:00
16:00
17:00
18:00
19:00
20:00
21:00

17 Mittwoch / Wednesday 8/11

Rote Kosmische Schlange: Lebenkraft, Überleben, Instinkt
Ton: Durchhalten, Transzendieren, Präsenz

Red Cosmic Serpent: Life Force, Survive, Instinct
Tone: Endure, Transcend, Presence

 Gelbe Resonante Sonne / Yellow Resonant Sun

12-21

07:00
08:00
09:00
10:00
11:00
12:00
13:00
14:00
15:00
16:00
17:00
18:00
19:00
20:00
21:00

18 Donnerstag / Thursday 8/12	19 Freitag / Friday 8/13	20 Samstag / Saturday 8/14
Weisser Magnetischer Weltenüberbrücker: Tod, Ausgleichen, Möglichkeiten **Ton:** Vereinheitlichen, Anziehen, Bestimmung	**Blaue Lunare Hand:** Vollendung, Wissen, Heilung **Ton:** Polarisieren, Stabilisieren, Herausforderung	**Gelber Elektrischer Stern:** Ästhetik, Verschönern, Kunst **Ton:** Aktivieren, Binden, Dienen
White Magnetic Worldbridger: Death, Equalize, Opportunity **Tone:** Unify, Attract, Purpose	**Blue Lunar Hand:** Accomplishment, Know, Healing **Tone:** Polarize, Stabilize, Challenge	**Yellow Electric Star:** Elegance, Beautify, Art **Tone:** Activate, Bond, Service
Roter Galaktischer Drache / Red Galactic Dragon	Weisser Solarer Wind / White Solar Wind	Blaue Planetare Nacht / Blue Planetary Night

Februar KW 7

18 Thursday — 07:00 – 21:00 (12–21)

19 Friday — 07:00 – 21:00 (12–21)

20 Saturday — 08:00 – 18:00 (12–21)

21 Sonntag / Sunday 8/15

 **Roter Selbstexistierender Mond:** Universelles Wasser, Reinigen, Flow **Ton:** Definieren, Messen, Form

Red Selfexisting Moon: Universal Water, Purify, Flow **Tone:** Define, Measure, Form

 Gelber Spektraler Same / Yellow Spectral Seed

12–21

107

Tag | Day	**22** Montag / Monday 8/16	**23** Dienstag / Tuesday 8/17	**24** Mittwoch / Wednesday 8/18
Dreamspell	 70 **Weisser Oberton Hund:** Herz, Lieben, Loyalität **Ton:** Ermächtigen, Befehlen, Strahlkraft — **White Overtone Dog:** Heart, Love, Loyalty **Tone:** Empowerment, Order, Radiance	71 **Blauer Rhythmischer Affe:** Magie, Spielen, Illusion **Ton:** Organisieren, Balancieren, Gleichheit . **Blue Rhythmic Monkey:** Magic, Play, Illusion **Tone:** Organize, Balance, Equality	 72 **Gelber Resonanter Mensch:** Freier Wille, Beeinflussen, Weisheit **Ton:** Kanalisieren, Inspirieren, Einstimmung ... **Yellow Resonant Human:** Free Will, Influence, Wisdom **Tone:** Channel, Inspire, Attunement
Long-count	 25 Rote Kristallene Schlange / Red Crystal Serpent	26 Weisser Kosmischer Weltenüberbrücker | White Cosmic Worldbridger	27 Blaue Magnetische Hand / Blue Magnetic Hand

07:00
08:00
09:00
10:00
11:00
12:00
13:00
14:00
15:00
16:00
17:00
18:00
19:00
20:00
21:00

25 Donnerstag / Thursday 8/19	**26** Freitag / Friday 8/20	**27** Samstag / Saturday 8/21
 **Roter Galaktischer Himmelswanderer:** Raum, Erforschen, Wachsamkeit **Ton:** Harmonisieren, Modellieren, Integrität	 **Weisser Solarer Magier:** Zeitlosigkeit, Verzaubern, Empfänglichkeit **Ton:** Pulsieren, Erkennen, Absicht	 **Blauer Planetarer Adler:** Vision, Erschaffen, Geist **Ton:** Perfektionieren, Produzieren, Manifestation
Red Galactic Skywalker: Space, Explore, Wakefullness **Tone:** Harmony, Model, Integrity	**White Solar Wizard:** Timelessness, Enchant, Receptivity **Tone:** Pulse, Realize, Intention	**Blue Planetary Eagle:** Vision, Create, Mind **Tone:** Perfect, Produce, Manifestation

Februar KW 8

 : Gelber Lunarer Stern / Yellow Lunar Star

 : Roter Elektrischer Mond / Red Electric Moon

 : Weisser Selbstexistierender Hund | White Selfexisting Dog

07:00
08:00
09:00
10:00
11:00
12:00
13:00
14:00
15:00
16:00
17:00
18:00
19:00
20:00
21:00

07:00
08:00
09:00
10:00
11:00
12:00
13:00
14:00
15:00
16:00
17:00
18:00
19:00
20:00
21:00

08:00
10:00
12:00
14:00
16:00
18:00

28 Sonntag / Sunday 8/22

Gelber Spektraler Krieger: Intelligenz, Fragen, Angstlosigkeit
Ton: Auflösen, Loslassen, Befreiung

Yellow Spectral Warrior: Intelligence, Question, Fearlessness
Tone: Dissolve, Release, Liberation

Blauer Oberton Affe / Blue Overtone Monkey

Für eine magische warme Cacao besuch unseren Shop

9. Solarer Mond | Solar Moon

1 7/3	2 8/3	3 9/3	4 10/3	5 11/3	6 12/3	7 13/3
8 14/3	9 15/3	10 16/3	11 17/3	12 18/3	13 19/3	14 20/3
15 21/3	16 22/3	17 23/3	18 24/3	19 25/3	20 26/3	21 27/3
22 28/3	23 29/3	24 30/3	25 31/3	26 1/4	27 2/4	28 3/4

Welche Entscheidungen stehen noch an?

Das Pulverfass ist gefüllt mit unserem Aktionspotenzial, das wir über die Schwelle des achten Mondes getragen haben. Jetzt wirds spannend! Das Streichholz wird entzündet, die Funken springen, die Lunte brennt – zZzisch … Die Rakete kann steigen. Der Solare Mond gibt uns 28 Tage Zeit, um uns für den Auftritt/Höhepunkt im zehnten Mond zu sammeln. Eine brennende Lunte muss nicht bedeuten, dass wir herumzäppeln müssen. Die meisten Schauspieler konzentrieren sich vor ihrem Auftritt, um ihren Geist zu leeren, damit sie das Zischen der Lunte genau hören! Denn im letzten Augenblick vor der Detonation – einem kurzen Moment der absoluten Stille – genau dann ist der pefekte Zeitpunkt gekommen, um auf die Bühne zu treten: selbstbewusst und zentriert! Daher stehen im 9. Mond wichtige Entscheidungen an, die nicht unbedingt spektakulär sein müssen. Aber sie unterstützen dich dabei, eine optimale Performance hinzulegen.

....

What decisions still have to be made ?

The powder keg is filled with our action potential, which we carried over the threshold of the eighth moon. Now it's getting exciting! The match is ignited, the sparks jump, the fuse burns – zZzisch … The rocket can rise. The Solar Moon gives us 28 days to gather ourselves for the performance/excitement in the tenth moon. A burning fuse does not have to mean that we have to fidget around. Most actors concentrate before their performance to empty their minds so they can hear the fizzle of the fuse! Because in the last moment before the detonation – a short moment of absolute silence – the perfect moment has come to step on stage: self-confident and centered! That's why important decisions, which don't necessarily have to be spectacular, have to be made in the 9th moon. But they help you to achieve an optimal performance.

Tag | Day
Dreamspell
Long-count

1 Montag / Monday 8/23

Rote Kristallene Erde: Führung, Entwickeln, Synchronisation
Ton: Hingabe, Verteilen, Zusammenarbeit

Red Crystal Earth: Navigation, Evolve, Synchronicity
Tone: Dedicate, Universalize, Cooperation

 | Gelber Rhythmischer Mensch
Yellow Rhythmic Human

77 / 32

07:00
08:00
09:00
10:00
11:00
12:00
13:00
14:00
15:00
16:00
17:00
18:00
19:00
20:00
21:00

2 Dienstag / Tuesday 8/24

Weisser Kosmischer Spiegel: Endlosigkeit, Reflektieren, Ordnung
Ton: Durchhalten, Transzendieren, Präsenz

White Cosmic Mirror: Endlessness, Reflect, Order
Tone: Endure, Transcend, Presence

 | Roter Resonanter Himmelswanderer | Red Resonant Skywalker

78 / 33

07:00
08:00
09:00
10:00
11:00
12:00
13:00
14:00
15:00
16:00
17:00
18:00
19:00
20:00
21:00

3 Mittwoch / Wednesday 8/25

Blauer Magnetischer Sturm: Selbsterneuerung, Katalysieren, Energie
Ton: Vereinheitlichen, Anziehen, Bestimmung

Blue Magnetic Storm: Self-generation, Catalyze, Energy
Tone: Unify, Attract, Purpose

 | Weisser Galaktischer Magier
White Galactic Wizard

79 / 34

07:00
08:00
09:00
10:00
11:00
12:00
13:00
14:00
15:00
16:00
17:00
18:00
19:00
20:00
21:00

4 Donnerstag / Thursday 8/26

 Gelbe Lunare Sonne: Universelles Feuer, Erleuchten, Leben
Ton: Polarisieren, Stabilisieren, Herausforderung

Yellow Lunar Sun: Universal Fire, Enlighten, Life
Tone: Polarize, Stabilize, Challenge

 Blauer Solarer Adler / Blue Solar Eagle

| 7:00 |
| 8:00 |
| 9:00 |
| 10:00 |
| 11:00 |
| 12:00 |
| 13:00 |
| 14:00 |
| 15:00 |
| 16:00 |
| 17:00 |
| 18:00 |
| 19:00 |
| 20:00 |
| 21:00 |

5 Freitag / Friday 8/27

 Roter Elektrischer Drache: Geburt, Nähren, Sein
Ton: Aktivieren, Binden, Dienen

Red Electric Dragon: Birth, Nurture, Being
Tone: Activate, Bond, Service

 Gelber Planetarer Krieger / Yellow Planetary Warrior

| 07:00 |
| 08:00 |
| 09:00 |
| 10:00 |
| 11:00 |
| 12:00 |
| 13:00 |
| 14:00 |
| 15:00 |
| 16:00 |
| 17:00 |
| 18:00 |
| 19:00 |
| 20:00 |
| 21:00 |

6 Samstag / Saturday 8/28

 **Weisser Selbstexistierender Wind:** Geist, Kommunikation, Atem
Ton: Definieren, Messen, Form

White Selfexisting Wind: Spirit, Communication, Breath
Tone: Define, Measure, Form

 Rote Spektrale Erde / Red Spectral Earth

| 08:00 |
| 10:00 |
| 12:00 |
| 14:00 |
| 16:00 |
| 18:00 |

7 Sonntag / Sunday 9/1

Blaue Oberton Nacht: Fülle, Träumen, Intuition
Ton: Ermächtigen, Befehlen, Strahlkraft

Blue Overtone Night: Abundance, Dream, Intuition
Tone: Empowerment, Order, Radiance

Weisser Kristallener Spiegel / White Crystal Mirror

März KW 9

Tag | Day

Dreamspell

Long-count

8 Montag / Monday 9/2

Gelber Rhythmischer Same: Erblühen, Zielen, Achtsamkeit
Ton: Organisieren, Balancieren, Gleichheit

Yellow Rhythmic Seed: Flowering, Target, Awareness
Tone: Organize, Balance, Equality

 Blauer Kosmischer Sturm / Blue Cosmic Storm — 39

9 Dienstag / Tuesday 9/3

Rote Resonante Schlange: Lebenkraft, Überleben, Instinkt
Ton: Kanalisieren, Inspirieren, Einstimmung

Red Resonant Serpent: Life Force, Survive, Instinct
Tone: Channel, Inspire, Attunement

 Gelbe Magnetische Sonne / Yellow Magnetic Sun — 40

10 Mittwoch / Wednesday 9/4

Weisser Galaktischer Weltenüberbrücker: Tod, Ausgleichen, Möglichkeiten
Ton: Harmonisieren, Modellieren, Integrität

White Galactic Worldbridger: Death, Equalize, Opportunity
Tone: Harmony, Model, Integrity

 Roter Lunarer Drache / Red Lunar Dragon — 41

Monday	Tuesday	Wednesday
07:00	07:00	07:00
08:00	08:00	08:00
09:00	09:00	09:00
10:00	10:00	10:00
11:00	11:00	11:00
12:00	12:00	12:00
13:00	13:00	13:00
14:00	14:00	14:00
15:00	15:00	15:00
16:00	16:00	16:00
17:00	17:00	17:00
18:00	18:00	18:00
19:00	19:00	19:00
20:00	20:00	20:00
21:00	21:00	21:00

11 Donnerstag / Thursday 9/5

 **Blaue Solare Hand:** Vollendung, Wissen, Heilung
Ton: Pulsieren, Erkennen, Absicht

Blue Solar Hand: Accomplishment, Know, Healing
Tone: Pulse, Realize, Intention

 Weisser Elektrischer Wind / White Electric Wind

07:00
08:00
09:00
10:00
11:00
12:00
13:00
14:00
15:00
16:00
17:00
18:00
19:00
20:00
21:00

12 Freitag / Friday   9/6

 **Gelber Planetarer Stern:** Ästhetik, Verschönern, Kunst
Ton: Perfektionieren, Produzieren, Manifestation

Yellow Planetary Star: Elegance, Beautify, Art
Tone: Perfect, Produce, Manifestation

 Blaue Selbstexistierende Nacht | Blue Selfexisting Night

12–21

07:00
08:00
09:00
10:00
11:00
12:00
13:00
14:00
15:00
16:00
17:00
18:00
19:00
20:00
21:00

13 Samstag / Saturday 9/7

 **Roter Spektraler Mond:** Universelles Wasser, Reinigen, Flow
Ton: Auflösen, Loslassen, Befreiung

Red Spectral Moon: Universal Water, Purify, Flow
Tone: Dissolve, Release, Liberation

 Gelber Oberton Same / Yellow Overtone Seed

12–21

08:00
10:00
12:00
14:00
16:00
18:00

14 Sonntag / Sunday 9/8

 **Weisser Kristallener Hund:** Herz, Lieben, Loyalität
Ton: Hingabe, Verteilen, Zusammenarbeit

White Crystal Dog: Heart, Love, Loyalty
Tone: Dedicate, Universalize, Cooperation

 Rote Rhythmische Schlange / Red Rhythmic Serpent

12–21

März KW 10

	15 Montag / Monday 9/9	**16** Dienstag / Tuesday 9/10	**17** Mittwoch / Wednesday 9/11
Dreamspell	 **Blauer Kosmischer Affe:** Magie, Spielen, Illusion **Ton:** Durchhalten, Transzendieren, Präsenz **Blue Cosmic Monkey:** Magic, Play, Illusion **Tone:** Endure, Transcend, Presence	**Gelber Lunarer Mensch:** Freier Wille, Beeinflussen, Weisheit **Ton:** Polarisieren, Stabilisieren, Herausforderung **Yellow Lunar Human:** Free Will, Influence, Wisdom **Tone:** Polarize, Stabilize, Challenge	 **Roter Lunarer Himmelswanderer:** Raum, Erforschen, Wachsamkeit **Ton:** Polarisieren, Stabilisieren, Herausforderung **Red Lunar Skywalker:** Space, Explore, Wakefullness **Tone:** Polarize, Stabilize, Challenge
Long-count	Weisser Resonanter Weltenüberbrücker | White Resonant Worldbridger	Blaue Galaktische Hand Blue Galactic Hand	Gelber Solarer Stern Yellow Solar Star

12–21   12–21   12–21

07:00
08:00
09:00
10:00
11:00
12:00
13:00
14:00
15:00
16:00
17:00
18:00
19:00
20:00
21:00

18 Donnerstag / Thursday 9/12	**19** Freitag / Friday 9/13	**20** Samstag / Saturday 9/14

 **Weisser Elektrischer Magier:** Zeitlosigkeit, Verzaubern, Empfänglichkeit
Ton: Aktivieren, Binden, Dienen

 Blauer Selbstexistierender Adler: Vision, Erschaffen, Geist
Ton: Definieren, Messen, Form

 **Gelber Oberton Krieger:** Intelligenz, Fragen, Angstlosigkeit
Ton: Ermächtigen, Befehlen, Strahlkraft

White Electric Wizard: Timelessness, Enchant, Receptivity
Tone: Activate, Bond, Service

Blue Selfexisting Eagle: Vision, Create, Mind
Tone: Define, Measure, Form

Yellow Overtone Warrior: Intelligence, Question, Fearlessness
Tone: Empowerment, Order, Radiance

März KW 11

Roter Planetarer Mond / Red Planetary Moon	**Weisser Spektraler Hund** / White Spectral Dog	**Blauer Kristallener Affe** / Blue Crystal Monkey

12–21

	07:00	08:00
	08:00	10:00
	09:00	12:00
	10:00	14:00
	11:00	16:00
	12:00	18:00
	13:00	
	14:00	

21 Sonntag / Sunday 9/15

 **Rote Rhythmische Erde:** Führung, Entwickeln, Synchronisation
Ton: Organisieren, Balancieren, Gleichheit

Red Rhythmic Earth: Navigation, Evolve, Synchronicity
Tone: Organize, Balance, Equality

 **Gelber Kosmischer Mensch** / Yellow Cosmic Human

Frühlingsäquinox | Sonnenfest

12–21

117

Tag | Day

22 Montag / Monday 9/16

98

Weisser Resonanter Spiegel: Endlosigkeit, Reflektieren, Ordnung
Ton: Kanalisieren, Inspirieren, Einstimmung

White Resonant Mirror: Endlessness, Reflect, Order
Tone: Channel, Inspire, Attunement

23 Dienstag / Tuesday 9/17

99

Blauer Galaktischer Sturm: Selbsterneuerung, Katalysieren, Energie
Ton: Harmonisieren, Modellieren, Integrität

Blue Galactic Storm: Self-generation, Catalyze, Energy
Tone: Harmony, Model, Integrity

24 Mittwoch / Wednesday 9/18

100

Gelbe Solare Sonne: Universelles Feuer, Erleuchten, Leben
Ton: Pulsieren, Erkennen, Absicht

Yellow Solar Sun: Universal Fire, Enlighten, Life
Tone: Pulse, Realize, Intention

Long-count

 53 • Roter Magnetischer Himmelswanderer | Red Magnetic Skywalker

 54 : Weisser Lunarer Magier / White Lunar Wizard

55 : Blauer Elektrischer Adler / Blue Electric Eagle

22 Mon	23 Tue	24 Wed
07:00	07:00	07:00
08:00	08:00	08:00
09:00	09:00	09:00
10:00	10:00	10:00
11:00	11:00	11:00
12:00	12:00	12:00
13:00	13:00	13:00
14:00	14:00	14:00
15:00	15:00	15:00
16:00	16:00	16:00
17:00	17:00	17:00
18:00	18:00	18:00
	19:00	19:00
	20:00	20:00
	21:00	21:00

Bald ist es soweit! Agenda 2022 zum «Early Bird» Preis

25 Donnerstag / Thursday 9/19

Roter Planetarer Drache: Geburt, Nähren, Sein
Ton: Perfektionieren, Produzieren, Manifestation

Red Planetary Dragon: Birth, Nurture, Being
Tone: Perfect, Produce, Manifestation

 Gelber Selbstexistierender Krieger | Yellow Selfexisting Warrior

26 Freitag / Friday 9/20

Weisser Spektraler Wind: Geist, Kommunikation, Atem
Ton: Auflösen, Loslassen, Befreiung

White Spectral Wind: Spirit, Communication, Breath
Tone: Dissolve, Release, Liberation

 57 | Rote Oberton Erde / Red Overtone Earth

07:00
08:00
09:00
10:00
11:00
12:00
13:00
14:00
15:00
16:00
17:00
18:00
19:00
20:00
21:00

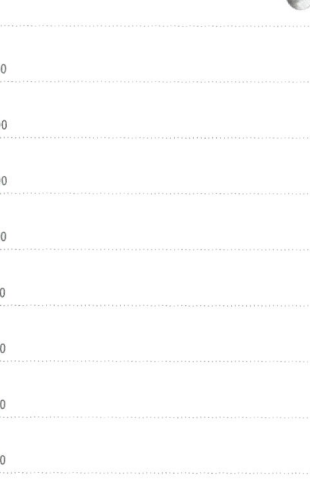

27 Samstag / Saturday 9/21

Blaue Kristallene Nacht: Fülle, Träumen, Intuition
Ton: Hingabe, Verteilen, Zusammenarbeit

Blue Crystal Night: Abundance, Dream, Intuition
Tone: Dedicate, Universalize, Cooperation

 58 | Weisser Rhythmischer Spiegel / White Rhythmic Mirror

08:00
10:00
12:00
14:00
16:00
18:00

28 Sonntag / Sunday 9/22

Gelber Kosmischer Same: Erblühen, Zielen, Achtsamkeit
Ton: Durchhalten, Transzendieren, Präsenz

Yellow Cosmic Seed: Flowering, Target, Awareness
Tone: Endure, Transcend, Presence

 59 | Blauer Resonanter Sturm / Blue Resonant Storm

Beginn der Sommerzeit

März KW 12

10. Planetarer Mond | Planetary Moon

1	2	3	4	5	6	7
4/4	5/4	6/4	7/4	8/4	9/4	10/4
8	9	10	11	12	13	14
11/4	12/4	13/4	14/4	15/4	16/4	17/4
15	16	17	18	19	20	21
18/4	19/4	20/4	21/4	22/4	23/4	24/4
22	23	24	25	26	27	28
25/4	26/4	27/4	28/4	29/4	30/4	1/5

Vorhang auf!

Vorhang auf, Bühne frei! Die folgenden 28 Tage sind da für dein «Meisterstück»! Egal wie die Vorbereitungen gelaufen sind, das Einzige, was jetzt noch zählt, ist der Augenblick! Und hier hast du immer alle Möglichkeiten offen! Spiele den Mann, die Frau, den Vater, die Mutter, die Tochter, den Sohn, das Kind, den Jugendlichen, den Erwachsenen, den Schüler und den Meister! Vergiss jedoch nicht den Alten, den Hässlichen, den Unvollkommenen, den Einfaltspinsel … und den (blauen) Affen. Aber spiel es gut und spiel vor allem authentisch! Sei du selber! Sei einfach! Sei! Dann ist dir der Applaus gewiss. Ehrlichkeit ist gefragt, Achtsamkeit, Grosszügigkeit, Offenheit, Freundlichkeit, Genauigkeit, Selbstsicherheit … Im 10. Mond wird das Ergebnis sichtbar, ob du willst oder nicht, ähnlich einer «Zwangsbeglückung» auf dem Höhepunkt der Reise.

Raise the curtain!

Curtain up, stage clear! The following 28 days are there for your «masterpiece»! No matter how the preparations went, the only thing that counts now is the moment! And here you always have all possibilities open! Play the man, the woman, the father, the mother, the daughter, the son, the child, the teenager, the adult, the disciple and the master! But don't forget the old man, the ugly one, the imperfect one, the simpleton … and the (blue) monkey. But play it well and, above all, play it authentically! Be yourself! Be simple! Then you can be sure of the applause. Honesty is in demand, attentiveness, generosity, openness, friendliness, accuracy, self-confidence … In the 10th moon the result becomes visible, whether you like it or not, similar to a «forced happiness» at the climax of the journey.

Tag | Day

Dreamspell

Long-count

	29 Montag / Monday 9/23	**30** Dienstag / Tuesday 9/24	**31** Mittwoch / Wednesday 9/25
	105  **Rote Magnetische Schlange:** Lebenkraft, Überleben, Instinkt **Ton:** Vereinheitlichen, Anziehen, Bestimmung	106 **Weisser Lunarer Weltenüberbrücker:** Tod, Ausgleichen, Möglichkeiten **Ton:** Polarisieren, Stabilisieren, Herausforderung	107 **Blaue Elektrische Hand:** Vollendung, Wissen, Heilung **Ton:** Aktivieren, Binden, Dienen
	Red Magnetic Serpent: Life Force, Survive, Instinct **Tone:** Unify, Attract, Purpose	**White Lunar Worldbridger:** Death, Equalize, Opportunity **Tone:** Polarize, Stabilize, Challenge	**Blue Electric Hand:** Accomplishment, Know, Healing **Tone:** Activate, Bond, Service
	60 Gelbe Galaktische Sonne / Yellow Galactic Sun	61 Roter Solarer Drache / Red Solar Dragon	62 Weisser Planetarer Wind / White Planetary Wind

07:00	07:00	07:00
08:00	08:00	08:00
09:00	09:00	09:00
10:00	10:00	10:00
11:00	11:00	11:00
12:00	12:00	12:00
13:00	13:00	13:00
14:00	14:00	14:00
15:00	15:00	15:00
16:00	16:00	16:00
17:00	17:00	17:00
18:00	18:00	18:00
19:00	19:00	19:00
20:00	20:00	20:00
21:00	21:00	21:00

1 Donnerstag / Thursday   9/26

 **Gelber Selbstexistie-render Stern:** Ästhetik, Verschönern, Kunst
Ton: Definieren, Messen, Form

Yellow Selfexisting Star: Elegance, Beautify, Art
Tone: Define, Measure, Form

2 Freitag / Friday   9/27

 Roter Oberton Mond: Universelles Wasser, Reinigen, Flow
Ton: Ermächtigen, Befehlen, Strahlkraft

Red Overtone Moon: Universal Water, Purify, Flow
Tone: Empowerment, Order, Radiance

3 Samstag / Saturday   9/28

 **Weisser Rhythmischer Hund:** Herz, Lieben, Loyalität
Ton: Organisieren, Balancieren, Gleichheit

White Rhythmic Dog: Heart, Love, Loyalty
Tone: Organize, Balance, Equality

 Blaue Spektrale Nacht / Blue Spectral Night

 Gelber Kristallener Same / Yellow Crystal Seed

 Rote Kosmische Schlange / Red Cosmic Serpent

April KW 13

	Karfreitag	
7:00	07:00	08:00
8:00	08:00	10:00
9:00	09:00	12:00
10:00	10:00	14:00
11:00	11:00	16:00
12:00	12:00	18:00
13:00	13:00	
14:00	14:00	

4 Sonntag / Sunday 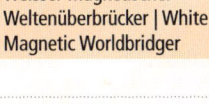 10/1

 **Blauer Resonanter Affe:** Magie, Spielen, Illusion
Ton: Kanalisieren, Inspirieren, Einstimmung
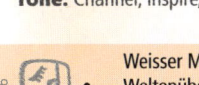

Blue Resonant Monkey: Magic, Play, Illusion
Tone: Channel, Inspire, Attunement

 **Weisser Magnetischer Weltenüberbrücker | White Magnetic Worldbridger**

15:00	15:00
16:00	16:00
17:00	17:00
18:00	18:00
19:00	19:00
20:00	20:00
21:00	21:00

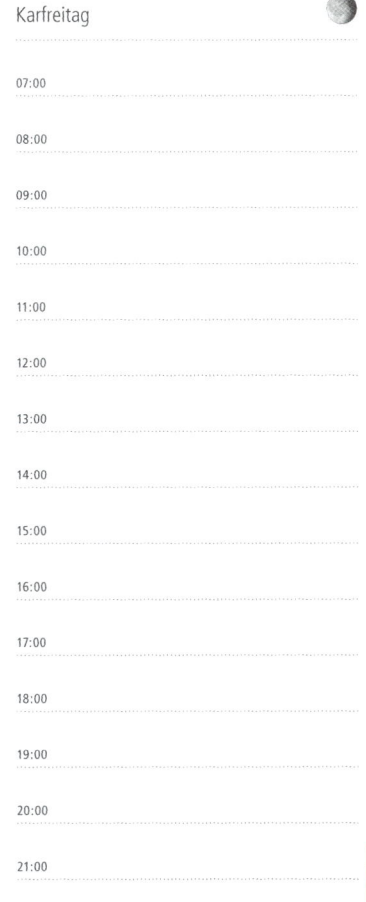

5 Montag / Monday   10/2

Gelber Galaktischer Mensch: Freier Wille, Beeinflussen, Weisheit
Ton: Harmonisieren, Modellieren, Integrität

Yellow Galactic Human:
Free Will, Influence, Wisdom
Tone: Harmony, Model, Integrity

Blaue Lunare Hand | Blue Lunar Hand

Ostermontag

07:00
08:00
09:00
10:00
11:00
12:00
13:00
14:00
15:00
16:00
17:00
18:00
19:00
20:00
21:00

6 Dienstag / Tuesday   10/3

Roter Solarer Himmelswanderer: Raum, Erforschen, Wachsamkeit
Ton: Pulsieren, Erkennen, Absicht

Red Solar Skywalker:
Space, Explore, Wakefullness
Tone: Pulse, Realize, Intention

Gelber Elektrischer Stern | Yellow Electric Star

07:00
08:00
09:00
10:00
11:00
12:00
13:00
14:00
15:00
16:00
17:00
18:00
19:00
20:00
21:00

7 Mittwoch / Wednesday 10/4

Weisser Planetarer Magier: Zeitlosigkeit, Verzaubern, Empfänglichkeit
Ton: Perfektionieren, Produzieren, Manifestation

White Planetary Wizard:
Timelessness, Enchant, Receptivity
Tone: Perfect, Produce, Manifestation

Roter Selbstexistierender Mond | Red Selfexisting Moon

07:00
08:00
09:00
10:00
11:00
12:00
13:00
14:00
15:00
16:00
17:00
18:00
19:00
20:00
21:00

8 Donnerstag / Thursday 10/5

Blauer Spektraler Adler: Vision, Erschaffen, Geist
Ton: Auflösen, Loslassen, Befreiung

Blue Spectral Eagle: Vision, Create, Mind
Tone: Dissolve, Release, Liberation

Weisser Oberton Hund / White Overtone Dog

- 7:00
- 8:00
- 9:00
- 10:00
- 11:00
- 12:00
- 13:00
- 14:00
- 15:00
- 16:00
- 17:00
- 18:00
- 19:00
- 20:00
- 21:00

9 Freitag / Friday 10/6

Gelber Kristallener Krieger: Intelligenz, Fragen, Angstlosigkeit
Ton: Hingabe, Verteilen, Zusammenarbeit

Yellow Crystal Warrior: Intelligence, Question, Fearlessness
Tone: Dedicate, Universalize, Cooperation

Blauer Rhythmischer Affe / Blue Rhythmic Monkey

- 07:00
- 08:00
- 09:00
- 10:00
- 11:00
- 12:00
- 13:00
- 14:00
- 15:00
- 16:00
- 17:00
- 18:00
- 19:00
- 20:00
- 21:00

10 Samstag / Saturday 10/7

Rote Kosmische Erde: Führung, Entwickeln, Synchronisation
Ton: Durchhalten, Transzendieren, Präsenz

Red Cosmic Earth: Navigation, Evolve, Synchronicity
Tone: Endure, Transcend, Presence

Gelber Resonanter Mensch / Yellow Resonant Human

- 08:00
- 10:00
- 12:00
- 14:00
- 16:00
- 18:00

11 Sonntag / Sunday 10/8

Weisser Magnetischer Spiegel: Endlosigkeit, Reflektieren, Ordnung
Ton: Vereinheitlichen, Anziehen, Bestimmung

White Magnetic Mirror: Endlessness, Reflect, Order
Tone: Unify, Attract, Purpose

Roter Galaktischer Himmelswanderer | Red Galactic Skywalker

April KW 14

12 Montag / Monday 10/9

Blauer Lunarer Sturm: Selbsterneuerung, Katalysieren, Energie
Ton: Polarisieren, Stabilisieren, Herausforderung

Blue Lunar Storm: Self-generation, Catalyze, Energy
Tone: Polarize, Stabilize, Challenge

 Weisser Solarer Magier / White Solar Wizard

12-21

07:00
08:00
09:00
10:00
11:00
12:00
13:00
14:00
15:00
16:00
17:00
18:00
19:00
20:00
21:00

13 Dienstag / Tuesday 10/10

Gelbe Elektrische Sonne: Universelles Feuer, Erleuchten, Leben
Ton: Aktivieren, Binden, Dienen

Yellow Electric Sun: Universal Fire, Enlighten, Life
Tone: Activate, Bond, Service

 Blauer Planetarer Adler / Blue Planetary Eagle

12-21

07:00
08:00
09:00
10:00
11:00
12:00
13:00
14:00
15:00
16:00
17:00
18:00
19:00
20:00
21:00

14 Mittwoch / Wednesday 10/11

Roter Selbstexistierender Drache: Geburt, Nähren, Sein
Ton: Definieren, Messen, Form

Red Selfexisting Dragon: Birth, Nurture, Being
Tone: Define, Measure, Form

  Gelber Spektraler Krieger / Yellow Spectral Warrior

12-21

07:00
08:00
09:00
10:00
11:00
12:00
13:00
14:00
15:00
16:00
17:00
18:00
19:00
20:00
21:00

15 Donnerstag / Thursday 10/12

Weisser Oberton Wind: Geist, Kommunikation, Atem
Ton: Ermächtigen, Befehlen, Strahlkraft

White Overtone Wind: Spirit, Communication, Breath
Tone: Empowerment, Order, Radiance

 Rote Kristallene Erde / Red Crystal Earth

12–21

07:00
08:00
09:00
10:00
11:00
12:00
13:00
14:00
15:00
16:00
17:00
18:00
19:00
20:00
21:00

16 Freitag / Friday 10/13

Blaue Rhythmische Nacht: Fülle, Träumen, Intuition
Ton: Organisieren, Balancieren, Gleichheit

Blue Rhythmic Night: Abundance, Dream, Intuition
Tone: Organize, Balance, Equality

Weisser Kosmischer Spiegel / White Cosmic Mirror

12–21

07:00
08:00
09:00
10:00
11:00
12:00
13:00
14:00
15:00
16:00
17:00
18:00
19:00
20:00
21:00

17 Samstag / Saturday 10/14

Gelber Resonanter Same: Erblühen, Zielen, Achtsamkeit
Ton: Kanalisieren, Inspirieren, Einstimmung

Yellow Resonant Seed: Flowering, Target, Awareness
Tone: Channel, Inspire, Attunement

 Blauer Magnetischer Sturm / Blue Magnetic Storm

12–21

08:00
10:00
12:00
14:00
16:00
18:00

18 Sonntag / Sunday 10/15

Rote Galaktische Schlange: Lebenkraft, Überleben, Instinkt
Ton: Harmonisieren, Modellieren, Integrität

Red Galactic Serpent: Life Force, Survive, Instinct
Tone: Harmony, Model, Integrity

Gelbe Lunare Sonne / Yellow Lunar Sun

12–21

April KW 15

Tag | Day — Dreamspell

19 Montag / Monday 10/16

Weisser Solarer Welten-überbrücker: Tod, Ausgleichen, Möglichkeiten
Ton: Pulsieren, Erkennen, Absicht

White Solar Worldbridger: Death, Equalize, Opportunity
Tone: Pulse, Realize, Intention

20 Dienstag / Tuesday 10/17

Blaue Planetare Hand: Vollendung, Wissen, Heilung
Ton: Perfektionieren, Produzieren, Manifestation

Blue Planetary Hand: Accomplishment, Know, Healing
Tone: Perfect, Produce, Manifestation

21 Mittwoch / Wednesday 10/18

Gelber Spektraler Stern: Ästhetik, Verschönern, Kunst
Ton: Auflösen, Loslassen, Befreiung

Yellow Spectral Star: Elegance, Beautify, Art
Tone: Dissolve, Release, Liberation

Long-count

81	Roter Elektrischer Drache / Red Electric Dragon
82	Weisser Selbstexistierender Wind / White Selfexisting Wind
83	Blaue Oberton Nacht / Blue Overtone Night

12–21

Monday
- 07:00
- 08:00
- 09:00
- 10:00
- 11:00
- 12:00
- 13:00
- 14:00
- 15:00
- 16:00
- 17:00
- 18:00
- 19:00
- 20:00
- 21:00

Tuesday
- 07:00
- 08:00
- 09:00
- 10:00
- 11:00
- 12:00
- 13:00
- 14:00
- 15:00
- 16:00
- 17:00
- 18:00
- 19:00
- 20:00
- 21:00

Wednesday
- 07:00
- 08:00
- 09:00
- 10:00
- 11:00
- 12:00
- 13:00
- 14:00
- 15:00
- 16:00
- 17:00
- 18:00
- 19:00
- 20:00
- 21:00

22 Donnerstag / Thursday 10/19	**23** Freitag / Friday 10/20	**24** Samstag / Saturday 10/21

 **Roter Kristallener Mond:** Universelles Wasser, Reinigen, Flow
Ton: Hingabe, Verteilen, Zusammenarbeit

 **Weisser Kosmischer Hund:** Herz, Lieben, Loyalität
Ton: Durchhalten, Transzendieren, Präsenz

 Blauer Magnetischer Affe: Magie, Spielen, Illusion
Ton: Vereinheitlichen, Anziehen, Bestimmung

Red Crystal Moon: Universal Water, Purify, Flow
Tone: Dedicate, Universalize, Cooperation

White Cosmic Dog: Heart, Love, Loyalty
Tone: Endure, Transcend, Presence

Blue Magnetic Monkey: Magic, Play, Illusion
Tone: Unify, Attract, Purpose

Gelber Rhythmischer Same / Yellow Rhythmic Seed	Rote Resonante Schlange / Red Resonant Serpent	Weisser Galaktischer Weltenüberbrücker / White Galactic Worldbridger

April KW 16

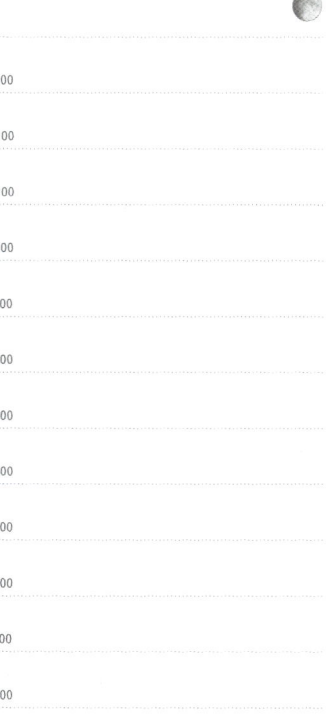

07:00
08:00
09:00
10:00
11:00
12:00
13:00
14:00
15:00
16:00
17:00
18:00
19:00
20:00
21:00

08:00
10:00
12:00
14:00
16:00
18:00

25 Sonntag / Sunday  10/22

Gelber Lunarer Mensch: Freier Wille, Beeinflussen, Weisheit
Ton: Polarisieren, Stabilisieren, Herausforderung

Yellow Lunar Human: Free Will, Influence, Wisdom
Tone: Polarize, Stabilize, Challenge

 Blaue Solare Hand / Blue Solar Hand

Kolibri

11. Spektraler Mond | Spectral Moon

1 2/5	2 3/5	3 4/5	4 5/5	5 6/5	6 7/5	7 8/5
8 9/5	9 10/5	10 11/5	11 12/5	12 13/5	13 14/5	14 15/5
15 16/5	16 17/5	17 18/5	18 19/5	19 20/5	20 21/5	21 22/5
22 23/5	23 24/5	24 25/5	25 26/5	26 27/5	27 28/5	28 29/5

Was lässt du alles los?
Der Vorhang fällt, tosender Applaus, Rufe, Pfiffe, Kreischen, standing Ovation! Wow – herzlichen Glückwunsch. Das wars! Es ist vollbracht! Der Applaus klingt ab, es wird ruhiger, die Leute machen sich auf den Weg nach Hause, hinter den Kulissen beginnt man mit dem Abbau. Du ziehst dich zurück, schminkst dich ab und machst dich frisch. Du lässt los, die Anspannung fällt dahin, dein Körper wird locker und leicht, du fühlst dich unbeschwert, frei wie ein Vogel. Du möchtest abheben und davonfliegen, doch bevor du das kannst, gilt es, den Kreis zu schliessen. Falls sich im 10. Mond ein positives Ergebnis offenbart hat, gilt es jetzt, alles loszulassen. Falls das Ergebnis jedoch nicht so ist, wie du es dir erhofft hast, dann hast du jetzt die Möglichkeit, das ganze Jahrespaket nochmals «aufzuschnüren», um am Ende des 13 Monde Jahres wenigstens «Ende gut – Alles gut» sagen zu können. Schau einfach nochmals ganz genau hin, nimm alles nochmals auseinander, denn der 11. Mond ist energetisch mit dem ersten verbunden, was dir hilft, wie ein Detektiv zu erforschen, warum es nicht optimal gelaufen ist

• •

What are you letting go of?
The curtain falls, thunderous applause, shouts, whistles, screams, standing ovation! Wow – congratulations. That's it! It's done! The applause fades away, it gets calmer, the people make their way home, behind the scenes you start dismantling. You retreat, make yourself up and freshen up. You let go, the tension goes away, your body becomes loose and light, you feel carefree, free like a bird! You want to take off and fly away, but before you can, you have to close the circle. If a positive result has been revealed in the 10th moon, now is the time to let go of everything. If, however, the result is not as you had hoped, then you now have the opportunity to «undo» the whole year's package again in order to be able to at least say «End good – all good» at the end of the 13 moon year. Just look again very carefully, take everything apart again, because the 11th moon is energetically connected to the first one, which helps you, like a detective, to explore why it did not run optimally.

	26 Montag / Monday 10/23	**27** Dienstag / Tuesday 10/24	**28** Mittwoch / Wednesday 10/25
Dreamspell	 **Roter Elektrischer Himmelswanderer:** Raum, Erforschen, Wachsamkeit **Ton:** Aktivieren, Binden, Dienen **Red Electric Skywalker:** Space, Explore, Wakefullness **Tone:** Activate, Bond, Service	**Weisser Selbstexistierender Magier:** Zeitlosigkeit, Verzaubern, Empfänglichkeit **Ton:** Definieren, Messen, Form **White Selfexisting Wizard:** Timelessness, Enchant, Receptivity **Tone:** Define, Measure, Form	 **Blauer Oberton Adler:** Vision, Erschaffen, Geist **Ton:** Ermächtigen, Befehlen, Strahlkraft **Blue Overtone Eagle:** Vision, Create, Mind **Tone:** Empowerment, Order, Radiance
Long-count	**Gelber Planetarer Stern** Yellow Planetary Star	**Roter Spektraler Mond** Red Spectral Moon	**Weisser Kristallener Hund** White Crystal Dog

07:00

08:00

09:00

10:00

11:00

12:00

13:00

14:00

15:00

16:00

17:00

18:00

19:00

20:00

21:00

29 Donnerstag / Thursday

 **Gelber Rhythmischer Krieger:** Intelligenz, Fragen, Angstlosigkeit
Ton: Organisieren, Balancieren, Gleichheit

Yellow Rhythmic Warrior: Intelligence, Question, Fearlessness
Tone: Organize, Balance, Equality

 Blauer Kosmischer Affe | Blue Cosmic Monkey

- 7:00
- 8:00
- 9:00
- 10:00
- 11:00
- 12:00
- 13:00
- 14:00
- 15:00
- 16:00
- 17:00
- 18:00
- 19:00
- 20:00
- 21:00

30 Freitag / Friday

 Rote Resonante Erde: Führung, Entwickeln, Synchronisation
Ton: Kanalisieren, Inspirieren, Einstimmung

Red Resonant Earth: Navigation, Evolve, Synchronicity
Tone: Channel, Inspire, Attunement

 Gelber Magnetischer Mensch | Yellow Magnetic Human

- 07:00
- 08:00
- 09:00
- 10:00
- 11:00
- 12:00
- 13:00
- 14:00
- 15:00
- 16:00
- 17:00
- 18:00
- 19:00
- 20:00
- 21:00

1 Samstag / Saturday

 **Weisser Galaktischer Spiegel:** Endlosigkeit, Reflektieren, Ordnung
Ton: Harmonisieren, Modellieren, Integrität

White Galactic Mirror: Endlessness, Reflect, Order
Tone: Harmony, Model, Integrity

 Roter Lunarer Himmelswanderer | Red Lunar Skywalker

Tag der Arbeit | Beltaine | Mondfest

- 08:00
- 10:00
- 12:00
- 14:00
- 16:00
- 18:00

2 Sonntag / Sunday 11/1

 **Blauer Solarer Sturm:** Selbsterneuerung, Katalysieren, Energie
Ton: Pulsieren, Erkennen, Absicht

Blue Solar Storm: Self-generation, Catalyze, Energy
Tone: Pulse, Realize, Intention

 Weisser Elektrischer Magier | White Electric Wizard

April KW 17

Tag | Day

Dreamspell

3 Montag / Monday 11/2

 140

Gelbe Planetare Sonne: Universelles Feuer, Erleuchten, Leben
Ton: Perfektionieren, Produzieren, Manifestation

Yellow Planetary Sun: Universal Fire, Enlighten, Life
Tone: Perfect, Produce, Manifestation

4 Dienstag / Tuesday 11/3

141

Roter Spektraler Drache: Geburt, Nähren, Sein
Ton: Auflösen, Loslassen, Befreiung

Red Spectral Dragon: Birth, Nurture, Being
Tone: Dissolve, Release, Liberation

5 Mittwoch / Wednesday 11/4

 142

Weisser Kristallener Wind: Geist, Kommunikation, Atem
Ton: Hingabe, Verteilen, Zusammenarbeit

White Crystal Wind: Spirit, Communication, Breath
Tone: Dedicate, Universalize, Cooperation

Long-count

 95 — **Blauer Selbstexistierender Adler | Blue Selfexisting Eagle**

 96 — **Gelber Oberton Krieger | Yellow Overtone Warrior**

 97 — **Rote Rhythmische Erde | Red Rhythmic Earth**

Monday	Tuesday	Wednesday
07:00	07:00	07:00
08:00	08:00	08:00
09:00	09:00	09:00
10:00	10:00	10:00
11:00	11:00	11:00
12:00	12:00	12:00
13:00	13:00	13:00
14:00	14:00	14:00
15:00	15:00	15:00
16:00	16:00	16:00
17:00	17:00	17:00
18:00	18:00	18:00
19:00	19:00	19:00
20:00	20:00	20:00
21:00	21:00	21:00

6 Donnerstag / Thursday — 11/5

Blaue Kosmische Nacht: Fülle, Träumen, Intuition
Ton: Durchhalten, Transzendieren, Präsenz

Blue Cosmic Night: Abundance, Dream, Intuition
Tone: Endure, Transcend, Presence

Weisser Resonanter Spiegel / White Resonant Mirror

07:00
08:00
09:00
10:00
11:00
12:00
13:00
14:00
15:00
16:00
17:00
18:00
19:00
20:00
21:00

7 Freitag / Friday — 11/6

Gelber Magnetischer Same: Erblühen, Zielen, Achtsamkeit
Ton: Vereinheitlichen, Anziehen, Bestimmung

Yellow Magnetic Seed: Flowering, Target, Awareness
Tone: Unify, Attract, Purpose

Blauer Galaktischer Sturm / Blue Galactic Storm

07:00
08:00
09:00
10:00
11:00
12:00
13:00
14:00
15:00
16:00
17:00
18:00
19:00
20:00
21:00

8 Samstag / Saturday — 11/7

Rote Lunare Schlange: Lebenkraft, Überleben, Instinkt
Ton: Polarisieren, Stabilisieren, Herausforderung

Red Lunar Serpent: Life Force, Survive, Instinct
Tone: Polarize, Stabilize, Challenge

Gelbe Solare Sonne / Yellow Solar Sun

08:00
10:00
12:00
14:00
16:00
18:00

9 Sonntag / Sunday — 11/8

Weisser Elektrischer Weltenüberbrücker: Tod, Ausgleichen, Möglichkeiten
Ton: Aktivieren, Binden, Dienen

White Electric Worldbridger: Death, Equalize, Opportunity
Tone: Activate, Bond, Service

Roter Planetarer Drache / Red Planetary Dragon

Muttertag

Mai KW 18

Tag | Day

10 Montag / Monday 11/9
11 Dienstag / Tuesday 11/10
12 Mittwoch / Wednesday 11/11

Dreamspell

 147
Blaue Selbstexistierende Hand: Vollendung, Wissen, Heilung
Ton: Definieren, Messen, Form

 148
Gelber Obertoner Stern: Ästhetik, Verschönern, Kunst
Ton: Ermächtigen, Befehlen, Strahlkraft

 149
Roter Rhythmischer Mond: Universelles Wasser, Reinigen, Flow
Ton: Organisieren, Balancieren, Gleichheit

Blue Selfexisting Hand: Accomplishment, Know, Healing
Tone: Define, Measure, Form

Yellow Overtone Star: Elegance, Beautify, Art
Tone: Empowerment, Order, Radiance

Red Rhythmic Moon: Universal Water, Purify, Flow
Tone: Organize, Balance, Equality

Long-count

 102
Weisser Spektraler Wind
White Spectral Wind

 103
Blaue Kristallene Nacht
Blue Crystal Night

 104
Gelber Kosmischer Same
Yellow Cosmic Seed

12–21

Time	Monday	Tuesday	Wednesday
07:00			
08:00			
09:00			
10:00			
11:00			
12:00			
13:00			
14:00			
15:00			
16:00			
17:00			
18:00			
19:00			
20:00			
21:00			

13 Donnerstag / Thursday  11/12

Weisser Resonanter Hund: Herz, Lieben, Loyalität
Ton: Kanalisieren, Inspirieren, Einstimmung

White Resonant Dog: Heart, Love, Loyality
Tone: Channel, Inspire, Attunement

14 Freitag / Friday  11/13

Blauer Galaktischer Affe: Magie, Spielen, Illusion
Ton: Harmonisieren, Modellieren, Integrität

Blue Galactic Monkey: Magic, Play, Illusion
Tone: Harmony, Model, Integrity

15 Samstag / Saturday   11/14

Gelber Solarer Mensch: Freier Wille, Beeinflussen, Weisheit
Ton: Pulsieren, Erkennen, Absicht

Yellow Solar Human: Free Will, Influence, Wisdom
Tone: Pulse, Realize, Intention

 Rote Magnetische Schlange / Red Magnetic Serpent

 Weisser Lunarer Weltenüberbrücker | White Lunar Worldbridger

 Blaue Elektrische Hand / Blue Electric Hand

Auffahrt

12–21 | 12–21 | 12–21

	07:00	08:00
	08:00	10:00
	09:00	12:00
	10:00	14:00
	11:00	16:00
	12:00	18:00
	13:00	
	14:00	

16 Sonntag / Sunday 11/15

Roter Planetarer Himmelswanderer: Raum, Erforschen, Wachsamkeit
Ton: Perfektionieren, Produzieren, Manifestation

Red Planetary Skywalker: Space, Explore, Wakefullness
Tone: Perfect, Produce, Manifestation

 Gelber Selbstexistierende Stern | Yellow Selfexisting Star

12–21

	15:00
	16:00
	17:00
	18:00
	19:00
	20:00
	21:00

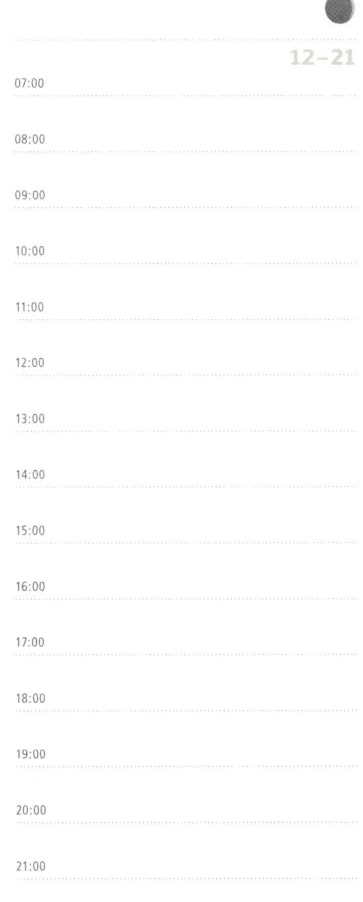

Mai KW 19

Tag | Day

Dreamspell

17 Montag / Monday  11/16

 154

Weisser Spektraler
Magier: Zeitlosigkeit, Verzaubern, Empfänglichkeit
Ton: Auflösen, Loslassen, Befreiung

White Spectral Wizard:
Timelessness, Enchant, Receptivity
Tone: Dissolve, Release, Liberation

18 Dienstag / Tuesday 11/17

 155

Blauer Kristallener
Adler: Vision, Erschaffen, Geist
Ton: Hingabe, Verteilen, Zusammenarbeit

Blue Crystal Eagle:
Vision, Create, Mind
Tone: Dedicate, Universalize, Cooperation

19 Mittwoch / Wednesday 11/18

156

Gelber Kosmischer
Krieger: Intelligenz, Fragen, Angstlosigkeit
Ton: Durchhalten, Transzendieren, Präsenz

Yellow Cosmic Warrior:
Intelligence, Question, Fearlessness
Tone: Endure, Transcend, Presence

Long-count

 109 | Roter Oberton Mond / Red Overtone Mond

110 | Weisser Rhythmischer Hund / White Rhythmic Dog

111 | Blauer Resonanter Affe / Blue Resonant Monkey

12–21 | 12–21 | 12–21

07:00 – 21:00 (all three days)

20 Donnerstag / Thursday — 11/19

 **Rote Magnetische Erde:** Führung, Entwickeln, Synchronisation
Ton: Vereinheitlichen, Anziehen, Bestimmung

Red Magnetic Earth: Navigation, Evolve, Synchronicity
Tone: Unify, Attract, Purpose

 Gelber Galaktischer Mensch / Yellow Galactic Human

12–21

7:00
8:00
9:00
10:00
11:00
12:00
13:00
14:00
15:00
16:00
17:00
18:00
19:00
20:00
21:00

21 Freitag / Friday — 11/20

 **Weisser Lunarer Spiegel:** Endlosigkeit, Reflektieren, Ordnung
Ton: Polarisieren, Stabilisieren, Herausforderung

White Lunar Mirror: Endlessness, Reflect, Order
Tone: Polarize, Stabilize, Challenge

 Roter Solarer Himmelswanderer | Red Solar Skywalker

12–21

07:00
08:00
09:00
10:00
11:00
12:00
13:00
14:00
15:00
16:00
17:00
18:00
19:00
20:00
21:00

22 Samstag / Saturday — 11/21

 **Blauer Elektrischer Sturm:** Selbsterneuerung, Katalysieren, Energie
Ton: Aktivieren, Binden, Dienen

Blue Electric Storm: Self-generation, Catalyze, Energy
Tone: Activate, Bond, Service

 Weisser Planetarer Magier / White Planetary Wizard

Check out Agenda 2022! Now with «Early Bird» price!

08:00
14:00
16:00
18:00

23 Sonntag / Sunday — 11/22

Gelbe Selbstexistierende Sonne: Universelles Feuer, Erleuchten, Leben
Ton: Definieren, Messen, Form

Yellow Selfexisting Sun: Universal Fire, Enlighten, Life
Tone: Define, Measure, Form

Blauer Spektraler Adler / Blue Spectral Eagle

Mai — KW 20

Monarchfalter

12. Kristallener Mond | Crystal Moon

1 30/5	2 31/5	3 1/6	4 2/6	5 3/6	6 4/6	7 5/6
8 6/6	9 7/6	10 8/6	11 9/6	12 10/6	13 11/6	14 12/6
15 13/6	16 14/6	17 15/6	18 16/6	19 17/6	20 18/6	21 19/6
22 20/6	23 21/6	24 22/6	25 23/6	26 24/6	27 25/6	28 26/6

Was ist die Essenz?

Nach einer kurzen Pause trifft man sich – ausnahmslos alle, die mitgewirkt haben: der Regisseur, der Kameramann, der Tontechniker, der Beleuchter, der Choreograph, der Bühenbildner, das Orchester, alle versammeln sich um den runden Tisch – ein Rückblick ist angesagt! Jeder erhält die Möglichkeit, alles auf den Tisch zu legen. Es gibt keine Tabus, Ehrlichkeit ist angesagt! Furchtlos und in einer wohlwollenden Atmosphäre wird «reiner Tisch» gemacht. Der Kristallene Mond sorgt für eine glasklare Kommunikation. Nichts bleibt ungeklärt, alles wird bereinigt. Nichts darf übrigbleiben – ausser der Essenz: ein funkelnder Kristall! Erst wenn dieser geschliffen und geputzt ist, geht es weiter zum letzten Mond dieser 13 Monde Welle.

....

What is the essence?

After a short break we meet – without exception everyone who has participated: the director, the cameraman, the sound engineer, the lighting technician, the choreographer, the set designer, the orchestra, everyone gathers around the round table – a look back is called for! Everyone has the opportunity to put everything on the table. There are no taboos, honesty is the order of the day! Fearless and in a benevolent atmosphere the air is cleared. The Crystal Moon ensures crystal-clear communication. Nothing remains unclear, everything is cleaned up. Nothing may remain – except the essence: a sparkling crystal! Only when this is polished and cleaned, it goes on to the last moon of this 13 moon wave.

Tag | Day

24 Montag / Monday   11/23

Roter Oberton Drache:
Geburt, Nähren, Sein
Ton: Ermächtigen, Befehlen, Strahlkraft

Red Overtone Dragon:
Birth, Nurture, Being
Tone: Empowerment, Order, Radiance

 Gelber Kristallener Krieger / Yellow Crystal Warrior

Pfingstmontag

- 07:00
- 08:00
- 09:00
- 10:00
- 11:00
- 12:00
- 13:00
- 14:00
- 15:00
- 16:00
- 17:00
- 18:00
- 19:00
- 20:00
- 21:00

25 Dienstag / Tuesday   11/24

Weisser Rhythmischer Wind: Geist, Kommunikation, Atem
Ton: Organisieren, Balancieren, Gleichheit

White Rhythmic Wind:
Spirit, Communication, Breath
Tone: Organize, Balance, Equality

 Rote Kosmische Erde / Red Cosmic Earth

- 07:00
- 08:00
- 09:00
- 10:00
- 11:00
- 12:00
- 13:00
- 14:00
- 15:00
- 16:00
- 17:00
- 18:00
- 19:00
- 20:00
- 21:00

26 Mittwoch / Wednesday   11/25

Blaue Resonante Nacht:
Fülle, Träumen, Intuition
Ton: Kanalisieren, Inspirieren, Einstimmung

Blue Resonant Night:
Abundance, Dream, Intuition
Tone: Channel, Inspire, Attunement

 Weisser Magnetischer Spiegel | White Magnetic Mirror

- 07:00
- 08:00
- 09:00
- 10:00
- 11:00
- 12:00
- 13:00
- 14:00
- 15:00
- 16:00
- 17:00
- 18:00
- 19:00
- 20:00
- 21:00

27 Donnerstag / Thursday — 11/26

Gelber Galaktischer Same: Erblühen, Zielen, Achtsamkeit
Ton: Harmonisieren, Modellieren, Integrität

Yellow Galactic Seed: Flowering, Target, Awareness
Tone: Harmony, Model, Integrity

 Blauer Lunarer Sturm / Blue Lunar Storm

07:00
08:00
09:00
10:00
11:00
12:00
13:00
14:00
15:00
16:00
17:00
18:00
19:00
20:00
21:00

28 Freitag / Friday — 11/27

Rote Solare Schlange: Lebenskraft, Überleben, Instinkt
Ton: Pulsieren, Erkennen, Absicht

Red Solar Serpent: Life Force, Survive, Instinct
Tone: Pulse, Realize, Intention

 Gelbe Elektrische Sonne / Yellow Electric Sun

07:00
08:00
09:00
10:00
11:00
12:00
13:00
14:00
15:00
16:00
17:00
18:00
19:00
20:00
21:00

29 Samstag / Saturday — 11/28

Weisser Planetarer Weltenüberbrücker: Tod, Ausgleichen, Möglichkeiten
Ton: Perfektionieren, Produzieren, Manifestation

White Planetary Worldbridger: Death, Equalize, Opportunity
Tone: Perfect, Produce, Manifestation

 Roter Selbstexistierender Drache | Red Selfexisting Dragon

08:00
10:00
12:00
14:00
16:00
18:00

30 Sonntag / Sunday — 12/1

Blaue Spektrale Hand: Vollendung, Wissen, Heilung
Ton: Auflösen, Loslassen, Befreiung

Blue Spectral Hand: Accomplishment, Know, Healing
Tone: Dissolve, Release, Liberation

 Weisser Oberton Wind / White Overtone Wind

Mai KW 21

Tag | Day

31 Montag / Monday 12/2

Gelber Kristallener Stern: Ästhetik, Verschönern, Kunst
Ton: Hingabe, Verteilen, Zusammenarbeit

Yellow Crystal Star: Elegance, Beautify, Art
Tone: Dedicate, Universalize, Cooperation

1 Dienstag / Tuesday 12/3

Roter Kosmischer Mond: Universelles Wasser, Reinigen, Flow
Ton: Durchhalten, Transzendieren, Präsenz

Red Cosmic Moon: Universal Water, Purify, Flow
Tone: Endure, Transcend, Presence

2 Mittwoch / Wednesday 12/4

Weisser Magnetischer Hund: Herz, Lieben, Loyalität
Ton: Vereinheitlichen, Anziehen, Bestimmung

White Magnetic Dog: Heart, Love, Loyality
Tone: Unify, Attract, Purpose

Long-count

123 | Blaue Rhythmische Nacht / Blue Rhythmic Night

124 | Gelber Resonanter Same / Yellow Resonant Seed

125 | Rote Galaktische Schlange / Red Galactic Serpent

Time	Monday	Tuesday	Wednesday
07:00			
08:00			
09:00			
10:00			
11:00			
12:00			
13:00			
14:00			
15:00			
16:00			
17:00			
18:00			
19:00			
20:00			
21:00			

Have you already subscribed to our cyclic Newsletter?

3 Donnerstag / Thursday 12/5

Blauer Lunarer Affe: Magie, Spielen, Illusion
Ton: Polarisieren, Stabilisieren, Herausforderung

Blue Lunar Monkey: Magic, Play, Illusion
Tone: Polarize, Stabilize, Challenge

	Weisser Solarer Weltenüberbrücker	White Solar Worldbridger

Fronleichnam

07:00
08:00
09:00
10:00
11:00
12:00
13:00
14:00
15:00
16:00
17:00
18:00
19:00
20:00
21:00

4 Freitag / Friday 12/6

Gelber Elektrischer Mensch: Freier Wille, Beeinflussen, Weisheit
Ton: Aktivieren, Binden, Dienen

Yellow Electric Human: Free Will, Influence, Wisdom
Tone: Activate, Bond, Service

	Blaue Planetare Hand / Blue Planetary Hand

07:00
08:00
09:00
10:00
11:00
12:00
13:00
14:00
15:00
16:00
17:00
18:00
19:00
20:00
21:00

5 Samstag / Saturday 12/7

Roter Selbstexistierender Himmelswanderer: Raum, Erforschen, Wachsamkeit
Ton: Definieren, Messen, Form

Red Selfexisting Skywalker: Space, Explore, Wakefullness
Tone: Define, Measure, Form

	Gelber Spektraler Stern / Yellow Spectral Star

08:00
10:00
12:00
14:00
16:00
18:00

6 Sonntag / Sunday 12/8

Weisser Obertoner Magier: Zeitlosigkeit, Verzaubern, Empfänglichkeit
Ton: Ermächtigen, Befehlen, Strahlkraft

White Overtone Wizard: Timelessness, Enchant, Receptivity
Tone: Empowerment, Order, Radiance

	Roter Kristallener Mond / Red Crystal Moon

Vatertag

Juni KW 22

Tag | Day
Dreamspell
Long-count

7 Montag / Monday 12/9

Blauer Rhythmischer Adler: Vision, Erschaffen, Geist
Ton: Organisieren, Balancieren, Gleichheit

Blue Rhythmic Eagle: Vision, Create, Mind
Tone: Organize, Balance, Equality

 Weisser Kosmischer Hund
White Cosmic Dog

07:00
08:00
09:00
10:00
11:00
12:00
13:00
14:00
15:00
16:00
17:00
18:00
19:00
20:00
21:00

8 Dienstag / Tuesday 12/10

Gelber Resonanter Krieger: Intelligenz, Fragen, Angstlosigkeit
Ton: Kanalisieren, Inspirieren, Einstimmung

Yellow Resonant Warrior: Intelligence, Question, Fearlessness
Tone: Channel, Inspire, Attunement

 Blauer Magnetischer Affe
Blue Magnetic Monkey

07:00
08:00
09:00
10:00
11:00
12:00
13:00
14:00
15:00
16:00
17:00
18:00
19:00
20:00
21:00

9 Mittwoch / Wednesday 12/11

Rote Galaktische Erde: Führung, Entwickeln, Synchronisation
Ton: Harmonisieren, Modellieren, Integrität

Red Galactic Earth: Navigation, Evolve, Synchronicity
Tone: Harmony, Model, Integrity

 Gelber Lunarer Mensch
Yellow Lunar Human

07:00
08:00
09:00
10:00
11:00
12:00
13:00
14:00
15:00
16:00
17:00
18:00
19:00
20:00
21:00

10 Donnerstag / Thursday — 12/12

Weisser Solarer Spiegel: Endlosigkeit, Reflektieren, Ordnung
Ton: Pulsieren, Erkennen, Absicht

White Solar Mirror: Endlessness, Reflect, Order
Tone: Pulse, Realize, Intention

 Roter Elektrischer Himmelswanderer | Red Electric Skywalker

07:00
08:00
09:00
10:00
11:00
12:00
13:00
14:00
15:00
16:00
17:00
18:00
19:00
20:00
21:00

11 Freitag / Friday — 12/13

Blauer Planetarer Sturm: Selbsterneuerung, Katalysieren, Energie
Ton: Perfektionieren, Produzieren, Manifestation

Blue Planetary Storm: Self-generation, Catalyze, Energy
Tone: Perfect, Produce, Manifestation

 Weisser Selbstexistierender Magier | White Selfexisting Wizard

07:00
08:00
09:00
10:00
11:00
12:00
13:00
14:00
15:00
16:00
17:00
18:00
19:00
20:00
21:00

12 Samstag / Saturday — 12/14

Gelbe Spektrale Sonne: Universelles Feuer, Erleuchten, Leben
Ton: Auflösen, Loslassen, Befreiung

Yellow Spectral Sun: Universal Fire, Enlighten, Life
Tone: Dissolve, Release, Liberation

 Blauer Oberton Adler / Blue Overton Eagle

12–21

08:00
10:00
12:00
14:00
16:00
18:00

13 Sonntag / Sunday — 12/15

Roter Kristallener Drache: Geburt, Nähren, Sein
Ton: Hingabe, Verteilen, Zusammenarbeit

Red Crystal Dragon: Birth, Nurture, Being
Tone: Dedicate, Universalize, Cooperation

 Gelber Rhythmischer Krieger / Yellow Rhythmic Warrior

12–21

Juni KW 23

Tag | Day

Dreamspell

14 Montag / Monday 12/16

182
Weisser Kosmischer Wind: Geist, Kommunikation, Atem
Ton: Durchhalten, Transzendieren, Präsenz

White Cosmic Wind:
Spirit, Communication, Breath
Tone: Endure, Transcend, Presence

15 Dienstag / Tuesday 12/17

183
Blaue Magnetische Nacht: Fülle, Träumen, Intuition
Ton: Vereinheitlichen, Anziehen, Bestimmung

Blue Magnetic Night:
Abundance, Dream, Intuition
Tone: Unify, Attract, Purpose

16 Mittwoch / Wednesday P 12/18

184
Gelber Lunarer Same: Erblühen, Zielen, Achtsamkeit
Ton: Polarisieren, Stabilisieren, Herausforderung

Yellow Lunar Seed:
Flowering, Target, Awareness
Tone: Polarize, Stabilize, Challenge

Long-count

137 | Rote Resonante Erde / Red Resonant Earth
138 | Weisser Galaktischer Spiegel / White Galactic Mirror
139 | Blauer Solarer Sturm / Blue Solar Storm

12–21

07:00
08:00
09:00
10:00
11:00
12:00
13:00
14:00
15:00
16:00
17:00
18:00
19:00
20:00
21:00

12–21

07:00
08:00
09:00
10:00
11:00
12:00
13:00
14:00
15:00
16:00
17:00
18:00
19:00
20:00
21:00

12–21

07:00
08:00
09:00
10:00
11:00
12:00
13:00
14:00
15:00
16:00
17:00
18:00
19:00
20:00
21:00

17 Donnerstag / Thursday 12/19

 **Rote Elektrische Schlange:** Lebenkraft, Überleben, Instinkt
Ton: Aktivieren, Binden, Dienen

Red Electric Serpent: Life Force, Survive, Instinct
Tone: Activate, Bond, Service

 Gelbe Planetare Sonne / Yellow Planetary Sun

12-21

07:00
08:00
09:00
10:00
11:00
12:00
13:00
14:00
15:00
16:00
17:00
18:00
19:00
20:00
21:00

18 Freitag / Friday 12/20

 **Weisser Selbstexistierender Weltenüberbrücker:** Tod, Ausgleichen, Möglichkeiten
Ton: Definieren, Messen, Form

White Selfexisting Worldbridger: Death, Equalize, Opportunity
Tone: Define, Measure, Form

 Roter Spektraler Drache / Red Spectral Dragon

12-21

07:00
08:00
09:00
10:00
11:00
12:00
13:00
14:00
15:00
16:00
17:00
18:00
19:00
20:00
21:00

19 Samstag / Saturday 12/21

 **Blaue Oberton Hand:** Vollendung, Wissen, Heilung
Ton: Ermächtigen, Befehlen, Strahlkraft

Blue Overtone Hand: Accomplishment, Know, Healing
Tone: Empowerment, Order, Radiance

 Weisser Kristallener Wind / White Crystal Wind

12-21

08:00
10:00
12:00
14:00
16:00
18:00

20 Sonntag / Sunday 12/22

 Gelber Rhythmischer Stern: Ästhetik, Verschönern, Kunst
Ton: Organisieren, Balancieren, Gleichheit

Yellow Rhythmic Star: Elegance, Beautify, Art
Tone: Organize, Balance, Equality

 Blaue Kosmische Nacht / Blue Cosmic Night

12-21

Juni — KW 24

Flamingo

13. Kosmischer Mond | Cosmic Moon

1 27/6	2 28/6	3 29/6	4 30/6	5 1/7	6 2/7	7 3/7
8 4/7	9 5/7	10 6/7	11 7/7	12 8/7	13 9/7	14 10/7
15 11/7	16 12/7	17 13/7	18 14/7	19 15/7	20 16/7	21 17/7
22 18/7	23 19/7	24 20/7	25 21/7	26 22/7	27 23/7	28 24/7

Bist du bereit für den magischen Flug?

Es ist soweit! Die Korken knallen, knackiger Beat ertönt, die Discokugel blitzt, «the Party is about to begin»! Endlich wird getanzt, gelacht, geschäkert, geplaudert und das Leben zelebriert. Denn alle sind in Bestform, alle einen grossen Schritt weiter im Leben durch Zeit und Raum. Diese 28 Tage wird gefeiert, in welcher Form auch immer. Einige ziehen es laut und lustig, andere still und leise vor. Auf jeden Fall wird Energie losgelassen, ausgeatmet, um dann noch tiefer einatmen zu können. Denn die Atmung ist wie der 13 Monde Kalender ein Rhythmus, welcher uns in Resonanz mit zahlreichen, äusserst lebendigen Rhythmen und Zyklen in und um uns herum bringt. Je mehr wir zu einem Resonanzkörper werden, umso mehr tritt innerer und äusserer Frieden ein – wir werden zu einem kosmischen Wesen und sind bereit für den magischen Flug, welcher uns in eine neue Jahreswelle führt.

....

Are you ready for the magic flight?

It's time! The corks pop, a crisp beat sounds, the disco ball flashes, «the Party is about to begin»! Finally there is dancing, laughing, flirting, chatting and celebrating life. Because everyone is in top form, everyone is one big step further in life through time and space. These 28 days are celebrated, in whatever form. Some prefer it loud and funny, others quiet and silent. In any case, energy is released, exhaled in order to be able to breathe in even deeper. Because the breathing is like the 13 Moon Calendar, a rhythm which brings us in resonance with numerous, extremely alive rhythms and cycles in and around us. The more we become a resonant body, the more inner and outer peace comes in – we become a cosmic being and are ready for the magic flight that takes us into a new wave of the year.

Tag | Day

21 Montag / Monday 12/23

 189

Roter Resonanter Mond: Universelles Wasser, Reinigen, Flow
Ton: Kanalisieren, Inspirieren, Einstimmung

Red Resonant Moon: Universal Water, Purify, Flow
Tone: Channel, Inspire, Attunement

22 Dienstag / Tuesday 12/24

 190

Weisser Galaktischer Hund: Herz, Lieben, Loyalität
Ton: Harmonisieren, Modellieren, Integrität

White Galactic Dog: Heart, Love, Loyalty
Tone: Harmony, Model, Integrity

23 Mittwoch / Wednesday 12/25

 191

Blauer Solarer Affe: Magie, Spielen, Illusion
Ton: Pulsieren, Erkennen, Absicht

Blue Solar Monkey: Magic, Play, Illusion
Tone: Pulse, Realize, Intention

Long-count

 144 • Gelber Magnetischer Same / Yellow Magnetic Seed

 145 : Rote Lunare Schlange / Red Lunar Serpent

 146 ⋮ Weisser Elektrischer Weltenüberbrücker | White Electric Worldbridger

---

Sommersonnenwende | Sonnenfest

12–21

Complete your collection: get the magical 13 Moon Wall Calendar!

10:00	07:00	07:00
11:00	08:00	08:00
12:00	09:00	09:00
13:00	10:00	10:00
14:00	11:00	11:00
15:00	12:00	12:00
16:00	13:00	13:00
17:00	14:00	14:00
18:00	15:00	15:00
19:00	16:00	16:00
20:00	17:00	17:00
21:00	18:00	18:00
	19:00	19:00
	20:00	20:00
	21:00	21:00

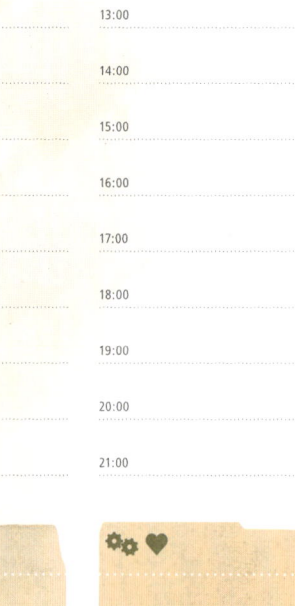

24 Donnerstag / Thursday  12/26

Gelber Planetarer Mensch: Freier Wille, Beeinflussen, Weisheit
Ton: Perfektionieren, Produzieren, Manifestation

Yellow Planetary Human: Free Will, Influence, Wisdom
Tone: Perfect, Produce, Manifestation

 Blaue Selbstexistierende Hand | Blue Selfexisting Hand

- 07:00
- 08:00
- 09:00
- 10:00
- 11:00
- 12:00
- 13:00
- 14:00
- 15:00
- 16:00
- 17:00
- 18:00
- 19:00
- 20:00
- 21:00

25 Freitag / Friday 12/27

Roter Spektraler Himmelswanderer: Raum, Erforschen, Wachsamkeit
Ton: Auflösen, Loslassen, Befreiung

Red Spectral Skywalker: Space, Explore, Wakefullness
Tone: Dissolve, Release, Liberation

 Gelber Oberton Stern | Yellow Overtone Star

- 07:00
- 08:00
- 09:00
- 10:00
- 11:00
- 12:00
- 13:00
- 14:00
- 15:00
- 16:00
- 17:00
- 18:00
- 19:00
- 20:00
- 21:00

26 Samstag / Saturday 12/28

Weisser Kristallener Magier: Zeitlosigkeit, Verzaubern, Empfänglichkeit
Ton: Hingabe, Verteilen, Zusammenarbeit

White Crystal Wizard: Timelessness, Enchant, Receptivity
Tone: Dedicate, Universalize, Cooperation

 Roter Rhythmischer Mond | Red Rhythmic Moon

- 08:00
- 10:00
- 12:00
- 14:00
- 16:00
- 18:00

27 Sonntag / Sunday 13/1

Blauer Kosmischer Adler: Vision, Erschaffen, Geist
Ton: Durchhalten, Transzendieren, Präsenz

Blue Cosmic Eagle: Vision, Create, Mind
Tone: Endure, Transcend, Presence

 Weisser Resonanter Hund | White Resonant Dog

Juni KW 25

Dreamspell

Long-count

28 Montag Monday 13/2

196 **Gelber Magnetischer Krieger:** Intelligenz, Fragen, Angstlosigkeit
Ton: Vereinheitlichen, Anziehen, Bestimmung

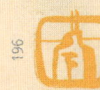

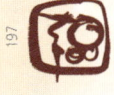

Yellow Magnetic Warrior: Intelligence, Question, Fearlessness
Tone: Unify, Attract, Purpose

151 Blauer Galaktischer Affe
Blue Galactic Monkey

07:00

08:00

09:00

10:00

11:00

12:00

13:00

14:00

15:00

16:00

17:00

18:00

19:00

20:00

21:00

29 Dienstag Tuesday P 13/3

197 **Rote Lunar Erde:** Führung, Entwickeln, Synchronisation
Ton: Polarisieren, Stabilisieren, Herausforderung

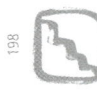

Red Lunar Earth: Navigation, Evolve, Synchronicity
Tone: Polarize, Stabilize, Challenge

152 Gelber Solarer Mensch
Yellow Solar Human

07:00

08:00

09:00

10:00

11:00

12:00

13:00

14:00

15:00

16:00

17:00

18:00

19:00

20:00

21:00

30 Mittwoch Wednesday 13/4

198 **Weisser Elektrischer Spiegel:** Endlosigkeit, Reflektieren, Ordnung
Ton: Aktivieren, Binden, Dienen

White Electric Mirror: Endlessness, Reflect, Order
Tone: Activate, Bond, Service

153 Roter Planetarer Himmelswanderer | Red Planetary Skywalker

07:00

08:00

09:00

10:00

11:00

12:00

13:00

14:00

15:00

16:00

17:00

18:00

19:00

20:00

21:00

1 Donnerstag / Thursday 13/5

Blauer Selbstexistierender Sturm: Selbsterneuerung, Katalysieren, Energie
Ton: Definieren, Messen, Form

Blue Selfexisting Storm: Self-generation, Catalyze, Energy
Tone: Define, Measure, Form

| Weisser Spektraler Magier / White Spectral Wizard |

2 Freitag / Friday 13/6

Gelbe Obertoner Sonne: Universelles Feuer, Erleuchten, Leben
Ton: Ermächtigen, Befehlen, Strahlkraft

Yellow Overtone Sun: Universal Fire, Enlighten, Life
Tone: Empowerment, Order, Radiance

| Blauer Kristallener Adler / Blue Crystal Eagle |

Mariä Himmelfahrt

07:00
08:00
09:00
10:00
11:00
12:00
13:00
14:00
15:00
16:00
17:00
18:00
19:00
20:00
21:00

3 Samstag / Saturday 13/7

Roter Rhythmischer Drache: Geburt, Nähren, Sein
Ton: Organisieren, Balancieren, Gleichheit

Red Rhythmic Serpent: Birth, Nurture, Being
Tone: Organize, Balance, Equality

| Gelber Kosmischer Krieger / Yellow Cosmic Warrior |

08:00
10:00
12:00
14:00
16:00
18:00

4 Sonntag / Sunday 13/8

Weisser Resonanter Wind: Geist, Kommunikation, Atem
Ton: Kanalisieren, Inspirieren, Einstimmung

White Resonant Wind: Spirit, Communication, Breath
Tone: Channel, Inspire, Attunement

| Rote Magnetische Erde / Red Magnetic Earth |

Juli KW 26

Have you already reserved your personal Agenda 2022 in our shop?

Tag | Day	**5** Montag / Monday 13/9	**6** Dienstag / Tuesday 13/10	**7** Mittwoch / Wednesday 13/11
Dreamspell	 203 **Blaue Galaktische Nacht:** Fülle, Träumen, Intuition **Ton:** Harmonisieren, Modellieren, Integrität	204 **Gelber Solarer Same:** Erblühen, Zielen, Achtsamkeit **Ton:** Pulsieren, Erkennen, Absicht	 205 **Rote Planetare Schlange:** Lebenskraft, Überleben, Instinkt **Ton:** Perfektionieren, Produzieren, Manifestation
	Blue Galactic Night: Abundance, Dream, Intuition **Tone:** Harmony, Model, Integrity	**Yellow Solar Seed:** Flowering, Target, Awareness **Tone:** Pulse, Realize, Intention	**Red Planetary Serpent:** Life Force, Survive, Instinct **Tone:** Perfect, Produce, Manifestation
Long-count	158 : Weisser Lunarer Spiegel / White Lunar Mirror	159 : Blauer Elektrischer Sturm / Blue Electric Storm	160 : Gelbe Selbstexistierende Sonne | Yellow Selfexisting Sun

07:00	07:00	07:00
08:00	08:00	08:00
09:00	09:00	09:00
10:00	10:00	10:00
11:00	11:00	11:00
12:00	12:00	12:00
13:00	13:00	13:00
14:00	14:00	14:00
15:00	15:00	15:00
16:00	16:00	16:00
17:00	17:00	17:00
18:00	18:00	18:00
19:00	19:00	19:00
20:00	20:00	20:00
21:00	21:00	21:00

8 Donnerstag / Thursday 13/12

Weisser Spektraler Weltenüberbrücker: Tod, Ausgleichen, Möglichkeiten
Ton: Auflösen, Loslassen, Befreiung

White Spectral Worldbridger: Death, Equalize, Opportunity
Tone: Dissolve, Release, Liberation

 Roter Oberton Drache / Red Overtone Dragon

- 06:00
- 07:00
- 08:00
- 09:00
- 10:00
- 11:00
- 12:00
- 13:00
- 14:00
- 15:00
- 16:00
- 17:00
- 18:00
- 19:00
- 20:00
- 21:00

9 Freitag / Friday 13/13

Blaue Kristallene Hand: Vollendung, Wissen, Heilung
Ton: Hingabe, Verteilen, Zusammenarbeit

Blue Crystal Hand: Accomplishment, Know, Healing
Tone: Dedicate, Universalize, Cooperation

 Weisser Rhythmischer Wind / White Rhythmic Wind

- 07:00
- 08:00
- 09:00
- 10:00
- 11:00
- 12:00
- 13:00
- 14:00
- 15:00
- 16:00
- 17:00
- 18:00
- 19:00
- 20:00
- 21:00

10 Samstag / Saturday 13/14

Gelber Kosmischer Stern: Ästhetik, Verschönern, Kunst
Ton: Durchhalten, Transzendieren, Präsenz

Yellow Cosmic Star: Elegance, Beautify, Art
Tone: Endure, Transcend, Presence

 Blaue Resonante Nacht / Blue Resonant Night

- 08:00
- 10:00
- 12:00
- 14:00
- 16:00
- 18:00

11 Sonntag / Sunday 13/15

Roter Magnetischer Mond: Universelles Wasser, Reinigen, Flow
Ton: Vereinheitlichen, Anziehen, Bestimmung

Red Magnetic Moon: Universal Water, Purify, Flow
Tone: Unify, Attract, Purpose

 Gelber Galaktischer Same / Yellow Galactic Seed

Juli KW 27

Tag | Day — Dreamspell / Long-count

12 Montag / Monday  13/16

 210

Weisser Lunarer Hund: Herz, Lieben, Loyalität
Ton: Polarisieren, Stabilisieren, Herausforderung

White Lunar Dog: Heart, Love, Loyalty
Tone: Polarize, Stabilize, Challenge

 165 **Rote Solare Schlange / Red Solar Serpent**

12–21

07:00
08:00
09:00
10:00
11:00
12:00
13:00
14:00
15:00
16:00
17:00
18:00

Coming soon 4rd Zuvuya Gathering: Subscribe to Newsletter!

13 Dienstag / Tuesday  13/17

 211

Blauer Elektrischer Affe: Magie, Spielen, Illusion
Ton: Aktivieren, Binden, Dienen

Blue Electric Monkey: Magic, Play, Illusion
Tone: Activate, Bond, Service

 166 **Weisser Planetarer Weltenüberbrücker | White Planetary Worldbridger**

12–21

07:00
08:00
09:00
10:00
11:00
12:00
13:00
14:00
15:00
16:00
17:00
18:00
19:00
20:00
21:00

14 Mittwoch / Wednesday 13/18

 212

Gelber Selbstexistierender Mensch: Freier Wille, Beeinflussen, Weisheit
Ton: Definieren, Messen, Form

Yellow Selfexisting Human: Free Will, Influence, Wisdom
Tone: Define, Measure, Form

 167 **Blaue Spektrale Hand / Blue Spectral Hand**

12–2

07:00
08:00
09:00
10:00
11:00
12:00
13:00
14:00
15:00
16:00
17:00
18:00
19:00
20:00
21:00

15 Donnerstag / Thursday 13/19

Roter Oberton Himmelswanderer: Raum, Erforschen, Wachsamkeit
Ton: Ermächtigen, Befehlen, Strahlkraft

Red Overtone Skywalker: Space, Explore, Wakefullness
Tone: Empowerment, Order, Radiance

  Gelber Kristallener Stern / Yellow Crystal Star

12–21

16 Freitag / Friday 13/20

Weisser Rhythmischer Magier: Zeitlosigkeit, Verzaubern, Empfänglichkeit
Ton: Organisieren, Balancieren, Gleichheit

White Rhythmic Wizard: Timelessness, Enchant, Receptivity
Tone: Organize, Balance, Equality

  Roter Kosmischer Mond / Red Cosmic Moon

07:00
08:00
09:00
10:00
11:00
12:00
13:00
14:00
15:00
16:00
17:00
18:00
19:00
20:00
21:00

12–21

17 Samstag / Saturday 13/21

Blauer Resonanter Adler: Vision, Erschaffen, Geist
Ton: Kanalisieren, Inspirieren, Einstimmung

Blue Resonant Eagle: Vision, Create, Mind
Tone: Channel, Inspire, Attunement

 Weisser Magnetischer Hund / White Magnetic Dog

08:00
10:00
12:00
14:00
16:00
18:00

12–21

18 Sonntag / Sunday 13/22

Gelber Galaktischer Krieger: Intelligenz, Fragen, Angstlosigkeit
Ton: Harmonisieren, Modellieren, Integrität

Yellow Galactic Warrior: Intelligence, Question, Fearlessness
Tone: Harmony, Model, Integrity

 Blauer Lunarer Affe / Blue Lunar Monkey

12–21

Juli KW 28

Hunab Ku

Hunab Ku ist das Mass aller Dinge. Die Mitte von allem, was existiert. Die einzige Quelle von Energie oder auch der Geber von Bewegung und Messung. Es ist ein riesiger, lebendinger Organismus, eine Energie im Zentrum unserer Galaxie, die uns alle einschliesst. Hunab-Ku ist die Essenz, die im Zentrum aller Dinge steht. Es ist auch das Herz unserer Galaxis und steht mit unserer Sonne (Kinich Ahau) in Verbindung. Wenn unsere Sonne, die Erde und das Zentrum der Galaxis in einer Achse stehen, sind wir im Einklang. Diese mündliche Überlieferung ist Basis der Maya-Kosmologie, der Himmelsbeobachtung und der Zeitrechnung.

Jedes zeremonielle Zentrum der Maya (Pyramide) ist eine Darstellung dieser Kosmologie, des vibrierenden Geistes der Sonne, der Venus und der Milchstrasse. Für die Maya haben die Natur und die Galaxis ein eigenes Bewusstsein und handeln selbstständig. Ihre Entscheidungen, im Einklang mit denen der Menschen, schaffen das Schicksal des Lebens.

Das Zeichen wird auch den Azteken zugeordnet und ist immer wieder neuen Interpretationen unterworfen. Im Dreamspell von Dr. José Argüelles symbolisiert es schlichtweg das Zentrum unserer Galaxie.

....

Hunab Ku is the measure of all things. The center of everything that exists, the only source of energy or the giver of movement and measurement. It is a huge, living organism, an energy in the center of our galaxy that includes us all. Hunab Ku is the essence that is at the center of all things. It is also the heart of our galaxy and is connected to our sun (Kinich Ahau). When our Sun, the Earth, and the center of the Galaxy are in one axis, we are in unison. This oral tradition is the basis of Mayan cosmology, sky observation and time calculation.

Each ceremonial center of the Maya (pyramid) is a representation of this cosmology, the vibrating spirit of the sun, Venus and the Milky Way. For the Maya, nature and the galaxy have their own consciousness and act independently. Their decisions, in harmony with those of humans, create the destiny of life.

The sign is also assigned to the Aztecs and is always subject to new interpretations. In the Dreamspell by Dr. José Argüelles it simply symbolizes the center of our galaxy.

25. Juli – Der Grüne Tag

Der letzte Tag im 13 Monde Kalender ist der «Tag ausserhalb der Zeit», da er weder zu einer Woche noch zu einem der 13 Monde gehört. Er stellt den nahezu unbekannten «+1 Faktor» dar, mit dem die Wachstumsspirale ausgelöst wird. Der Kreis, der aus 12 Einheiten (12 x 30° = 360°) besteht, wird durch die wichtige Primzahl 13 zur Spirale, ein neuer Reigen wird initiiert. In alten Zeiten wurde dieser Tag benutzt, um Schulden zu begleichen (oder zu löschen), Vergehen zu vergeben und Altes loszulassen. Damit wurde die Energie freigesetzt, die für einen schwungvollen Neustart benötigt wurde.

Der Tag ausserhalb der Zeit, auch «Grüner Tag» genannt, wird seit einigen Jahrzehnten weltweit von Millionen von Menschen gefeiert. Friedliche und kunstvolle Events werden rund um den Grünen Tag organisiert und im Kollektiv zelebriert. Einzelne Länder haben diesen Tag bereits zum Nationalfeiertag ernannt, um ein Zeichen zu setzen für eine friedliche Zukunft.

....

July 25th – The Green Day

The last day in the 13 Moon Calendar is the «Day out of Time», since it belongs neither to a week nor to one of the 13 moons. It represents the almost unknown «+1 factor» that triggers the growth spiral. The circle, which consists of 12 units (12 x 30° = 360°), becomes a spiral by the important prime number 13, a new round dance is initiated. In old times this day was used to settle debts (or to cancel them), to forgive offences and to let go of old things. This released the energy needed for a bouncy restart.

The Day out of Time, also called «Green Day», has been celebrated by millions of people worldwide for several decades. Peaceful and artistic events are organized around the Green Day and celebrated collectively. Some countries have already declared this day a national holiday in order to set an example for a peaceful future.

Tag | Day

19 Montag / Monday 13/23

Rote Solare Erde: Führung, Entwickeln, Synchronisation
Ton: Pulsieren, Erkennen, Absicht

Red Solar Earth: Navigation, Evolve, Synchronicity
Tone: Pulse, Realize, Intention

 Gelber Elektrischer Mensch | Yellow Electric Human

20 Dienstag / Tuesday 13/24

Weisser Planetarer Spiegel: Endlosigkeit, Reflektieren, Ordnung
Ton: Perfektionieren, Produzieren, Manifestation

White Planetary Mirror: Endlessness, Reflect, Order
Tone: Perfect, Produce, Manifestation

 Roter Selbstexistierender Himmelswanderer | Red Selfexisting Skywalker

21 Mittwoch / Wednesday 13/25

Blauer Spektraler Sturm: Selbsterneuerung, Katalysieren, Energie
Ton: Auflösen, Loslassen, Befreiung

Blue Spectral Storm: Self-generation, Catalyze, Energy
Tone: Dissolve, Release, Liberation

 Weisser Oberton Magier | White Overtone Wizard

12-21

07:00	07:00	07:00
08:00	08:00	08:00
09:00	09:00	09:00
10:00	10:00	10:00
11:00	11:00	11:00
12:00	12:00	12:00
13:00	13:00	13:00
14:00	14:00	14:00
15:00	15:00	15:00
16:00	16:00	16:00
17:00	17:00	17:00
18:00	18:00	18:00
19:00	19:00	19:00
20:00	20:00	20:00
21:00	21:00	21:00

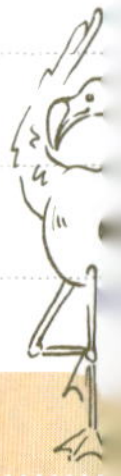

22 Donnerstag / Thursday — 13/26

Gelbe Kristallene
Sonne: Universelles Feuer, Erleuchten, Leben
Ton: Hingabe, Verteilen, Zusammenarbeit

Yellow Crystal Sun:
Universal Fire, Enlighten, Life
Tone: Dedicate, Universalize, Cooperation

 Blauer Rhythmischer Adler / Blue Rhythmic Eagle 176

23 Freitag / Friday — 13/27

Roter Kosmischer
Drache: Geburt, Nähren, Sein
Ton: Durchhalten, Transzendieren, Präsenz

Red Cosmic Dragon:
Birth, Nurture, Being
Tone: Endure, Transcend, Presence

 Gelber Resonanter Krieger / Yellow Resonant Warrior 177

24 Samstag / Saturday — P 13/28

Weisser Magnetischer
Wind: Geist, Kommunikation, Atem
Ton: Vereinheitlichen, Anziehen, Bestimmung

White Magnetic Wind:
Spirit, Communication, Breath
Tone: Unify, Attract, Purpose

 Rote Galaktische Erde / Red Galactic Earth

Juli · KW 29

:00	07:00	08:00
:00	08:00	10:00
:00	09:00	12:00
:00	10:00	14:00
:00	11:00	16:00
:00	12:00	18:00
:00	13:00	
:00	14:00	

25 Sonntag / Sunday

Blaue Lunare Nacht:
Fülle, Träumen, Intuition
Ton: Polarisieren, Stabilisieren, Herausforderung

Blue Lunar Night:
Abundance, Dream, Intuition
Tone: Polarize, Stabilize, Challenge

 Weisser Solarer Spiegel / White Solar Mirror 178

Grüner Tag

:00	15:00
:00	16:00
:00	17:00
:00	18:00
:00	19:00
:00	20:00
:00	21:00

Unser magischer 13 Monde Wandkalender im Shop erhältlich!

Pirania

1. Magnetischer Mond | Magnetic Moon

1	2	3	4	5	6	7
26/7	27/7	28/7	29/7	30/7	31/7	1/8
8	9	10	11	12	13	14
2/8	3/8	4/8	5/8	6/8	7/8	8/8
15	16	17	18	19	20	21
9/8	10/8	11/8	12/8	13/8	14/8	15/8
22	23	24	25	26	27	28
16/8	17/8	18/8	19/8	20/8	21/8	22/8

Was ziehe ich an?

Dr. José Argüelles hat den ersten Mond «Magnetisch» genannt, weil dieser in diesen ersten 28 Tagen wie ein Magnet in das/dein Quantenfeld der Zeit hintaucht und die Themen an die Oberfläche holt, welche von der Zeitdynamik her an der Reihe sind. Als fortgeschrittener Zuvuya°Surfer wirst du jedoch mehr und mehr auch selbst bewusst wählen können, wie du das Jahresthema anpacken und umsetzen möchtest. Der weltweit gültige 13 Monde Kalender, der am 26. Juli beginnt, dauert 13 x 28 Tage. Wie eine Welle türmen sich diese 13 x 28 Tage auf, um anschliessend wieder zusammenzufallen, bevor die Jahreswelle von neuem beginnt. Das ist der solare Zyklus der Zeit, da wir dabei einmal um die Sonne kreisen. Dieser Magnetische Mond gilt auch für deinen individuellen 13 Monde Zyklus, welcher jeweils mit deinem Geburtstag und Jahres°KIN beginnt und damit das aktuelle Jahresthema vorgibt.

What do I attract?

Dr. José Argüelles called the first moon «Magnetic» because in these first 28 days it plunges like a magnet into the quantum field of time and brings to the surface the themes which are next in terms of time dynamics. As an advanced Zuvuya°Surfer you will be able to choose more and more consciously how you want to tackle and implement the theme of the year. The worldwide valid 13 Moon Calendar, which starts on July 26th, lasts 13 x 28 days. These 13 x 28 days pile up like a wave and then collapse again before the annual wave begins anew. This is the solar cycle of time, as we circle once around the sun. This magnetic moon is also valid for your individual 13 moon cycle, which begins with your birthday and year°KIN and thus defines the current theme of the year.

26 Montag / Monday 1/1

Gelber Elektrischer Same: Erblühen, Zielen, Achtsamkeit
Ton: Aktivieren, Binden, Dienen

Yellow Electric Seed: Flowering, Target, Awareness
Tone: Activate, Bond, Service

27 Dienstag / Tuesday 1/2

Rote Selbstexistierende Schlange: Lebenskraft, Überleben, Instinkt
Ton: Definieren, Messen, Form

Red Selfexisting Serpent: Life Force, Survive, Instinct
Tone: Define, Measure, Form

28 Mittwoch / Wednesday 1/3

Weisser Oberton Weltenüberbrücker: Tod, Ausgleichen, Möglichkeiten
Ton: Ermächtigen, Befehlen, Strahlkraft

White Overtone Worldbridger: Death, Equalize, Opportunity
Tone: Empowerment, Order, Radiance

 Blauer Planetarer Sturm / Blue Planetary Storm — 179

 Gelbe Spektrale Sonne / Yellow Spectral Sun — 180

 Roter Kristallener Drache / Red Crystal Dragon — 181

---

13 Monde Kalender «Neujahr»

26 Montag	27 Dienstag	28 Mittwoch
07:00	07:00	07:00
08:00	08:00	08:00
09:00	09:00	09:00
10:00	10:00	10:00
11:00	11:00	11:00
12:00	12:00	12:00
13:00	13:00	13:00
14:00	14:00	14:00
15:00	15:00	15:00
16:00	16:00	16:00
17:00	17:00	17:00
18:00	18:00	18:00
19:00	19:00	19:00
20:00	20:00	20:00
21:00	21:00	21:00

29 Donnerstag / Thursday 1/4

Blaue Rhythmische Hand: Vollendung, Wissen, Heilung
Ton: Organisieren, Balancieren, Gleichheit

Blue Rhythmic Hand: Accomplishment, Know, Healing
Tone: Organize, Balance, Equality

Weisser Kosmischer Wind / White Cosmic Wind — 183

7:00
8:00
9:00
10:00
11:00
12:00
13:00
14:00
15:00
16:00
17:00
18:00
19:00
20:00
21:00

30 Freitag / Friday 1/5

Gelber Resonanter Stern: Ästhetik, Verschönern, Kunst
Ton: Kanalisieren, Inspirieren, Einstimmung

Yellow Resonant Star: Elegance, Beautify, Art
Tone: Channel, Inspire, Attunement

Blaue Magnetische Nacht / Blue Magnetic Night — 184

07:00
08:00
09:00
10:00
11:00
12:00
13:00
14:00
15:00
16:00
17:00
18:00
19:00
20:00
21:00

31 Samstag / Saturday 1/6

Roter Galaktischer Mond: Universelles Wasser, Reinigen, Flow
Ton: Harmonisieren, Modellieren, Integrität

Red Galactic Moon: Universal Water, Purify, Flow
Tone: Harmony, Model, Integrity

Gelber Lunarer Same / Yellow Lunar Seed

08:00
10:00
12:00
14:00
16:00
18:00

1 Sonntag / Sunday 1/7

Weisser Solarer Hund: Herz, Lieben, Loyalität
Ton: Pulsieren, Erkennen, Absicht

White Solar Dog: Heart, Love, Loyality
Tone: Pulse, Realize, Intention

Rote Elektrische Schlange / Red Electric Serpent — 185

Lughnasadh | Mondfest

Juli — KW 30

	2 Montag / Monday 1/8	**3** Dienstag / Tuesday 1/9	**4** Mittwoch / Wednesday 1/10
Dreamspell	 231 **Blauer Planetarer Affe:** Magie, Spielen, Illusion **Ton:** Perfektionieren, Produzieren, Manifestation	 232 **Gelber Spektraler Mensch:** Freier Wille, Beeinflussen, Weisheit **Ton:** Auflösen, Loslassen, Befreiung	 233 **Roter Kristallener Himmelswanderer:** Raum, Erforschen, Wachsamkeit **Ton:** Hingabe, Verteilen, Zusammenarbeit
	Blue Planetary Monkey: Magic, Play, Illusion **Tone:** Perfect, Produce, Manifestation	**Yellow Spectral Human:** Free Will, Influence, Wisdom **Tone:** Dissolve, Release, Liberation	**Red Crystal Skywalker:** Space, Explore, Wakefullness **Tone:** Dedicate, Universalize, Cooperation
Long-count	 186 Weisser Selbstexistierender Weltenübrbrücker | White Selfexisting Worldbridger	187 Blaue Oberton Hand Blue Overtone Hand	188 Gelber Rhythmischer Stern Yellow Rhythmic Star

07:00
08:00
09:00
10:00
11:00
12:00
13:00
14:00
15:00
16:00
17:00
18:00
19:00
20:00
21:00

5 Donnerstag / Thursday 1/11

Weisser Kosmischer Magier: Zeitlosigkeit, Verzaubern, Empfänglichkeit
Ton: Durchhalten, Transzendieren, Präsenz

White Cosmic Wizard: Timelessness, Enchant, Receptivity
Tone: Endure, Transcend, Presence

 | Roter Resonanter Mond / Red Resonant Moon

07:00
08:00
09:00
10:00
11:00
12:00
13:00
14:00
15:00
16:00
17:00
18:00
19:00
20:00
21:00

6 Freitag / Friday 1/12

Blauer Magnetischer Adler: Vision, Erschaffen, Geist
Ton: Vereinheitlichen, Anziehen, Bestimmung

Blue Magnetic Eagle: Vision, Create, Mind
Tone: Unify, Attract, Purpose

 | Weisser Galaktischer Hund / White Galactic Dog

07:00
08:00
09:00
10:00
11:00
12:00
13:00
14:00
15:00
16:00
17:00
18:00
19:00
20:00
21:00

7 Samstag / Saturday 1/13

Gelber Lunarer Krieger: Intelligenz, Fragen, Angstlosigkeit
Ton: Polarisieren, Stabilisieren, Herausforderung

Yellow Lunar Warrior: Intelligence, Question, Fearlessness
Tone: Polarize, Stabilize, Challenge

  | Blauer Solarer Affe / Blue Solar Monkey

08:00
10:00
12:00
14:00
16:00
18:00

8 Sonntag / Sunday 1/14

Rote Elektrische Erde: Führung, Entwickeln, Synchronisation
Ton: Aktivieren, Binden, Dienen

Red Electric Earth: Navigation, Evolve, Synchronicity
Tone: Activate, Bond, Service

 | Gelber Planetarer Mensch / Yellow Planetary Human

August KW 31

9 Montag / Monday 1/15

 238

Weisser Selbstexistierender Spiegel: Endlosigkeit, Reflektieren, Ordnung
Ton: Definieren, Messen, Form

White Selfexisting Mirror: Endlessness, Reflect, Order
Tone: Define, Measure, Form

 193

Roter Spektraler Himmelswanderer | Red Spectral Skywalker

07:00
08:00
09:00
10:00
11:00
12:00
13:00
14:00
15:00
16:00
17:00
18:00
19:00
20:00
21:00

10 Dienstag / Tuesday [P] 1/16

 239

Blauer Oberton Sturm: Selbsterneuerung, Katalysieren, Energie
Ton: Ermächtigen, Befehlen, Strahlkraft

Blue Overtone Storm: Self-generation, Catalyze, Energy
Tone: Empowerment, Order, Radiance

194 **Weisser Kristallener Magier / White Crystal Wizard**

07:00
08:00
09:00
10:00
11:00
12:00
13:00
14:00
15:00
16:00
17:00
18:00
19:00
20:00
21:00

11 Mittwoch / Wednesday 1/17

 240

Gelbe Rhythmische Sonne: Universelles Feuer, Erleuchten, Leben
Ton: Organisieren, Balancieren, Gleichheit

Yellow Rhythmic Sun: Universal Fire, Enlighten, Life
Tone: Organize, Balance, Equality

195 **Blauer Kosmischer Adler / Blue Cosmic Eagle**

07:00
08:00
09:00
10:00
11:00
12:00
13:00
14:00
15:00
16:00
17:00
18:00
19:00
20:00
21:00

12 Donnerstag / Thursday 1/18

 **Roter Resonanter Drache:** Geburt, Nähren, Sein
Ton: Kanalisieren, Inspirieren, Einstimmung

Red Resonant Dragon: Birth, Nurture, Being
Tone: Channel, Inspire, Attunement

 Gelber Magnetischer Krieger / Yellow Magnetic Warrior

12–21

07:00
08:00
09:00
10:00
11:00
12:00
13:00
14:00
15:00
16:00
17:00
18:00
19:00
20:00
21:00

13 Freitag / Friday 1/19

 **Weisser Galaktischer Wind:** Geist, Kommunikation, Atem
Ton: Harmonisieren, Modellieren, Integrität

White Galactic Wind: Spirit, Communication, Breath
Tone: Harmony, Model, Integrity

 Rote Lunare Erde / Red Lunar Earth

12–21

07:00
08:00
09:00
10:00
11:00
12:00
13:00
14:00
15:00
16:00
17:00
18:00
19:00
20:00
21:00

14 Samstag / Saturday 1/20

 **Blaue Solare Nacht:** Fülle, Träumen, Intuition
Ton: Pulsieren, Erkennen, Absicht

Blue Solar Night: Abundance, Dream, Intuition
Tone: Pulse, Realize, Intention

 Weisser Elektrischer Spiegel / White Electric Mirror

12–21

08:00
10:00
12:00
14:00
16:00
18:00

15 Sonntag / Sunday 1/21

 **Gelber Planetarer Same:** Erblühen, Zielen, Achtsamkeit
Ton: Perfektionieren, Produzieren, Manifestation

Yellow Planetary Seed: Flowering, Target, Awareness
Tone: Perfect, Produce, Manifestation

 Blauer Selbstexistierender Sturm | Blue Selfexisting Storm

12–21

August KW 32

Tag | Day

Dreamspell

16 Montag / Monday 1/22

245

Rote Spektrale Schlange: Lebenkraft, Überleben, Instinkt
Ton: Auflösen, Loslassen, Befreiung

Red Spectral Serpent: Life Force, Survive, Instinct
Tone: Dissolve, Release, Liberation

17 Dienstag / Tuesday 1/23

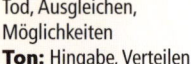

246

Weisser Kristallener Weltenüberbrücker: Tod, Ausgleichen, Möglichkeiten
Ton: Hingabe, Verteilen, Zusammenarbeit

White Crystal Worldbridger: Death, Equalize, Opportunity
Tone: Dedicate, Universalize, Cooperation

18 Mittwoch / Wednesday 1/24

247

Blaue Kosmische Hand: Vollendung, Wissen, Heilung
Ton: Durchhalten, Transzendieren, Präsenz

Blue Cosmic Hand: Accomplishment, Know, Healing
Tone: Endure, Transcend, Presence

Long-count

 200 | Gelbe Oberton Sonne / Yellow Overtone Sun

 201 | Roter Rhythmischer Drache / Red Rhythmic Dragon

 202 | Weisser Resonanter Wind / White Resonant Wind

12–21

16 Montag	17 Dienstag	18 Mittwoch
07:00	07:00	07:00
08:00	08:00	08:00
09:00	09:00	09:00
10:00	10:00	10:00
11:00	11:00	11:00
12:00	12:00	12:00
13:00	13:00	13:00
14:00	14:00	14:00
15:00	15:00	15:00
16:00	16:00	16:00
17:00	17:00	17:00
18:00	18:00	18:00
19:00	19:00	19:00
20:00	20:00	20:00
21:00	21:00	21:00

19 Donnerstag / Thursday 1/25

Gelber Magnetischer Stern: Ästhetik, Verschönern, Kunst
Ton: Vereinheitlichen, Anziehen, Bestimmung

Yellow Magnetic Star: Elegance, Beautify, Art
Tone: Unify, Attract, Purpose

 Blaue Galaktische Nacht | Blue Galactic Night

	12–21
07:00	
08:00	
09:00	
10:00	
11:00	
12:00	
13:00	
14:00	
15:00	
16:00	
17:00	
18:00	
19:00	
20:00	
21:00	

20 Freitag / Friday 1/26

Roter Lunarer Mond: Universelles Wasser, Reinigen, Flow
Ton: Polarisieren, Stabilisieren, Herausforderung

Red Lunar Moon: Universal Water, Purify, Flow
Tone: Polarize, Stabilize, Challenge

 Gelber Solarer Same | Yellow Solar Seed

	12–21
07:00	
08:00	
09:00	
10:00	
11:00	
12:00	
13:00	
14:00	
15:00	
16:00	
17:00	
18:00	
19:00	
20:00	
21:00	

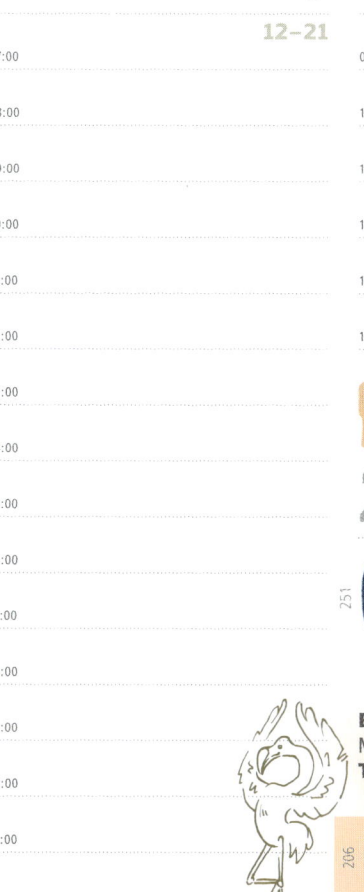

21 Samstag / Saturday 1/27

Weisser Elektrischer Hund: Herz, Lieben, Loyalität
Ton: Aktivieren, Binden, Dienen

White Electric Dog: Heart, Love, Loyalty
Tone: Activate, Bond, Service

 Rote Planetare Schlange | Red Planetary Serpent

	12–21
08:00	
10:00	
12:00	
14:00	
16:00	
18:00	

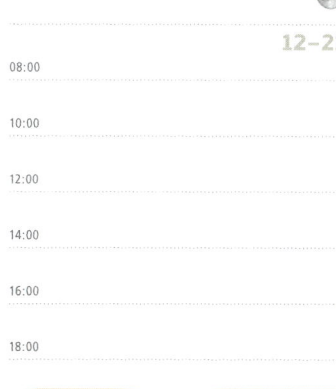

22 Sonntag / Sunday 1/28

Blauer Selbstexistierender Affe: Magie, Spielen, Illusion
Ton: Definieren, Messen, Form

Blue Selfexisting Monkey: Magic, Play, Illusion
Tone: Define, Measure, Form

 Weisser Spektraler Weltenüberbrücker | White Spectral Worldbridger

August KW 33

Schauer-Klapperschlange

2. Lunarer Mond | Lunar Moon

1 23/8	2 24/8	3 25/8	4 26/8	5 27/8	6 28/8	7 29/8	🟥
8 30/8	9 31/8	10 1/9	11 2/9	12 3/9	13 4/9	14 5/9	⬜
15 6/9	16 7/9	17 8/9	18 9/9	19 10/9	20 11/9	21 12/9	🟦
22 13/9	23 14/9	24 15/9	25 16/9	26 17/9	27 18/9	28 19/9	🟨

Was erzeugt genügend Spannung?

Die Würfel sind gefallen, jetzt geht es los! Um möglichst viel Schwung für die bevorstehende Jahresreise zu haben, ist es wichtig, genügend «Spannung» aufzubauen. Die Formel ist übrigens ganz einfach: Je grösser die Herausforderung, desto näher zu den Sternen gelangen wir – wie ein Pfeilbogen, der stark gespannt ist, damit der Pfeil möglichst weit fliegen kann. Mit dem Lunaren Mond werden die Themen des ersten Mondes ausgebreitet, damit wir besser sehen und verstehen können, worum es in diesem Jahr wirklich geht. Stell dir einen Fischer vor, der im ersten Mond sein Netz ausgeworfen hat und es nun im zweiten Mond einholt und seinen Fang begutachtet. Allenfalls wird ein wenig aussortiert, damit lediglich die wirklich grossen Fische (spannende Themen) übrigbleiben. Einige Themen werden im zweiten Mond aktiviert/verstärkt, was wiederum bereits zu Spannung(en) führen kann. Dies sorgt für ein gutes «Aktionspotential» für die restliche Reise.

••••••••••••••••••••••••••••••

What generates enough voltage?

The dice have been thrown, here we go! In order to have as much momentum as possible for the forthcoming trip of the year, it is important to build up enough «tension». By the way, the formula is quite simple: The bigger the challenge the closer we get to the stars – like a bow, which is strongly stretched, so that the arrow can fly as far as possible. With the Lunar Moon, the themes of the first moon are spread out so that we can better see and understand what this year is really about. Imagine a fisherman who has cast out his net in the first moon and now hauls it in in the second moon and inspects his catch. At best, a little is sorted out, so that only the really big fish (exciting topics) remain. Some themes are activated/enhanced in the second moon, which can already lead to tension(s). This provides a good «action potential» for the rest of the journey.

Tag | Day	**23** Montag / Monday	**24** Dienstag / Tuesday	**25** Mittwoch / Wednesday
Dreamspell	 252 **Gelber Oberton** **Mensch:** Freier Wille, Beeinflussen, Weisheit **Ton:** Ermächtigen, Befehlen, Strahlkraft	 253 **Roter Rhythmischer Himmelswanderer:** Raum, Erforschen, Wachsamkeit **Ton:** Organisieren, Balancieren, Gleichheit	 254 **Weisser Resonanter Magier:** Zeitlosigkeit, Verzaubern, Empfänglichkeit **Ton:** Kanalisieren, Inspirieren, Einstimmung
	Yellow Overtone Human: Free Will, Influence, Wisdom **Tone:** Empowerment, Order, Radiance	**Red Rhythmic Skywalker:** Space, Explore, Wakefullness **Tone:** Organize, Balance, Equality	**White Resonant Wizard:** Timelessness, Enchant, Receptivity **Tone:** Channel, Inspire, Attunement
Long-count	207 Blaue Kristallene Hand / Blue Crystal Hand	208 Gelber Kosmischer Stern / Yellow Cosmic Star	209 Roter Magnetischer Mond / Red Magnetic Moon

07:00	07:00	07:00
08:00	08:00	08:00
09:00	09:00	09:00
10:00	10:00	10:00
11:00	11:00	11:00
12:00	12:00	12:00
13:00	13:00	13:00
14:00	14:00	14:00
15:00	15:00	15:00
16:00	16:00	16:00
17:00	17:00	17:00
18:00	18:00	18:00
19:00	19:00	19:00
20:00	20:00	20:00
21:00	21:00	21:00

26 Donnerstag / Thursday 2/4

 **Blauer Galaktischer Adler:** Vision, Erschaffen, Geist
Ton: Harmonisieren, Modellieren, Integrität

Blue Galactic Eagle: Vision, Create, Mind
Tone: Harmony, Model, Integrity

 : Weisser Lunarer Hund / White Lunar Dog

07:00
08:00
09:00
10:00
11:00
12:00
13:00
14:00
15:00
16:00
17:00
18:00
19:00
20:00
21:00

27 Freitag / Friday 2/5

 **Gelber Solarer Krieger:** Intelligenz, Fragen, Angstlosigkeit
Ton: Pulsieren, Erkennen, Absicht

Yellow Solar Warrior: Intelligence, Question, Fearlessness
Tone: Pulse, Realize, Intention

 : Blauer Elektrischer Affe / Blue Electric Monkey

07:00
08:00
09:00
10:00
11:00
12:00
13:00
14:00
15:00
16:00
17:00
18:00
19:00
20:00
21:00

28 Samstag / Saturday 2/6

 Rote Planetare Erde: Führung, Entwickeln, Synchronisation
Ton: Perfektionieren, Produzieren, Manifestation

Red Planetary Earth: Navigation, Evolve, Synchronicity
Tone: Perfect, Produce, Manifestation

 : Gelber Selbstexistierender Mensch | Yellow Selfexisting Human

08:00
10:00
12:00
14:00
16:00
18:00

29 Sonntag / Sunday 2/7

 **Weisser Spektraler Spiegel:** Endlosigkeit, Reflektieren, Ordnung
Ton: Auflösen, Loslassen, Befreiung

White Spectral Mirror: Endlessness, Reflect, Order
Tone: Dissolve, Release, Liberation

 Roter Oberton Himmelswanderer | Red Overtone Skywalker

August KW 34

Tag | Day · Dreamspell · Long-count

30 Montag / Monday 2/8

Blauer Kristallener Sturm: Selbsterneuerung, Katalysieren, Energie
Ton: Hingabe, Verteilen, Zusammenarbeit

259

Blue Crystal Storm: Self-generation, Catalyze, Energy
Tone: Dedicate, Universalize, Cooperation

 214 | Weisser Rhythmischer Magier / White Rhythmic Wizard

31 Dienstag / Tuesday 2/9

Gelbe Kosmische Sonne: Universelles Feuer, Erleuchten, Leben
Ton: Durchhalten, Transzendieren, Präsenz

260

Yellow Cosmic Sun: Universal Fire, Enlighten, Life
Tone: Endure, Transcend, Presence

 215 | Blauer Resonanter Adler / Blue Resonant Eagle

1 Mittwoch / Wednesday 2/10

Roter Magnetischer Drache: Geburt, Nähren, Sein
Ton: Vereinheitlichen, Anziehen, Bestimmung

1

Red Magnetic Dragon: Birth, Nurture, Being
Tone: Unify, Attract, Purpose

 216 | Gelber Galaktischer Krieger / Yellow Galactic Warrior

Monday	Tuesday	Wednesday
07:00	07:00	07:00
08:00	08:00	08:00
09:00	09:00	09:00
10:00	10:00	10:00
11:00	11:00	11:00
12:00	12:00	12:00
13:00	13:00	13:00
14:00	14:00	14:00
15:00	15:00	15:00
16:00	16:00	16:00
17:00	17:00	17:00
18:00	18:00	18:00
19:00	19:00	19:00
20:00	20:00	20:00
21:00	21:00	21:00

2 **Donnerstag / Thursday** 2/11

Weisser Lunarer Wind: Geist, Kommunikation, Atem
Ton: Polarisieren, Stabilisieren, Herausforderung

White Lunar Wind: Spirit, Communication, Breath
Tone: Polarize, Stabilize, Challenge

 Rote Solare Erde / Red Solar Earth

7:00
8:00
9:00
10:00
11:00
12:00
13:00
14:00
15:00
16:00
17:00
18:00
19:00
20:00
21:00

---

3 **Freitag / Friday** 2/12

Blaue Elektrische Nacht: Fülle, Träumen, Intuition
Ton: Aktivieren, Binden, Dienen

Blue Electric Night: Abundance, Dream, Intuition
Tone: Activate, Bond, Service

218 Weisser Planetarer Spiegel / White Planetary Mirror

07:00
08:00
09:00
10:00
11:00
12:00
13:00
14:00
15:00
16:00
17:00
18:00
19:00
20:00
21:00

---

4 **Samstag / Saturday** 2/13

Gelber Selbstexistierender Same: Erblühen, Zielen, Achtsamkeit
Ton: Definieren, Messen, Form

Yellow Selfexisting Seed: Flowering, Target, Awareness
Tone: Define, Measure, Form

219 Blauer Spektraler Sturm / Blue Spectral Storm

08:00
10:00
12:00
14:00
16:00
18:00

---

5 **Sonntag / Sunday** 2/14

Rote Oberton Schlange: Lebenkraft, Überleben, Instinkt
Ton: Ermächtigen, Befehlen, Strahlkraft

Red Overtone Serpent: Life Force, Survive, Instinct
Tone: Empowerment, Order, Radiance

220  Gelbe Kristallene Sonne / Yellow Crystal Sun

September KW 35

Tag | Day

Dreamspell

6 Montag / Monday 2/15

Weisser Rhythmischer Weltenüberbrücker: Tod, Ausgleichen, Möglichkeiten
Ton: Organisieren, Balancieren, Gleichheit

White Rhythmic Worldbridger: Death, Equalize, Opportunity
Tone: Organize, Balance, Equality

Long-count 221 Roter Kosmischer Drache / Red Cosmic Dragon

7 Dienstag / Tuesday 2/16

Blaue Resonante Hand: Vollendung, Wissen, Heilung
Ton: Kanalisieren, Inspirieren, Einstimmung

Blue Resonant Hand: Accomplishment, Know, Healing
Tone: Channel, Inspire, Attunement

222 Weisser Magnetischer Wind / White Magnetic Wind

8 Mittwoch / Wednesday 2/17

Gelber Galaktischer Stern: Ästhetik, Verschönern, Kunst
Ton: Harmonisieren, Modellieren, Integrität

Yellow Galactic Star: Elegance, Beautify, Art
Tone: Harmony, Model, Integrity

223 Blaue Lunare Nacht / Blue Lunar Night

07:00	07:00	07:00
08:00	08:00	08:00
09:00	09:00	09:00
10:00	10:00	10:00
11:00	11:00	11:00
12:00	12:00	12:00
13:00	13:00	13:00
14:00	14:00	14:00
15:00	15:00	15:00
16:00	16:00	16:00
17:00	17:00	17:00
18:00	18:00	18:00
19:00	19:00	19:00
20:00	20:00	20:00
21:00	21:00	21:00

Falls du deine Agenda 2022 noch nicht bestellt hast > Nur solange Vorrat!

If you haven't ordered your Agenda 2022 yet > Only while stocks last!

9 Donnerstag / Thursday 2/18

Roter Solarer Mond: Universelles Wasser, Reinigen, Flow
Ton: Pulsieren, Erkennen, Absicht

Red Solar Moon: Universal Water, Purify, Flow
Tone: Pulse, Realize, Intention

 Gelber Elektrischer Same / Yellow Electric Seed

- 7:00
- 8:00
- 9:00
- 10:00
- 11:00
- 12:00
- 13:00
- 14:00
- 15:00
- 16:00
- 17:00
- 18:00
- 19:00
- 20:00
- 21:00

10 Freitag / Friday 2/19

Weisser Planetarer Hund: Herz, Lieben, Loyalität
Ton: Perfektionieren, Produzieren, Manifestation

White Planetary Dog: Heart, Love, Loyalty
Tone: Perfect, Produce, Manifestation

 Rote Selbstexistierende Schlange | Red Selfexisting Serpent

- 07:00
- 08:00
- 09:00
- 10:00
- 11:00
- 12:00
- 13:00
- 14:00
- 15:00
- 16:00
- 17:00
- 18:00
- 19:00
- 20:00
- 21:00

11 Samstag / Saturday 2/20

Blauer Spektraler Affe: Magie, Spielen, Illusion
Ton: Auflösen, Loslassen, Befreiung

Blue Spectral Monkey: Magic, Play, Illusion
Tone: Dissolve, Release, Liberation

 Weisser Oberton Weltenüberbrücker | White Overtone Worldbridger

- 08:00
- 10:00
- 12:00
- 14:00
- 16:00
- 18:00

12 Sonntag / Sunday 2/21

Gelber Kristallener Mensch: Freier Wille, Beeinflussen, Weisheit
Ton: Hingabe, Verteilen, Zusammenarbeit

Yellow Crystal Human: Free Will, Influence, Wisdom
Tone: Dedicate, Universalize, Cooperation

 Blaue Rhythmische Hand / Blue Rhythmic Hand

12–21

September KW 36

Tag | Day

Dreamspell

13 Montag / Monday

Roter Kosmischer Himmelswanderer: Raum, Erforschen, Wachsamkeit
Ton: Durchhalten, Transzendieren, Präsenz

Red Cosmic Skywalker: Space, Explore, Wakefullness
Tone: Endure, Transcend, Presence

14 Dienstag / Tuesday

Weisser Magnetischer Magier: Zeitlosigkeit, Verzaubern, Empfänglichkeit
Ton: Vereinheitlichen, Anziehen, Bestimmung

White Magnetic Wizard: Timelessness, Enchant, Receptivity
Tone: Unify, Attract, Purpose

15 Mittwoch / Wednesday

Blauer Lunarer Adler: Vision, Erschaffen, Geist
Ton: Polarisieren, Stabilisieren, Herausforderung

Blue Lunar Eagle: Vision, Create, Mind
Tone: Polarize, Stabilize, Challenge

Long-count

Gelber Resonanter Stern / Yellow Resonant Star	**Roter Galaktischer Mond** / Red Galactic Moon	**Weisser Solarer Hund** / White Solar Dog

12–21

Monday	Tuesday	Wednesday
07:00	07:00	07:00
08:00	08:00	08:00
09:00	09:00	09:00
10:00	10:00	10:00
11:00	11:00	11:00
12:00	12:00	12:00
13:00	13:00	13:00
14:00	14:00	14:00
15:00	15:00	15:00
16:00	16:00	16:00
17:00	17:00	17:00
18:00	18:00	18:00
19:00	19:00	19:00
20:00	20:00	20:00
21:00	21:00	21:00

16 Donnerstag / Thursday 2/25

Gelber Elektrischer Krieger: Intelligenz, Fragen, Angstlosigkeit
Ton: Aktivieren, Binden, Dienen

Yellow Electric Warrior: Intelligence, Question, Fearlessness
Tone: Activate, Bond, Service

 Blauer Planetarer Affe / Blue Planetary Monkey

12–21

- 00
- 00
- 00
- 00
- 00
- 00
- 00
- 00
- 00
- 00
- 00
- 00
- 00
- 00

17 Freitag / Friday 2/26

Rote Selbstexistierende Erde: Führung, Entwickeln, Synchronisation
Ton: Definieren, Messen, Form

Red Selfexisting Earth: Navigation, Evolve, Synchronicity
Tone: Define, Measure, Form

 Gelber Spektraler Mensch / Yellow Spectral Human

12–21

- 07:00
- 08:00
- 09:00
- 10:00
- 11:00
- 12:00
- 13:00
- 14:00
- 15:00
- 16:00
- 17:00
- 18:00
- 19:00
- 20:00
- 21:00

18 Samstag / Saturday 2/27

Weisser Oberton Spiegel: Endlosigkeit, Reflektieren, Ordnung
Ton: Ermächtigen, Befehlen, Strahlkraft

White Overtone Mirror: Endlessness, Reflect, Order
Tone: Empowerment, Order, Radiance

 Roter Kristallener Himmelswanderer | Red Crystal Skywalker

12–21

- 08:00
- 10:00
- 12:00
- 14:00
- 16:00
- 18:00

19 Sonntag / Sunday 2/28

Blauer Rhythmischer Sturm: Selbsterneuerung, Katalysieren, Energie
Ton: Organisieren, Balancieren, Gleichheit

Blue Rhythmic Storm: Self-generation, Catalyze, Energy
Tone: Organize, Balance, Equality

 Weisser Kosmischer Magier / White Cosmic Wizard

12–21

September KW 37

Steinadler

3. Elektrischer Mond | Electric Moon

1	2	3	4	5	6	7
20/9	21/9	22/9	23/9	24/9	25/9	26/9
8	9	10	11	12	13	14
27/9	28/9	29/9	30/9	1/10	2/10	3/10
15	16	17	18	19	20	21
4/10	5/10	6/10	7/10	8/10	9/10	10/10
22	23	24	25	26	27	28
11/10	12/10	13/10	14/10	15/10	16/10	17/10

Was bringt das Ganze zum Laufen?

Wo viel Energie ist, beginnt es zu knistern. Im Elektrischen Mond werden die Themen regelrecht aktiviert und verstärkt, was zum Teil bereits sehr intensiv werden kann. Daher gilt es, diese 28 Tage zu nutzen, um mit dieser «Elektrizität» deinen Tank zu füllen, damit du für das restliche Jahresprogramm genügend Energie zur Verfügung hast. Wir werden so oder so am Ziel ankommen – die Frage ist nur: Wie? Völlig erschöpft, Zunge heraushängend, ausgemergelt und leichenblass? Oder wie ein Zuvuya-Surfer ins Ziel rauschen – mit einem entspannten Lächeln? Damit das möglich ist, muss ich wissen, WIE ich es tun muss! Wenn du auf der sicheren Seite stehen willst, gibt's ein untrügliches GPS: Wenn es sich gut anfühlt und innere Freude verursacht, dann zeigt der Daumen nach oben! Alles andere ist nicht optimal oder sogar hinderlich! Und noch etwas: Im dritten Mond lohnt es sich auch zu fragen, wie ich meinen Mitmenschen oder der Erde dienen kann. Denn damit sorgst du dafür, dass mehr Energie zurückfliesst, als du investierst.

What's making this work?

Where there is a lot of energy, it begins to crackle. In the Electric Moon the themes are activated and amplified, which can become very intense. Therefore it is important to use these 28 days to fill your tank with this «electricity» so that you have enough energy available for the rest of the year. Either way, we will arrive at our destination – the only question is: How? Totally exhausted, tongue hanging out, emaciated and pale as a ghost? Or how a Zuvuya°Surfer rushes into the finish line – with a relaxed smile? To make this possible, I have to know HOW to do it! If you want to be on the safe side, there's an unmistakable GPS: If it feels good and causes inner joy, then your thumb is pointing upwards! Everything else is not optimal or even obstructive! And something else: In the third moon it is worth asking yourself how I can serve my fellow men or the earth. Because with it you make sure that more energy flows back than you invest.

Tag | Day — Dreamspell — Long-count

20 Montag / Monday 3/1

Gelbe Resonante Sonne: Universelles Feuer, Erleuchten, Leben
Ton: Kanalisieren, Inspirieren, Einstimmung

Yellow Resonant Sun: Universal Fire, Enlighten, Life
Tone: Channel, Inspire, Attunement

 235 Blauer Magnetischer Adler / Blue Magnetic Eagle

12–21

07:00
08:00
09:00
10:00
11:00
12:00
13:00
14:00
15:00
16:00
17:00
18:00
19:00
20:00
21:00

21 Dienstag / Tuesday 3/2

Roter Galaktischer Drache: Geburt, Nähren, Sein
Ton: Harmonisieren, Modellieren, Integrität

Red Galactic Dragon: Birth, Nurture, Being
Tone: Harmony, Model, Integrity

 236 Gelber Lunarer Krieger / Yellow Lunar Warrior

12–21

07:00
08:00
09:00
10:00
11:00
12:00
13:00
14:00
15:00
16:00
17:00
18:00
19:00
20:00
21:00

22 Mittwoch / Wednesday 3/3

Weisser Solarer Wind: Geist, Kommunikation, Atem
Ton: Pulsieren, Erkennen, Absicht

White Solar Wind: Spirit, Communication, Breath
Tone: Pulse, Realize, Intention

 237 Rote Elektrische Erde / Red Electric Earth

07:00
08:00
09:00
10:00
11:00
12:00
13:00
14:00
15:00
16:00
17:00
18:00
19:00
20:00
21:00

23 Donnerstag / Thursday 3/4

Blaue Planetare Nacht:
Fülle, Träumen, Intuition
Ton: Perfektionieren, Produzieren, Manifestation

Blue Planetary Night:
Abundance, Dream, Intuition
Tone: Perfect, Produce, Manifestation

 Weisser Selbstexistierender Spiegel | White Selfexisting Mirror

Herbstäquinox | Sonnenfest

| 07:00 |
| 08:00 |
| 09:00 |
| 10:00 |
| 11:00 |
| 12:00 |
| 13:00 |
| 14:00 |
| 15:00 |
| 16:00 |
| 17:00 |
| 18:00 |
| 19:00 |
| 20:00 |
| 21:00 |

24 Freitag / Friday 3/5

Gelber Spektraler Same: Erblühen, Zielen, Achtsamkeit
Ton: Auflösen, Loslassen, Befreiung

Yellow Spectral Seed:
Flowering, Target, Awareness
Tone: Dissolve, Release, Liberation

 Blauer Oberton Sturm / Blue Overtone Storm

| 07:00 |
| 08:00 |
| 09:00 |
| 10:00 |
| 11:00 |
| 12:00 |
| 13:00 |
| 14:00 |
| 15:00 |
| 16:00 |
| 17:00 |
| 18:00 |
| 19:00 |
| 20:00 |
| 21:00 |

25 Samstag / Saturday 3/6

Rote Kristallene Schlange: Lebenskraft, Überleben, Instinkt
Ton: Hingabe, Verteilen, Zusammenarbeit

Red Crystal Serpent:
Life Force, Survive, Instinct
Tone: Dedicate, Universalize, Cooperation

 Gelbe Rhythmische Sonne / Yellow Rhythmic Sun

| 08:00 |
| 10:00 |
| 12:00 |
| 14:00 |
| 16:00 |
| 18:00 |

26 Sonntag / Sunday 3/7

Weisser Kosmischer Weltenüberbrücker: Tod, Ausgleichen, Möglichkeiten
Ton: Durchhalten, Transzendieren, Präsenz

White Cosmic Worldbridger:
Death, Equalize, Opportunity
Tone: Endure, Transcend, Presence

 Roter Resonanter Drache / Red Resonant Dragon

September KW 38

Tag / Day			
Dreamspell	**27** Montag / Monday 3/8  **Blaue Magnetische Hand:** Vollendung, Wissen, Heilung **Ton:** Vereinheitlichen, Anziehen, Bestimmung **Blue Magnetic Hand:** Accomplishment, Know, Healing **Tone:** Unify, Attract, Purpose	**28** Dienstag / Tuesday 3/9 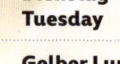 **Gelber Lunarer Stern:** Ästhetik, Verschönern, Kunst **Ton:** Polarisieren, Stabilisieren, Herausforderung **Yellow Lunar Star:** Elegance, Beautify, Art **Tone:** Polarize, Stabilize, Challenge	**29** Mittwoch / Wednesday 3/10  **Roter Elektrischer Mond:** Universelles Wasser, Reinigen, Flow **Ton:** Aktivieren, Binden, Dienen **Red Electric Moon:** Universal Water, Purify, Flow **Tone:** Activate, Bond, Service
Long-count	242 — Weisser Galaktischer Wind / White Galactic Wind	243 — Blaue Solare Nacht / Blue Solar Night	244 — Gelber Planetarer Same / Yellow Planetary Seed

Monday 27	Tuesday 28	Wednesday 29
07:00	07:00	07:00
08:00	08:00	08:00
09:00	09:00	09:00
10:00	10:00	10:00
11:00	11:00	11:00
12:00	12:00	12:00
13:00	13:00	13:00
14:00	14:00	14:00
15:00	15:00	15:00
16:00	16:00	16:00
17:00	17:00	17:00
18:00	18:00	18:00
19:00	19:00	19:00
20:00	20:00	20:00
21:00	21:00	21:00

30 Donnerstag / Thursday 3/11

Weisser Selbstexistierender Hund:
Herz, Lieben, Loyalität
Ton: Definieren, Messen, Form

White Selfexisting Dog:
Heart, Love, Loyalty
Tone: Define, Measure, Form

1 Freitag / Friday 3/12

Blauer Oberton Affe:
Magie, Spielen, Illusion
Ton: Ermächtigen, Befehlen, Strahlkraft

Blue Overtone Monkey:
Magic, Play, Illusion
Tone: Empowerment, Order, Radiance

2 Samstag / Saturday 3/13

Gelber Rhythmischer Mensch: Freier Wille, Beeinflussen, Weisheit
Ton: Organisieren, Balancieren, Gleichheit

Yellow Rhythmic Human:
Free Will, Influence, Wisdom
Tone: Organize, Balance, Equality

September KW 39

 Rote Spektrale Schlange / Red Spectral Serpent

246 Weisser Kristallener Weltenüberbrücker | White Crystal Worldbridger

247 Blaue Kosmische Hand / Blue Cosmic Hand

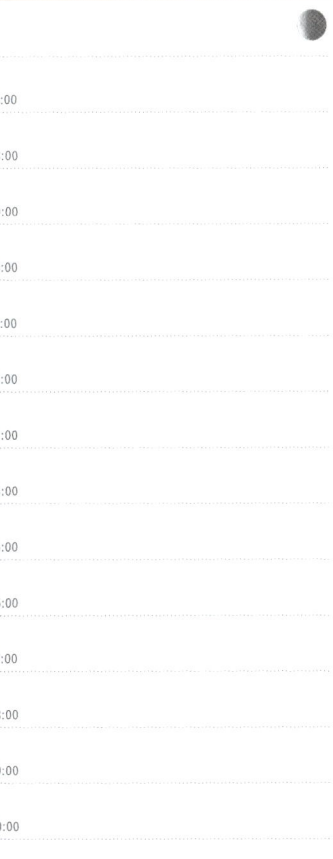

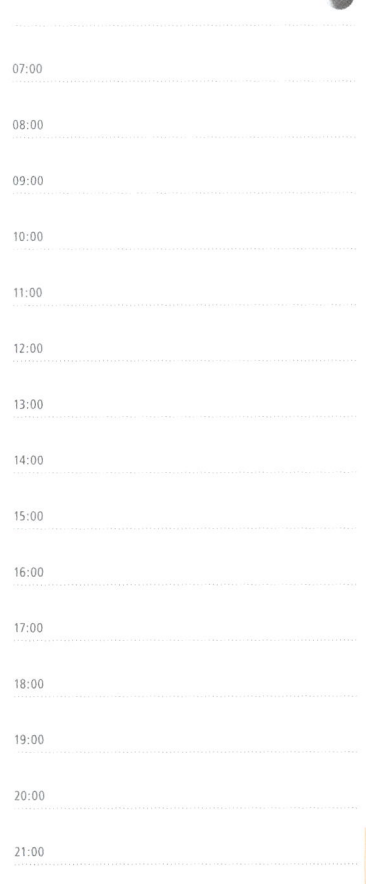

3 Sonntag / Sunday 3/14

Roter Resonanter Himmelswanderer:
Raum, Erforschen, Wachsamkeit
Ton: Kanalisieren, Inspirieren, Einstimmung

Red Resonant Skywalker:
Space, Explore, Wakefullness
Tone: Channel, Inspire, Attunement

248 Gelber Magnetischer Stern / Yellow Magnetic Star

Tag | Day

Dreamspell

4 Montag / Monday 3/15

Weisser Galaktischer Magier: Zeitlosigkeit, Verzaubern, Empfänglichkeit
Ton: Harmonisieren, Modellieren, Integrität

White Galactic Wizard: Timelessness, Enchant, Receptivity
Tone: Harmony, Model, Integrity

5 Dienstag / Tuesday 3/16

Blauer Solarer Adler: Vision, Erschaffen, Geist
Ton: Pulsieren, Erkennen, Absicht

Blue Solar Eagle: Vision, Create, Mind
Tone: Pulse, Realize, Intention

6 Mittwoch / Wednesday 3/17

Gelber Planetarer Krieger: Intelligenz, Frager Angstlosigkeit
Ton: Perfektionieren, Produzieren, Manifestation

Yellow Planetary Warrior: Intelligence, Question, Fearlessness
Tone: Perfect, Produce, Manifestation

Long-count

249 — Roter Lunarer Mond / Red Lunar Moon

250 — Weisser Elektrischer Hund / White Electric Dog

251 — Blauer Selbstexistierender Affe | Blue Selfexisting Monkey

---

07:00
08:00
09:00
10:00
11:00
12:00
13:00
14:00
15:00
16:00
17:00
18:00
19:00
20:00
21:00

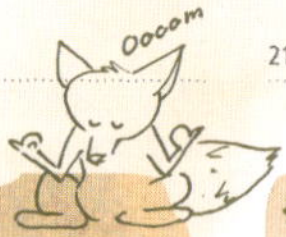

7 Donnerstag / Thursday 3/18

Rote Spektrale Erde: Führung, Entwickeln, Synchronisation
Ton: Auflösen, Loslassen, Befreiung

Red Spectral Earth: Navigation, Evolve, Synchronicity
Tone: Dissolve, Release, Liberation

 Gelber Oberton Mensch | Yellow Overtone Human

8 Freitag / Friday 3/19

Weisser Kristallener Spiegel: Endlosigkeit, Reflektieren, Ordnung
Ton: Hingabe, Verteilen, Zusammenarbeit

White Crystal Mirror: Endlessness, Reflect, Order
Tone: Dedicate, Universalize, Cooperation

 Roter Rhythmischer Himmelswanderer | Red Rhythmic Skywalker

07:00
08:00
09:00
10:00
11:00
12:00
13:00
14:00
15:00
16:00
17:00
18:00
19:00
20:00
21:00

9 Samstag / Saturday 3/20

Blauer Kosmischer Sturm: Selbsterneuerung, Katalysieren, Energie
Ton: Durchhalten, Transzendieren, Präsenz

Blue Cosmic Storm: Self-generation, Catalyze, Energy
Tone: Endure, Transcend, Presence

 Weisser Resonanter Magier | White Resonant Wizard

08:00
10:00
12:00
14:00
16:00
18:00

10 Sonntag / Sunday 3/21

Gelbe Magnetische Sonne: Universelles Feuer, Erleuchten, Leben
Ton: Vereinheitlichen, Anziehen, Bestimmung

Yellow Magnetic Sun: Universal Fire, Enlighten, Life
Tone: Unify, Attract, Purpose

Blauer Galaktischer Adler | Blue Galactic Eagle

Oktober KW 40

Tag | Day

11 Montag / Monday   3/22

 41

Roter Lunarer Drache: Geburt, Nähren, Sein
Ton: Polarisieren, Stabilisieren, Herausforderung

Red Lunar Dragon: Birth, Nurture, Being
Tone: Polarize, Stabilize, Challenge

12 Dienstag / Tuesday 3/23

 42

Weisser Elektrischer Wind: Geist, Kommunikation, Atem
Ton: Aktivieren, Binden, Dienen

White Electric Wind: Spirit, Communication, Breath
Tone: Activate, Bond, Service

13 Mittwoch / Wednesday   3/24

 43

Blaue Selbstexistierende Nacht: Fülle, Träumen, Intuition
Ton: Definieren, Messen, Form

Blue Selfexisting Night: Abundance, Dream, Intuition
Tone: Define, Measure, Form

Dreamspell

Long-count

xxx | Gelber Solarer Krieger / Yellow Solar Warrior

257 | Rote Planetare Erde / Red Planetary Earth

258 | Weisser Spektraler Spiegel / White Spectral Mirror

	Monday	Tuesday 12-21	Wednesday 12-2
07:00			
08:00			
09:00			
10:00			
11:00			
12:00			
13:00			
14:00			
15:00			
16:00			
17:00			
18:00			
19:00			
20:00			
21:00			

For cozy nigh Raw Cacao (bio in our sho

14 Donnerstag / Thursday 3/25

Gelber Oberton Same: Erblühen, Zielen, Achtsamkeit
Ton: Ermächtigen, Befehlen, Strahlkraft

Yellow Overtone Seed: Flowering, Target, Awareness
Tone: Empowerment, Order, Radiance

 Blauer Kristallener Sturm / Blue Crystal Storm

	12–21
7:00	
8:00	
9:00	
10:00	
11:00	
12:00	
13:00	
14:00	
15:00	
16:00	
17:00	
18:00	
19:00	
20:00	
21:00	

15 Freitag / Friday 3/26

Rote Rhythmische Schlange: Lebenkraft, Überleben, Instinkt
Ton: Organisieren, Balancieren, Gleichheit

Red Rhythmic Serpent: Life Force, Survive, Instinct
Tone: Organize, Balance, Equality

 Gelbe Kosmischer Sonne / Yellow Cosmic Sun

	12–21
07:00	
08:00	
09:00	
10:00	
11:00	
12:00	
13:00	
14:00	
15:00	
16:00	
17:00	
18:00	
19:00	
20:00	
21:00	

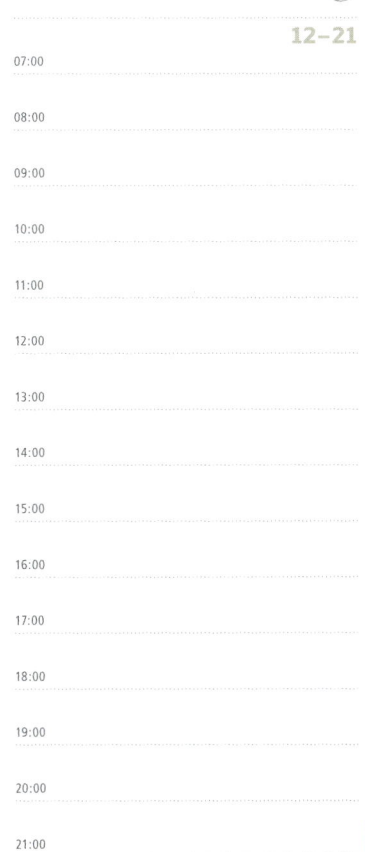

16 Samstag / Saturday 3/27

Weisser Resonanter Weltenüberbrücker: Tod, Ausgleichen, Möglichkeiten
Ton: Kanalisieren, Inspirieren, Einstimmung

White Resonant Worldbridger: Death, Equalize, Opportunity
Tone: Channel, Inspire, Attunement

 Roter Magnetischer Drache / Red Magnetic Dragon

	12–21
08:00	
10:00	
12:00	
14:00	
16:00	
18:00	

17 Sonntag / Sunday 3/28

Blaue Galaktische Hand: Vollendung, Wissen, Heilung
Ton: Harmonisieren, Modellieren, Integrität

Blue Galactic Hand: Accomplishment, Know, Healing
Tone: Harmony, Model, Integrity

 Weisser Lunarer Wind / White Lunar Wind

	12–21

Oktober KW 41

4. Selbstexistierender Mond | Self-existing Moon

1 18/10	2 19/10	3 20/10	4 21/10	5 22/10	6 23/10	7 24/10
8 25/10	9 26/10	10 27/10	11 28/10	12 29/10	13 30/10	14 31/10
15 1/11	16 2/11	17 3/11	18 4/11	19 5/11	20 6/11	21 7/11
22 8/11	23 9/11	24 10/11	25 11/11	26 12/11	27 13/11	28 14/11

Wie soll das Ganze aussehen?
So, jetzt fehlt noch die ideale FORM, dann kann es losgehen! Mit Form wird im Wavespell alles Strukturgebende bezeichnet: Das Vorgehen, der Plan, die Methodik, die Strategie! Denn ohne diese formgebende Struktur ist die Gefahr gross, dass es etwas Unstrukturiertes, Formloses, Beliebiges, Unverständliches, Befremdendes oder sogar Bedrohliches wird! Um die Form zu bilden, sind Entscheidungen notwendig: Links oder rechts, hoch oder tief? Oder hoch UND tief? Ständig müssen wir beobachten, interpretieren, fühlen, entscheiden, bestimmen, erklären, beurteilen oder bewerten! Erst wenn wir diese Macht der Entscheidung voll und ganz annehmen, können wir unseren Weg auch selbstbewusst und absichtsvoll gehen! Daher gilt es, im vierten Mond etwas Stabiles aufzubauen, das in sich selbst stabil = selbstbestehend ist. Mit diesem vierten Mond fassen wir die ersten drei Monde zusammen und schliessen den ersten von drei Unterzyklen ab. Wie bei einer Redaktionskonferenz wird hier entschieden, was wichtig/unwichtig ist. Mit den wichtigen Themen bauen wir uns ein stabiles Fundament, auf dem der nächste Zyklus aufbauen kann.

What's it supposed to look like?
So, now the ideal FORM is still missing, then it can start! The form of the Wavespell is the term used to describe everything that gives structure: The procedure, the plan, the methodology, the strategy! Because without this shaping structure there is a great danger that it will be something unstructured, formless, arbitrary, incomprehensible, alienating or even threatening! In order to form the form, decisions are necessary: Left or right, high or low? Or high AND deep? We must constantly observe, interpret, feel, decide, determine, explain, judge or evaluate! Only when we fully accept this power of decision can we go our way self-confidently and intentionally! Therefore it is necessary to build something stable in the fourth moon, which is stable in itself = self-existing. With this fourth moon we summarize the first three moons and complete the first of three sub cycles. As at an editorial conference it is decided here what is important/unimportant. With the important topics we build ourselves a stable foundation on which the next cycle can build.

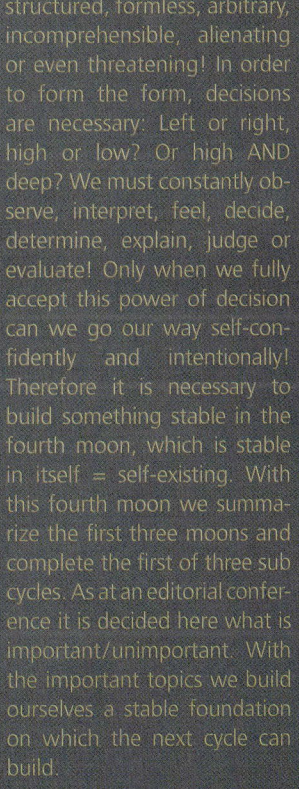

18 Montag / Monday 4/1

Gelber Solarer Stern: Ästhetik, Verschönern, Kunst
Ton: Pulsieren, Erkennen, Absicht

Yellow Solar Star: Elegance, Beautify, Art
Tone: Pulse, Realize, Intention

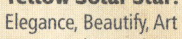 Blaue Elektrische Nacht / Blue Electric Night

12-21

07:00
08:00
09:00
10:00
11:00
12:00
13:00
14:00
15:00
16:00
17:00
18:00
19:00
20:00
21:00

19 Dienstag / Tuesday 4/2

Roter Planetarer Mond: Universelles Wasser, Reinigen, Flow
Ton: Perfektionieren, Produzieren, Manifestation

Red Planetary Moon: Universal Water, Purify, Flow
Tone: Perfect, Produce, Manifestation

 Gelber Selbstexistierender Same | Yellow Selfexisting Seed

12-21

07:00
08:00
09:00
10:00
11:00
12:00
13:00
14:00
15:00
16:00
17:00
18:00
19:00
20:00
21:00

20 Mittwoch / Wednesday P 4/3

Weisser Spektraler Hund: Herz, Lieben, Loyalität
Ton: Auflösen, Loslassen, Befreiung

White Spectral Dog: Heart, Love, Loyalty
Tone: Dissolve, Release, Liberation

 Rote Oberton Schlange / Red Overtone Serpent

12-21

07:00
08:00
09:00
10:00
11:00
12:00
13:00
14:00
15:00
16:00
17:00
18:00
19:00
20:00
21:00

21 Donnerstag / Thursday 4/4

Blauer Kristallener Affe: Magie, Spielen, Illusion
Ton: Hingabe, Verteilen, Zusammenarbeit

Blue Crystal Monkey: Magic, Play, Illusion
Tone: Dedicate, Universalize, Cooperation

 Weisser Rhythmischer Weltenüberbrücker | White Rhythmic Worldbridger

12–21

22 Freitag / Friday 4/5

Gelber Kosmischer Mensch: Freier Wille, Beeinflussen, Weisheit
Ton: Durchhalten, Transzendieren, Präsenz

Yellow Cosmic Human: Free Will, Influence, Wisdom
Tone: Endure, Transcend, Presence

 Blaue Resonante Hand / Blue Resonant Hand

07:00
08:00
09:00
10:00
11:00
12:00
13:00
14:00
15:00
16:00
17:00
18:00
19:00
20:00
21:00

23 Samstag / Saturday 4/6

Roter Magnetischer Himmelswanderer: Raum, Erforschen, Wachsamkeit
Ton: Vereinheitlichen, Anziehen, Bestimmung

Red Magnetic Skywalker: Space, Explore, Wakefullness
Tone: Unify, Attract, Purpose

 Gelber Galaktischer Stern / Yellow Galactic Star

08:00
10:00
12:00
14:00
16:00
18:00

24 Sonntag / Sunday 4/7

Weisser Lunarer Magier: Zeitlosigkeit, Verzaubern, Empfänglichkeit
Ton: Polarisieren, Stabilisieren, Herausforderung

White Lunar Wizard: Timelessness, Enchant, Receptivity
Tone: Polarize, Stabilize, Challenge

 Roter Solarer Mond / Red Solar Moon

Oktober KW 42

	25 Montag / Monday 4/8	26 Dienstag / Tuesday 4/9	27 Mittwoch / Wednesday 4/10
	 **Blauer Elektrischer Adler:** Vision, Erschaffen, Geist **Ton:** Aktivieren, Binden, Dienen •••	 **Gelber Selbstexistierender Krieger:** Intelligenz, Fragen, Angstlosigkeit **Ton:** Definieren, Messen, Form ••••	 **Rote Oberton Erde:** Führung, Entwickeln, Synchronisation **Ton:** Ermächtigen, Befehlen, Strahlkraft —
	Blue Electric Eagle: Vision, Create, Mind **Tone:** Activate, Bond, Service	**Yellow Selfexisting Warrior:** Intelligence, Question, Fearlessness **Tone:** Define, Measure, Form	**Red Overtone Earth:** Navigation, Evolve, Synchronicity **Tone:** Empowerment, Order, Radiance
	Weisser Planetarer Hund / White Planetary Dog	Blauer Spektraler Affe / Blue Spectral Monkey	Gelber Kristallener Mensch / Yellow Crystal Human

Tag | Day — Dreamspell / Long-count

07:00	07:00	07:00
08:00	08:00	08:00
09:00	09:00	09:00
10:00	10:00	10:00
11:00	11:00	11:00
12:00	12:00	12:00
13:00	13:00	13:00
14:00	14:00	14:00
15:00	15:00	15:00
16:00	16:00	16:00
17:00	17:00	17:00
18:00	18:00	18:00
19:00	19:00	19:00
20:00	20:00	20:00
21:00	21:00	21:00

28 Donnerstag / Thursday 4/11

Weisser Rhythmischer Spiegel: Endlosigkeit, Reflektieren, Ordnung
Ton: Organisieren, Balancieren, Gleichheit

White Rhythmic Mirror: Endlessness, Reflect, Order
Tone: Organize, Balance, Equality

Roter Kosmischer Himmelswanderer | Red Cosmic Skywalker

07:00
08:00
09:00
10:00
11:00
12:00
13:00
14:00
15:00
16:00
17:00
18:00
19:00
20:00
21:00

29 Freitag / Friday 4/12

Blauer Resonanter Sturm: Selbsterneuerung, Katalysieren, Energie
Ton: Kanalisieren, Inspirieren, Einstimmung

Blue Resonant Storm: Self-generation, Catalyze, Energy
Tone: Channel, Inspire, Attunement

Weisser Magnetischer Magier / White Magnetic Wizard

07:00
08:00
09:00
10:00
11:00
12:00
13:00
14:00
15:00
16:00
17:00
18:00
19:00
20:00
21:00

30 Samstag / Saturday 4/13

Gelbe Galaktische Sonne: Universelles Feuer, Erleuchten, Leben
Ton: Harmonisieren, Modellieren, Integrität

Yellow Galactic Sun: Universal Fire, Enlighten, Life
Tone: Harmony, Model, Integrity

Blauer Lunarer Adler / Blue Lunar Eagle

08:00
10:00
12:00
14:00
16:00
18:00

31 Sonntag / Sunday 4/14

Roter Solarer Drache: Geburt, Nähren, Sein
Ton: Pulsieren, Erkennen, Absicht

Red Solar Dragon: Birth, Nurture, Being
Tone: Pulse, Realize, Intention

Gelber Elektrischer Krieger / Yellow Electric Warrior

Halloween | Ende der Sommerzeit

Oktober KW 43

1 Montag / Monday 4/15

Weisser Planetarer Wind: Geist, Kommunikation, Atem
Ton: Perfektionieren, Produzieren, Manifestation

White Planetary Wind:
Spirit, Communication, Breath
Tone: Perfect, Produce, Manifestation

 | Rote Selbstexistierende Erde
Red Selfexisting Earth

Allerheiligen | Samhain | Mondfest

07:00	
08:00	
09:00	
10:00	
11:00	
12:00	
13:00	
14:00	
15:00	
16:00	
17:00	
18:00	
19:00	
20:00	
21:00	

2 Dienstag / Tuesday 4/16

Blaue Spektrale Nacht: Fülle, Träumen, Intuition
Ton: Auflösen, Loslassen, Befreiung

Blue Spectral Night:
Abundance, Dream, Intuition
Tone: Dissolve, Release, Liberation

 | Weisser Oberton Spiegel
White Overtone Mirror

07:00	
08:00	
09:00	
10:00	
11:00	
12:00	
13:00	
14:00	
15:00	
16:00	
17:00	
18:00	
19:00	
20:00	
21:00	

3 Mittwoch / Wednesday 4/17

Gelber Kristallener Same: Erblühen, Zielen, Achtsamkeit
Ton: Hingabe, Verteilen, Zusammenarbeit

Yellow Crystal Seed:
Flowering, Target, Awareness
Tone: Dedicate, Universalize, Cooperation

 | Blauer Rhythmischer Sturm
Blue Rhythmic Storm

07:00	
08:00	
09:00	
10:00	
11:00	
12:00	
13:00	
14:00	
15:00	
16:00	
17:00	
18:00	
19:00	
20:00	
21:00	

4 Donnerstag / Thursday 4/18

Rote Kosmische Schlange: Lebenskraft, Überleben, Instinkt
Ton: Durchhalten, Transzendieren, Präsenz

Red Cosmic Serpent:
Life Force, Survive, Instinct
Tone: Endure, Transcend, Presence

 Gelbe Resonante Sonne / Yellow Resonant Sun

07:00
08:00
09:00
10:00
11:00
12:00
13:00
14:00
15:00
16:00
17:00
18:00
19:00
20:00
21:00

5 Freitag / Friday 4/19

Weisser Magnetischer Weltenüberbrücker: Tod, Ausgleichen, Möglichkeiten
Ton: Vereinheitlichen, Anziehen, Bestimmung

White Magnetic Worldbridger:
Death, Equalize, Opportunity
Tone: Unify, Attract, Purpose

 Roter Galaktischer Drache / Red Galactic Dragon

07:00
08:00
09:00
10:00
11:00
12:00
13:00
14:00
15:00
16:00
17:00
18:00
19:00
20:00
21:00

6 Samstag / Saturday 4/20

Blaue Lunare Hand: Vollendung, Wissen, Heilung
Ton: Polarisieren, Stabilisieren, Herausforderung

Blue Lunar Hand:
Accomplishment, Know, Healing
Tone: Polarize, Stabilize, Challenge

  Weisser Solarer Wind / White Solar Wind

08:00
10:00
12:00
14:00
16:00
18:00

7 Sonntag / Sunday 4/21

Gelber Elektrischer Stern: Ästhetik, Verschönern, Kunst
Ton: Aktivieren, Binden, Dienen

Yellow Electric Star:
Elegance, Beautify, Art
Tone: Activate, Bond, Service

 Blaue Planetare Nacht / Blue Planetary Night

November KW 44

Tag | Day

Dreamspell

8 Montag / Monday 4/22

 69

Roter Selbstexistierender Mond: Universelles Wasser, Reinigen, Flow
Ton: Definieren, Messen, Form

Red Selfexisting Moon: Universal Water, Purify, Flow
Tone: Define, Measure, Form

9 Dienstag / Tuesday 4/23

 70

Weisser Oberton Hund: Herz, Lieben, Loyalität
Ton: Ermächtigen, Befehlen, Strahlkraft

White Overtone Dog: Heart, Love, Loyality
Tone: Empowerment, Order, Radiance

10 Mittwoch / Wednesday 4/24

 71

Blauer Rhythmischer Affe: Magie, Spielen, Illusion
Ton: Organisieren, Balancieren, Gleichheit

Blue Rhythmic Monkey: Magic, Play, Illusion
Tone: Organize, Balance, Equality

Long-count

24 ‖ Gelber Spektraler Same / Yellow Spectral Seed

25 ‖ Rote Kristallene Schlange / Red Crystal Serpent

26 ‖ Weisser Kosmischer Weltenüberbrücker | White Cosmic Worldbridger

---

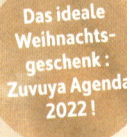

Das ideale Weihnachtsgeschenk: Zuvuya Agenda 2022!

Monday	Tuesday	Wednesday
	07:00	07:00
	08:00	08:00
	09:00	09:00
10:00	10:00	10:00
11:00	11:00	11:00
12:00	12:00	12:00
13:00	13:00	13:00
14:00	14:00	14:00
15:00	15:00	15:00
16:00	16:00	16:00
17:00	17:00	17:00
18:00	18:00	18:00
19:00	19:00	19:00
20:00	20:00	20:00
21:00	21:00	21:00

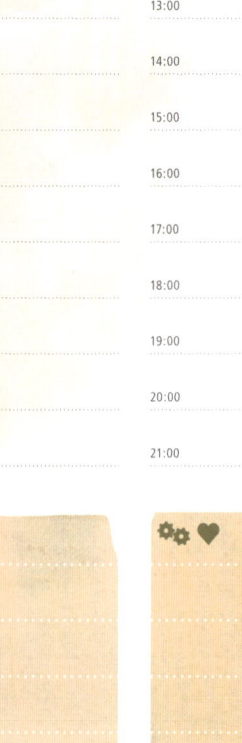

11 Donnerstag / Thursday 4/25

Gelber Resonanter Mensch: Freier Wille, Beeinflussen, Weisheit
Ton: Kanalisieren, Inspirieren, Einstimmung

Yellow Resonant Human: Free Will, Influence, Wisdom
Tone: Channel, Inspire, Attunement

12 Freitag / Friday 4/26

Roter Galaktischer Himmelswanderer: Raum, Erforschen, Wachsamkeit
Ton: Harmonisieren, Modellieren, Integrität

Red Galactic Skywalker: Space, Explore, Wakefullness
Tone: Harmony, Model, Integrity

13 Samstag / Saturday 4/27

Weisser Solarer Magier: Zeitlosigkeit, Verzaubern, Empfänglichkeit
Ton: Pulsieren, Erkennen, Absicht

White Solar Wizard: Timelessness, Enchant, Receptivity
Tone: Pulse, Realize, Intention

 Blaue Magnetische Hand / Blue Magnetic Hand

 28 Gelber Lunarer Stern / Yellow Lunar Star

 29 Roter Elektrischer Mond / Red Electric Moon

November KW 45

07:00	07:00	12–21
08:00	08:00	08:00
09:00	09:00	10:00
10:00	10:00	12:00
11:00	11:00	14:00
12:00	12:00	16:00
13:00	13:00	18:00
14:00	14:00	
15:00	15:00	
16:00	16:00	
17:00	17:00	
18:00	18:00	
19:00	19:00	
20:00	20:00	
21:00	21:00	

14 Sonntag / Sunday 4/28

Blauer Planetarer Adler: Vision, Erschaffen, Geist
Ton: Perfektionieren, Produzieren, Manifestation

Blue Planetary Eagle: Vision, Create, Mind
Tone: Perfect, Produce, Manifestation

30 Weisser Selbstexistierender Hund | White Selfexisting Dog

12–21

Tukan

5. Oberton Mond | Overtone Moon

1	2	3	4	5	6	7
15/11	16/11	17/11	18/11	19/11	20/11	21/11
8	9	10	11	12	13	14
22/11	23/11	24/11	25/11	26/11	27/11	28/11
15	16	17	18	19	20	21
29/11	30/11	1/12	2/12	3/12	4/12	5/12
22	23	24	25	26	27	28
6/12	7/12	8/12	9/12	10/12	11/12	12/12

Wo soll es hingehen?
So, jetzt geht´s los – aber richtig! Denn bisher haben wir uns vorbereitet, Ziele bestimmt, Aktionspotential aufgebaut, vollgetankt, einen Routenplan bestimmt. Wir sitzen im Wagen und die Lokomotive beginnt zu rollen. Der Oberton ist ein Ton, der über dem Grundton schwingt! Alles hat einen Oberton! Wenn wir reden, lachen, singen oder sogar tanzen – nie schwingt irgendetwas nur auf einer Frequenz! Wenn wir diese Stimme in/über/unter/um uns herum wahrnehmen können, spüren wir die Kraft und Führung des Obertons. Wenn wir dieser Stimme folgen, kann nichts mehr schiefgehen! Im fünften Mond gilt es daher, bewusst eine Richtung zu wählen, auf die innere Stimme zu hören, mutig Entscheide zu treffen und schliesslich in die gewünschte Richtung loszulaufen. Unser Abenteuer kann beginnen …

....

Where do you want to go?
So, here we go – but right! Because so far we have prepared ourselves, determined goals, built up action potential, filled up the tank, determined a route plan. We are sitting in the car and the locomotive starts to roll. The overtone is a tone that vibrates above the basic tone! Everything has an overtone! When we talk, laugh, sing or even dance – nothing ever vibrates on a single frequency! If we can perceive this voice in/over/under/around us, we feel the power and guidance of the overtone. If we follow this voice, nothing can go wrong! In the fifth moon it is therefore necessary to consciously choose a direction, listen to the inner voice, make courageous decisions and finally run in the desired direction. Our adventure can begin ...

	Montag / Monday 5/1	Dienstag / Tuesday 5/2	Mittwoch / Wednesday 5/3
	15	**16**	**17**
Dreamspell	 76 **Gelber Spektraler Krieger:** Intelligenz, Fragen, Angstlosigkeit **Ton:** Auflösen, Loslassen, Befreiung **Yellow Spectral Warrior:** Intelligence, Question, Fearlessness **Tone:** Dissolve, Release, Liberation	 77 **Rote Kristallene Erde:** Führung, Entwickeln, Synchronisation **Ton:** Hingabe, Verteilen, Zusammenarbeit **Red Crystal Earth:** Navigation, Evolve, Synchronicity **Tone:** Dedicate, Universalize, Cooperation	 78 **Weisser Kosmischer Spiegel:** Endlosigkeit, Reflektieren, Ordnung **Ton:** Durchhalten, Transzendieren, Präsenz **White Cosmic Mirror:** Endlessness, Reflect, Order **Tone:** Endure, Transcend, Presence
Long-count	31 Blauer Oberton Affe / Blue Overtone Monkey	32 Gelber Rhythmischer Mensch / Yellow Rhythmic Human	33 Roter Resonanter Himmelswanderer / Red Resonant Skywalker

	Monday 12-21	Tuesday 12-21	Wednesday 12-21
07:00			
08:00			
09:00			
10:00			
11:00			
12:00			
13:00			
14:00			
15:00			
16:00			
17:00			
18:00			
19:00			
20:00			
21:00			

18 **Donnerstag** / Thursday 5/4	19 **Freitag** / Friday 5/5	20 **Samstag** / Saturday 5/6
 **Blauer Magnetischer Sturm:** Selbsterneuerung, Katalysieren, Energie **Ton:** Vereinheitlichen, Anziehen, Bestimmung	 **Gelbe Lunare Sonne:** Universelles Feuer, Erleuchten, Leben **Ton:** Polarisieren, Stabilisieren, Herausforderung	 **Roter Elektrischer Drache:** Geburt, Nähren, Sein **Ton:** Aktivieren, Binden, Dienen

Blue Magnetic Storm:
Self-generation, Catalyze, Energy
Tone: Unify, Attract, Purpose

Yellow Lunar Sun:
Universal Fire, Enlighten, Life
Tone: Polarize, Stabilize, Challenge

Red Electric Dragon:
Birth, Nurture, Being
Tone: Activate, Bond, Service

 | **Weisser Galaktischer Magier** / White Galactic Wizard

 | **Blauer Solarer Adler** / Blue Solar Eagle

 | **Gelber Planetarer Krieger** / Yellow Planetary Warrior

12–21

07:00	07:00	08:00
08:00	08:00	10:00
09:00	09:00	12:00
10:00	10:00	14:00
11:00	11:00	16:00
12:00	12:00	18:00
13:00	13:00	
14:00	14:00	
15:00	15:00	**21 Sonntag** / Sunday 5/7
16:00	16:00	 **Weisser Selbstexistierender Wind:** Geist, Kommunikation, Atem **Ton:** Definieren, Messen, Form
17:00	17:00	
18:00	18:00	**White Selfexisting Wind:** Spirit, Communication, Breath **Tone:** Define, Measure, Form
19:00	19:00	
20:00	20:00		**Rote Spektrale Erde** / Red Spectral Earth
21:00	21:00	
		12–21

November KW 46

22 Montag / Monday 5/8

Blaue Oberton Nacht: Fülle, Träumen, Intuition
Ton: Ermächtigen, Befehlen, Strahlkraft

Blue Overtone Night: Abundance, Dream, Intuition
Tone: Empowerment, Order, Radiance

 Weisser Kristallener Spiegel / White Crystal Mirror

23 Dienstag / Tuesday 5/9

Gelber Rhythmischer Same: Erblühen, Zielen, Achtsamkeit
Ton: Organisieren, Balancieren, Gleichheit

Yellow Rhythmic Seed: Flowering, Target, Awareness
Tone: Organize, Balance, Equality

 Blauer Kosmischer Sturm / Blue Cosmic Storm

24 Mittwoch / Wednesday 5/10

Rote Resonante Schlange: Lebenkraft, Überleben, Instinkt
Ton: Kanalisieren, Inspirieren, Einstimmung

Red Resonant Serpent: Life Force, Survive, Instinct
Tone: Channel, Inspire, Attunement

 Gelbe Magnetischer Sonne / Yellow Magnetic Sun

22 Monday	23 Tuesday	24 Wednesday
07:00	07:00	07:00
08:00	08:00	08:00
09:00	09:00	09:00
10:00	10:00	10:00
11:00	11:00	11:00
12:00	12:00	12:00
13:00	13:00	13:00
14:00	14:00	14:00
15:00	15:00	15:00
16:00	16:00	16:00
17:00	17:00	17:00
18:00	18:00	18:00
19:00	19:00	19:00
20:00	20:00	20:00
21:00	21:00	21:00

25 Donnerstag / Thursday 5/11

Weisser Galaktischer Weltenüberbrücker: Tod, Ausgleichen, Möglichkeiten
Ton: Harmonisieren, Modellieren, Integrität

White Galactic Worldbridger: Death, Equalize, Opportunity
Tone: Harmony, Model, Integrity

 Roter Lunarer Drache / Red Lunar Dragon

07:00
08:00
09:00
10:00
11:00
12:00
13:00
14:00
15:00
16:00
17:00
18:00
19:00
20:00
21:00

26 Freitag / Friday 5/12

Blaue Solare Hand: Vollendung, Wissen, Heilung
Ton: Pulsieren, Erkennen, Absicht

Blue Solar Hand: Accomplishment, Know, Healing
Tone: Pulse, Realize, Intention

 Weisser Elektrischer Wind / White Electric Wind

07:00
08:00
09:00
10:00
11:00
12:00
13:00
14:00
15:00
16:00
17:00
18:00
19:00
20:00
21:00

27 Samstag / Saturday 5/13

Gelber Planetarer Stern: Ästhetik, Verschönern, Kunst
Ton: Perfektionieren, Produzieren, Manifestation

Yellow Planetary Star: Elegance, Beautify, Art
Tone: Perfect, Produce, Manifestation

 Blaue Selbstexistierende Nacht | Blue Selfexisting Night

08:00
10:00
12:00
14:00
16:00
18:00

28 Sonntag / Sunday 5/14

Roter Spektraler Mond: Universelles Wasser, Reinigen, Flow
Ton: Auflösen, Loslassen, Befreiung

Red Spectral Moon: Universal Water, Purify, Flow
Tone: Dissolve, Release, Liberation

 Gelber Oberton Same / Yellow Overtone Seed

1. Advent

November KW 47

Tag | Day

Dreamspell

29 Montag / Monday 5/15
Weisser Kristallener Hund: Herz, Lieben, Loyalität
Ton: Hingabe, Verteilen, Zusammenarbeit

White Crystal Dog:
Heart, Love, Loyality
Tone: Dedicate, Universalize, Cooperation

30 Dienstag / Tuesday 5/16
Blauer Kosmischer Affe: Magie, Spielen, Illusion
Ton: Durchhalten, Transzendieren, Präsenz

Blue Cosmic Monkey:
Magic, Play, Illusion
Tone: Endure, Transcend, Presence

1 Mittwoch / Wednesday 5/17
Gelber Magnetischer Mensch: Freier Wille, Beeinflussen, Weisheit
Ton: Vereinheitlichen, Anziehen, Bestimmung

Yellow Magnetic Human:
Free Will, Influence, Wisdom
Tone: Unify, Attract, Purpose

Long-count

 Rote Rhythmische Schlange / Red Rhythmic Serpent

 Weisser Resonanter Weltenüberbrücker | White Resonant Worldbridger

 Blaue Galaktische Hand / Blue Galactic Hand

29 Montag	30 Dienstag	1 Mittwoch
07:00	07:00	07:00
08:00	08:00	08:00
09:00	09:00	09:00
10:00	10:00	10:00
11:00	11:00	11:00
12:00	12:00	12:00
13:00	13:00	13:00
14:00	14:00	14:00
15:00	15:00	15:00
16:00	16:00	16:00
17:00	17:00	17:00
18:00	18:00	18:00
19:00	19:00	19:00
20:00	20:00	20:00
21:00	21:00	21:00

2 Donnerstag / Thursday 5/18

Roter Lunarer Himmelswanderer: Raum, Erforschen, Wachsamkeit
Ton: Polarisieren, Stabilisieren, Herausforderung

Red Lunar Skywalker: Space, Explore, Wakefullness
Tone: Polarize, Stabilize, Challenge

 Gelber Solarer Stern / Yellow Solar Star

07:00
08:00
09:00
10:00
11:00
12:00
13:00
14:00
15:00
16:00
17:00
18:00
19:00
20:00
21:00

3 Freitag / Friday 5/19

Weisser Elektrischer Magier: Zeitlosigkeit, Verzaubern, Empfänglichkeit
Ton: Aktivieren, Binden, Dienen

White Electric Wizard: Timelessness, Enchant, Receptivity
Tone: Activate, Bond, Service

 Roter Planetarer Mond / Red Planetary Moon

07:00
08:00
09:00
10:00
11:00
12:00
13:00
14:00
15:00
16:00
17:00
18:00
19:00
20:00
21:00

4 Samstag / Saturday 5/20

Blauer Selbstexistierender Adler: Vision, Erschaffen, Geist
Ton: Definieren, Messen, Form

Blue Selfexisting Eagle: Vision, Create, Mind
Tone: Define, Measure, Form

 Weisser Spektraler Hund / White Spectral Dog

08:00
10:00
12:00
14:00
16:00
18:00

5 Sonntag / Sunday 5/21

Gelber Oberton Krieger: Intelligenz, Fragen, Angstlosigkeit
Ton: Ermächtigen, Befehlen, Strahlkraft

Yellow Overtone Warrior: Intelligence, Question, Fearlessness
Tone: Empowerment, Order, Radiance

 Blauer Kristallener Affe / Blue Crystal Monkey

2. Advent

Dezember KW 48

Tag | Day

Dreamspell

6 Montag / Monday   5/22

Rote Rhythmische Erde: Führung, Entwickeln, Synchronisation
Ton: Organisieren, Balancieren, Gleichheit

Red Rhythmic Earth: Navigation, Evolve, Synchronicity
Tone: Organize, Balance, Equality

7 Dienstag / Tuesday   5/23

Weisser Resonanter Spiegel: Endlosigkeit, Reflektieren, Ordnung
Ton: Kanalisieren, Inspirieren, Einstimmung

White Resonant Mirror: Endlessness, Reflect, Order
Tone: Channel, Inspire, Attunement

8 Mittwoch / Wednesday  5/24

Blauer Galaktischer Sturm: Selbsterneuerung, Katalysieren, Energie
Ton: Harmonisieren, Modellieren, Integrität

Blue Galactic Storm: Self-generation, Catalyze, Energy
Tone: Harmony, Model, Integrity

Long-count

 52 — Gelber Kosmischer Mensch / Yellow Cosmic Human

 53 — Roter Magnetischer Himmelswanderer | Red Magnetic Skywalker

 54 — Weisser Lunarer Magier / White Lunar Wizard

Ein nachhaltiges Weihnachtsgeschenk?
Zuvuya Agenda 2022

A sustainable Christmas present?
Zuvuya Agenda 2022

Monday 6	Tuesday 7	Wednesday 8
	07:00	07:00
	08:00	08:00
	09:00	09:00
	10:00	10:00
11:00	11:00	11:00
12:00	12:00	12:00
13:00	13:00	13:00
14:00	14:00	14:00
15:00	15:00	15:00
16:00	16:00	16:00
17:00	17:00	17:00
18:00	18:00	18:00
19:00	19:00	19:00
20:00	20:00	20:00
21:00	21:00	21:00

9 Donnerstag / Thursday — 5/25

Gelbe Solare Sonne: Universelles Feuer, Erleuchten, Leben
Ton: Pulsieren, Erkennen, Absicht

Yellow Solar Sun: Universal Fire, Enlighten, Life
Tone: Pulse, Realize, Intention

 Blauer Elektrischer Adler / Blue Electric Eagle

07:00
08:00
09:00
10:00
11:00
12:00
13:00
14:00
15:00
16:00
17:00
18:00
19:00
20:00
21:00

10 Freitag / Friday — 5/26

Roter Planetarer Drache: Geburt, Nähren, Sein
Ton: Perfektionieren, Produzieren, Manifestation

Red Planetary Dragon: Birth, Nurture, Being
Tone: Perfect, Produce, Manifestation

 Gelber Selbstexistierender Krieger | Yellow Selfexisting Warrior

07:00
08:00
09:00
10:00
11:00
12:00
13:00
14:00
15:00
16:00
17:00
18:00
19:00
20:00
21:00

11 Samstag / Saturday — 5/27

Weisser Spektraler Wind: Geist, Kommunikation, Atem
Ton: Auflösen, Loslassen, Befreiung

White Spectral Wind: Spirit, Communication, Breath
Tone: Dissolve, Release, Liberation

 Rote Oberton Erde / Red Overtone Earth

08:00
10:00
12:00
14:00
16:00
18:00

12 Sonntag / Sunday — 5/28

Blaue Kristallene Nacht: Fülle, Träumen, Intuition
Ton: Hingabe, Verteilen, Zusammenarbeit

Blue Crystal Night: Abundance, Dream, Intuition
Tone: Dedicate, Universalize, Cooperation

 Weisser Rhythmischer Spiegel / White Rhythmic Mirror

3. Advent

12–21

Dezember — KW 49

Weissrüssel-Nasenbär

6. Rhythmischer Mond | Rhythmic Moon

1 13/12	2 14/12	3 15/12	4 16/12	5 17/12	6 18/12	7 19/12
8 20/12	9 21/12	10 22/12	11 23/12	12 24/12	13 25/12	14 26/12
15 27/12	16 28/12	17 29/12	18 30/12	19 31/12	20 1/1	21 2/1
22 3/1	23 4/1	24 5/1	25 6/1	26 7/1	27 8/1	28 9/1

Was gibt es auszubalancieren?

Wir lassen die vertraute Umgebung hinter uns, der Horizont vor uns erstreckt sich weit, wir laufen der Sonne nach! Wenn wir wirklich in uns ruhen, jeden Schritt spüren und geniessen – die Natur um uns herum und die Welt in uns drinnen – dann werden wir auf einmal merken, wie alles sich immer mehr und mehr aufeinander einschwingt! Es ist, als ob unser Herzschlag, die Atmung, die Schritte sich mit dem Zirpen der Grillen, dem Muhen der Kühe, dem Summen der Bienen, ja, sogar dem Rascheln der Blätter synchron bewegt! Das ist – gelinde ausgedrückt ekstatisch! Falls du jedoch in diesen 28 Tagen spürst, dass ein paar Dinge noch nicht im Lot/Balance sind, dann ermöglicht dir dieser Mond, noch Korrekturen anzubringen und Dinge auszubalancieren. Frage dich ganz einfach, wo es noch hakt und versuche, mit Aufmerksamkeit und Intelligenz, gezielt ein paar Tropfen Öl anzubringen, damit alles wieder reibungslos rollen/flowen kann.

What is there to balance?

We leave the familiar surroundings behind us, the horizon in front of us stretches far, we follow the sun! If we really rest in ourselves, feel and enjoy every step – the nature around us and the world inside us – then we will suddenly notice how everything becomes more and more resonant with each other! It is as if our heartbeat, our breathing, our steps move synchronously with the chirping of the crickets, the mooing of the cows, the humming of the bees, even the rustling of the leaves! That is – to put it mildly – ecstatic! However, if you feel during these 28 days that a few things are not in balance yet, then this moon will allow you to make corrections and balance things. Just ask yourself where it is still resinous and try to apply a few drops of oil with attention and intelligence, so that everything can roll/flow smoothly again.

	13 Montag / Monday 6/1	**14** Dienstag / Tuesday 6/2	**15** Mittwoch / Wednesday ⓟ 6/3

Dreamspell

 **Gelber Kosmischer Same:** Erblühen, Zielen, Achtsamkeit
Ton: Durchhalten, Transzendieren, Präsenz

Yellow Cosmic Seed: Flowering, Target, Awareness
Tone: Endure, Transcend, Presence

 Rote Magnetische Schlange: Lebenskraft, Überleben, Instinkt
Ton: Vereinheitlichen, Anziehen, Bestimmung

Red Magnetic Serpent: Life Force, Survive, Instinct
Tone: Unify, Attract, Purpose

 **Weisser Lunarer Weltenüberbrücker:** Tod, Ausgleichen, Möglichkeiten
Ton: Polarisieren, Stabilisieren, Herausforderung

White Lunar Worldbridger: Death, Equalize, Opportunity
Tone: Polarize, Stabilize, Challenge

Long-count

 Blauer Resonanter Sturm / Blue Resonant Storm (59)

 Gelbe Galaktische Sonne / Yellow Galactic Sun (60)

 Roter Solarer Drache / Red Solar Dragon (61)

12–21

Montag	Dienstag	Mittwoch
07:00	07:00	07:00
08:00	08:00	08:00
09:00	09:00	09:00
10:00	10:00	10:00
11:00	11:00	11:00
12:00	12:00	12:00
13:00	13:00	13:00
14:00	14:00	14:00
15:00	15:00	15:00
16:00	16:00	16:00
17:00	17:00	17:00
18:00	18:00	18:00
19:00	19:00	19:00
20:00	20:00	20:00
21:00	21:00	21:00

16 Donnerstag / Thursday 6/4

Blaue Elektrische Hand: Vollendung, Wissen, Heilung
Ton: Aktivieren, Binden, Dienen

Blue Electric Hand: Accomplishment, Know, Healing
Tone: Activate, Bond, Service

 Weisser Planetarer Wind / White Planetary Wind

12-21

7:00
8:00
9:00
10:00
11:00
12:00
13:00
14:00
15:00
16:00
17:00
18:00
19:00
20:00
21:00

17 Freitag / Friday 6/5

Gelber Selbstexistierender Stern: Ästhetik, Verschönern, Kunst
Ton: Definieren, Messen, Form

Yellow Selfexisting Star: Elegance, Beautify, Art
Tone: Define, Measure, Form

 Blaue Spektrale Nacht / Blue Spectral Night

12-21

07:00
08:00
09:00
10:00
11:00
12:00
13:00
14:00
15:00
16:00
17:00
18:00
19:00
20:00
21:00

18 Samstag / Saturday 6/6

Roter Oberton Mond: Universelles Wasser, Reinigen, Flow
Ton: Ermächtigen, Befehlen, Strahlkraft

Red Overtone Moon: Universal Water, Purify, Flow
Tone: Empowerment, Order, Radiance

 Gelber Kristallener Same / Yellow Crystal Seed

12-21

08:00
10:00
12:00
14:00
16:00
18:00

19 Sonntag / Sunday 6/7

Weisser Rhythmischer Hund: Herz, Lieben, Loyalität
Ton: Organisieren, Balancieren, Gleichheit

White Rhythmic Dog: Heart, Love, Loyality
Tone: Organize, Balance, Equality

 Rote Kosmische Schlange / Red Cosmic Serpent

4. Advent

12-21

Dezember KW 50

Tag | Day			
Dreamspell	**20** Montag / Monday 6/8	**21** Dienstag / Tuesday 6/9	**22** Mittwoch / Wednesday 6/10
	 **Blauer Resonanter Affe:** Magie, Spielen, Illusion **Ton:** Kanalisieren, Inspirieren, Einstimmung	 **Gelber Galaktischer Mensch:** Freier Wille, Beeinflussen, Weisheit **Ton:** Harmonisieren, Modellieren, Integrität	 **Roter Solarer Himmelswanderer:** Raum, Erforschen, Wachsamkeit **Ton:** Pulsieren, Erkennen, Absicht
	Blue Resonant Monkey: Magic, Play, Illusion **Tone:** Channel, Inspire, Attunement	**Yellow Galactic Human:** Free Will, Influence, Wisdom **Tone:** Harmony, Model, Integrity	**Red Solar Skywalker:** Space, Explore, Wakefullness **Tone:** Pulse, Realize, Intention
Long-count	Weisser Magnetischer Weltenüberbrücker | White Magnetic Worldbridger	Blaue Lunare Hand / Blue Lunar Hand	Gelber Elektrischer Stern / Yellow Electric Star
		Wintersonnenwende | Sonnenfest	
	12-21	12-21	

07:00	07:00	07:00
08:00	08:00	08:00
09:00	09:00	09:00
10:00	10:00	10:00
11:00	11:00	11:00
12:00	12:00	12:00
13:00	13:00	13:00
14:00	14:00	14:00
15:00	15:00	15:00
16:00	16:00	16:00
17:00	17:00	17:00
18:00	18:00	18:00
19:00	19:00	19:00
20:00	20:00	20:00
21:00	21:00	21:00

23 Donnerstag / Thursday 6/11	**24** Freitag / Friday 6/12	**25** Samstag / Saturday 6/13
 **Weisser Planetarer Magier:** Zeitlosigkeit, Verzaubern, Empfänglichkeit **Ton:** Perfektionieren, Produzieren, Manifestation	**Blauer Spektraler Adler:** Vision, Erschaffen, Geist **Ton:** Auflösen, Loslassen, Befreiung	 **Gelber Kristallener Krieger:** Intelligenz, Fragen, Angstlosigkeit **Ton:** Hingabe, Verteilen, Zusammenarbeit

Dezember KW 51

White Planetary Wizard:
Timelessness, Enchant, Receptivity
Tone: Perfect, Produce, Manifestation

Blue Spectral Eagle:
Vision, Create, Mind
Tone: Dissolve, Release, Liberation

Yellow Crystal Warrior:
Intelligence, Question, Fearlessness
Tone: Dedicate, Universalize, Cooperation

Roter Selbstexistierender Mond | Red Selfexisting Moon	Weisser Oberton Hund / White Overtone Dog	Blauer Rhythmischer Affe / Blue Rhythmic Monkey

Weihnachten

	07:00	08:00
	08:00	10:00
	09:00	12:00
10:00	10:00	14:00
11:00	11:00	16:00
12:00	12:00	18:00
13:00	13:00	
14:00	14:00	
15:00	15:00	**26** Sonntag / Sunday 6/14
16:00	16:00	 **Rote Kosmische Erde:** Führung, Entwickeln, Synchronisation **Ton:** Durchhalten, Transzendieren, Präsenz
17:00	17:00	
18:00	18:00	
19:00	19:00	**Red Cosmic Earth:** Navigation, Evolve, Synchronicity **Tone:** Endure, Transcend, Presence
20:00	20:00	
21:00	21:00	 Gelber Resonanter Mensch / Yellow Resonant Human

Tag | Day

Dreamspell

Long-count

27 Montag / Monday 6/15

118

Weisser Magnetischer Spiegel: Endlosigkeit, Reflektieren, Ordnung
Ton: Vereinheitlichen, Anziehen, Bestimmung

White Magnetic Mirror: Endlessness, Reflect, Order
Tone: Unify, Attract, Purpose

73 Roter Galaktischer Himmelswanderer | Red Galactic Skywalker

07:00
08:00
09:00
10:00
11:00
12:00
13:00
14:00
15:00
16:00
17:00
18:00
19:00
20:00
21:00

28 Dienstag / Tuesday 6/16

119

Blauer Lunarer Sturm: Selbsterneuerung, Katalysieren, Energie
Ton: Polarisieren, Stabilisieren, Herausforderung

Blue Lunar Storm: Self-generation, Catalyze, Energy
Tone: Polarize, Stabilize, Challenge

74 Weisser Solarer Magier / White Solar Wizard

07:00
08:00
09:00
10:00
11:00
12:00
13:00
14:00
15:00
16:00
17:00
18:00
19:00
20:00
21:00

29 Mittwoch / Wednesday 6/17

120

Gelbe Elektrische Sonne: Universelles Feuer, Erleuchten, Leben
Ton: Aktivieren, Binden, Dienen

Yellow Electric Sun: Universal Fire, Enlighten, Life
Tone: Activate, Bond, Service

75 Blauer Planetarer Adler / Blue Planetary Eagle

07:00
08:00
09:00
10:00
11:00
12:00
13:00
14:00
15:00
16:00
17:00
18:00
19:00
20:00
21:00

30 Donnerstag / Thursday 6/18

 **Roter Selbstexistierender Drache:** Geburt, Nähren, Sein
Ton: Definieren, Messen, Form

Red Selfexisting Dragon: Birth, Nurture, Being
Tone: Define, Measure, Form

 Gelber Spektraler Krieger / Yellow Spectral Warrior

- 07:00
- 08:00
- 09:00
- 10:00
- 11:00
- 12:00
- 13:00
- 14:00
- 15:00
- 16:00
- 17:00
- 18:00
- 19:00
- 20:00
- 21:00

31 Freitag / Friday 6/19

 **Weisser Oberton Wind:** Geist, Kommunikation, Atem
Ton: Ermächtigen, Befehlen, Strahlkraft

White Overtone Wind: Spirit, Communication, Breath
Tone: Empowerment, Order, Radiance

 Rote Kristallene Erde / Red Crystal Earth

- 07:00
- 08:00
- 09:00
- 10:00
- 11:00
- 12:00
- 13:00
- 14:00
- 15:00
- 16:00
- 17:00
- 18:00
- 19:00
- 20:00
- 21:00

1 Samstag / Saturday 6/20

 Blaue Rhythmische Nacht: Fülle, Träumen, Intuition
Ton: Organisieren, Balancieren, Gleichheit

Blue Rhythmic Night: Abundance, Dream, Intuition
Tone: Organize, Balance, Equality

 Weisser Kosmischer Spiegel / White Cosmic Mirror

- 08:00
- 10:00
- 12:00
- 14:00
- 16:00
- 18:00

2 Sonntag / Sunday 6/21

 **Gelber Resonanter Same:** Erblühen, Zielen, Achtsamkeit
Ton: Kanalisieren, Inspirieren, Einstimmung

Yellow Resonant Seed: Flowering, Target, Awareness
Tone: Channel, Inspire, Attunement

Blauer Magnetischer Sturm / Blue Magnetic Storm

Dezember KW 52

3 Montag / Monday 6/22

Rote Galaktische Schlange: Lebenkraft, Überleben, Instinkt
Ton: Harmonisieren, Modellieren, Integrität

Red Galactic Serpent: Life Force, Survive, Instinct
Tone: Harmony, Model, Integrity

 Gelbe Lunare Sonne / Yellow Lunar Sun

| 07:00 |
| 08:00 |
| 09:00 |
| 10:00 |
| 11:00 |
| 12:00 |
| 13:00 |
| 14:00 |
| 15:00 |
| 16:00 |
| 17:00 |
| 18:00 |
| 19:00 |
| 20:00 |
| 21:00 |

4 Dienstag / Tuesday 6/23

Weisser Solarer Weltenüberbrücker: Tod, Ausgleichen, Möglichkeiten
Ton: Pulsieren, Erkennen, Absicht

White Solar Worldbridger: Death, Equalize, Opportunity
Tone: Pulse, Realize, Intention

 Roter Elektrischer Drache / Red Electric Dragon

| 07:00 |
| 08:00 |
| 09:00 |
| 10:00 |
| 11:00 |
| 12:00 |
| 13:00 |
| 14:00 |
| 15:00 |
| 16:00 |
| 17:00 |
| 18:00 |
| 19:00 |
| 20:00 |
| 21:00 |

5 Mittwoch / Wednesday 6/24

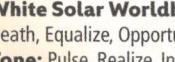

Blaue Planetare Hand: Vollendung, Wissen, Heilung
Ton: Perfektionieren, Produzieren, Manifestation

Blue Planetary Hand: Accomplishment, Know, Healing
Tone: Perfect, Produce, Manifestation

 Weisser Selbstexistierender Wind | White Selfexisting Wind

| 07:00 |
| 08:00 |
| 09:00 |
| 10:00 |
| 11:00 |
| 12:00 |
| 13:00 |
| 14:00 |
| 15:00 |
| 16:00 |
| 17:00 |
| 18:00 |
| 19:00 |
| 20:00 |
| 21:00 |

6 **Donnerstag** / **Thursday** 6/25 **7** **Freitag** / **Friday** 6/26 **8** **Samstag** / **Saturday** 6/27

 **Gelber Spektraler**
Stern: Ästhetik, Verschönern, Kunst
Ton: Auflösen, Loslassen, Befreiung

 **Roter Kristallener**
Mond: Universelles Wasser, Reinigen, Flow
Ton: Hingabe, Verteilen, Zusammenarbeit

 **Weisser Kosmischer**
Hund: Herz, Lieben, Loyalität
Ton: Durchhalten, Transzendieren, Präsenz

Yellow Spectral Star:
Elegance, Beautify, Art
Tone: Dissolve, Release, Liberation

Red Crystal Moon:
Universal Water, Purify, Flow
Tone: Dedicate, Universalize, Cooperation

White Cosmic Dog:
Heart, Love, Loyality
Tone: Endure, Transcend, Presence

 Blaue Oberton Nacht / Blue Overtone Night

 Gelber Rhythmischer Same / Yellow Rhythmic Seed

 Rote Resonante Schlange / Red Resonant Serpent

Heilige drei Könige

07:00	07:00	08:00
08:00	08:00	10:00
09:00	09:00	12:00
10:00	10:00	14:00
11:00	11:00	16:00
12:00	12:00	18:00
13:00	13:00	
14:00	14:00	

9 **Sonntag** / **Sunday** 6/28

 **Blauer Magnetischer**
Affe: Magie, Spielen, Illusion
Ton: Vereinheitlichen, Anziehen, Bestimmung

15:00	15:00
16:00	16:00
17:00	17:00

Blue Magnetic Monkey:
Magic, Play, Illusion
Tone: Unify, Attract, Purpose

18:00	18:00
19:00	19:00
20:00	20:00
21:00	21:00

 Weisser Galaktischer Weltenüberbrücker | White Galactic Worldbridger

Januar KW 1

Rotkopf-Amazonenpapagei

7. Resonanter Mond | Resonant Moon

1 10/1	2 11/1	3 12/1	4 13/1	5 14/1	6 15/1	7 16/1
8 17/1	9 18/1	10 19/1	11 20/1	12 21/1	13 22/1	14 23/1
15 24/1	16 25/1	17 26/1	18 27/1	19 28/1	20 29/1	21 30/1
22 31/1	23 1/2	24 2/2	25 3/2	26 4/2	27 5/2	28 6/2

Nimm die Zügel selbst in die Hand!

Zwischendurch lohnt es sich, die Zeitungen zu lesen, damit wir ein bisschen mitplaudern können im Kontakt mit den «anderen»! Aber eigentlich reicht es, wenn wir unsere Mitte halten. Das bedeutet, zentriert zu sein – und was zentriert ist, schwingt resonant mit allem! Wenn du resonant bist mit allem, was dich umgibt, gibt es keine Fragen mehr, nur noch Antworten! Die 28 Tage des Resonanten Mondes bilden die Mitte des 13 Monde Zyklus (und natürlich auch die Mitte deines individuellen 13 Monde Jahres: Halbzeit!) Es ist die Brücke von der ersten Halbzeit zur zweiten ... Es ist die Pause, wenn du so willst – der Trainer hat dir ein paar wichtige Beobachtungen und Informationen mitzuteilen! Und ja, bis hierhin hat die Zeitdynamik die Zügel in den Händen gehalten, welche für die zweite Halbzeit dir übergeben werden. Oder nochmals anders ausgedrückt: Mit dem 6. Mond sind wir in einen Kreisverkehr hineingefahren und im 7. Mond bestimmst du selber, welche Ausfahrt (Richtung) du nehmen möchtest. Falls du bisher aufmerksam warst, wirst du mit Sicherheit eine gute Entscheidung treffen.

....

Take the reins into your own hands!

In the meanwhile it is worth reading the newspapers, so that we can chat a little in contact with the «others»! But actually it is enough if we keep our middle. That means to be centered – and what is centered resonates with everything! If you are resonant with everything that surrounds you, there are no more questions, only answers! The 28 days of the resonant moon form the middle of the 13 moon cycle (and of course the middle of your individual 13 moon year: halftime!) It is the bridge from the first halftime to the second ... It is the break, if you like – the trainer has some important observations and information to share with you! And yes, so far the time dynamics have held the reins in their hands, which will be handed over to you for the second half. Or to put it another way: with the 6th moon we entered a roundabout and in the 7th moon you decide yourself which exit (direction) you want to take. If you have been attentive so far, you will certainly make a good decision.

Tag | Day

Dreamspell

Long-count

10 Montag / Monday 7/1

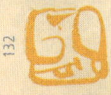

132 **Gelber Lunarer Mensch:** Freier Wille, Beeinflussen, Weisheit
Ton: Polarisieren, Stabilisieren, Herausforderung

Yellow Lunar Human: Free Will, Influence, Wisdom
Tone: Polarize, Stabilize, Challenge

87 Blaue Solare Hand
Blue Solar Hand

07:00
08:00
09:00
10:00
11:00
12:00
13:00
14:00
15:00
16:00
17:00
18:00
19:00
20:00
21:00

11 Dienstag / Tuesday 7/2

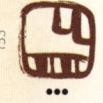

133 **Roter Elektrischer Himmelswanderer:** Raum, Erforschen, Wachsamkeit
Ton: Aktivieren, Binden, Dienen

Red Electric Skywalker: Space, Explore, Wakefullness
Tone: Activate, Bond, Service

88 Gelber Planetarer Stern
Yellow Planetary Star

07:00
08:00
09:00
10:00
11:00
12:00
13:00
14:00
15:00
16:00
17:00
18:00
19:00
20:00
21:00

12 Mittwoch / Wednesday 7/3

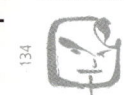

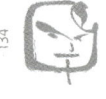

134 **Weisser Selbstexistierender Magier:** Zeitlosigkeit, Verzaubern, Empfänglichkeit
Ton: Definieren, Messen, Form

White Selfexisting Wizard: Timelessness, Enchant, Receptivity
Tone: Define, Measure, Form

89 Roter Spektraler Mond
Red Spectral Moon

12–21

07:00
08:00
09:00
10:00
11:00
12:00
13:00
14:00
15:00
16:00
17:00
18:00
19:00
20:00
21:00

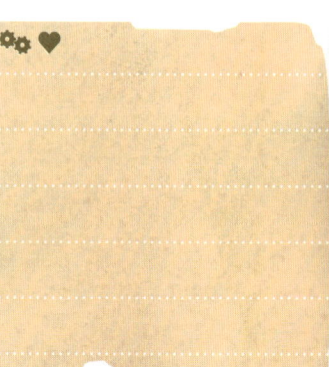

13 Donnerstag / Thursday 7/4

Blauer Oberton Adler: Vision, Erschaffen, Geist
Ton: Ermächtigen, Befehlen, Strahlkraft

Blue Overtone Eagle: Vision, Create, Mind
Tone: Empowerment, Order, Radiance

 Weisser Kristallener Hund / White Crystal Dog

12–21

- 07:00
- 08:00
- 09:00
- 10:00
- 11:00
- 12:00
- 13:00
- 14:00
- 15:00
- 16:00
- 17:00
- 18:00
- 19:00
- 20:00
- 21:00

14 Freitag / Friday 7/5

Gelber Rhythmischer Krieger: Intelligenz, Fragen, Angstlosigkeit
Ton: Organisieren, Balancieren, Gleichheit

Yellow Rhythmic Warrior: Intelligence, Question, Fearlessness
Tone: Organize, Balance, Equality

 Blauer Kosmischer Affe / Blue Cosmic Monkey

12–21

- 07:00
- 08:00
- 09:00
- 10:00
- 11:00
- 12:00
- 13:00
- 14:00
- 15:00
- 16:00
- 17:00
- 18:00
- 19:00
- 20:00
- 21:00

15 Samstag / Saturday 7/6

Rote Resonante Erde: Führung, Entwickeln, Synchronisation
Ton: Kanalisieren, Inspirieren, Einstimmung

Red Resonant Earth: Navigation, Evolve, Synchronicity
Tone: Channel, Inspire, Attunement

 Gelber Magnetischer Mensch / Yellow Magnetic Human

12–21

- 08:00
- 10:00
- 12:00
- 14:00
- 16:00
- 18:00

16 Sonntag / Sunday 7/7

Weisser Galaktischer Spiegel: Endlosigkeit, Reflektieren, Ordnung
Ton: Harmonisieren, Modellieren, Integrität

White Galactic Mirror: Endlessness, Reflect, Order
Tone: Harmony, Model, Integrity

 Roter Lunarer Himmelswanderer | Red Lunar Skywalker

12–21

Januar KW 2

Tag | Day	Montag / Monday 7/8	Dienstag / Tuesday 7/9	Mittwoch / Wednesday 7/10
	17	**18**	**19**

 **Blauer Solarer Sturm:** Selbsterneuerung, Katalysieren, Energie
Ton: Pulsieren, Erkennen, Absicht

 **Gelbe Planetare Sonne:** Universelles Feuer, Erleuchten, Leben
Ton: Perfektionieren, Produzieren, Manifestation

 **Roter Spektraler Drache:** Geburt, Nähren, Sein
Ton: Auflösen, Loslassen, Befreiung

Blue Solar Storm: Self-generation, Catalyze, Energy
Tone: Pulse, Realize, Intention

Yellow Planetary Sun: Universal Fire, Enlighten, Life
Tone: Perfect, Produce, Manifestation

Red Spectral Dragon: Birth, Nurture, Being
Tone: Dissolve, Release, Liberation

 Weisser Elektrischer Magier
White Electric Wizard

 Blauer Selbstexistierender Adler | Blue Selfexisting Eagle

 Gelber Oberton Krieger
Yellow Overtone Warrior

12–21 | 12–21 | 12–21

07:00
08:00
09:00
10:00
11:00
12:00
13:00
14:00
15:00
16:00
17:00
18:00
19:00
20:00
21:00

20 Donnerstag / Thursday 7/11

Weisser Kristallener Wind: Geist, Kommunikation, Atem
Ton: Hingabe, Verteilen, Zusammenarbeit

White Crystal Wind:
Spirit, Communication, Breath
Tone: Dedicate, Universalize, Cooperation

21 Freitag / Friday 7/12

Blaue Kosmische Nacht: Fülle, Träumen, Intuition
Ton: Durchhalten, Transzendieren, Präsenz

Blue Cosmic Night:
Abundance, Dream, Intuition
Tone: Endure, Transcend, Presence

22 Samstag / Saturday 7/13

Gelber Magnetischer Same: Erblühen, Zielen, Achtsamkeit
Ton: Vereinheitlichen, Anziehen, Bestimmung

Yellow Magnetic Seed:
Flowering, Target, Awareness
Tone: Unify, Attract, Purpose

Januar · KW 3

 | Rote Rhythmische Erde / Red Rhythmic Earth
 | Weisser Resonanter Spiegel / White Resonant Mirror
 | Blauer Galaktischer Sturm / Blue Galactic Storm

12–21

07:00	07:00	08:00
08:00	08:00	10:00
09:00	09:00	12:00
10:00	10:00	14:00
11:00	11:00	16:00
12:00	12:00	18:00
13:00	13:00	
14:00	14:00	

23 Sonntag / Sunday 7/14

Rote Lunare Schlange: Lebenkraft, Überleben, Instinkt
Ton: Polarisieren, Stabilisieren, Herausforderung

Red Lunar Serpent:
Life Force, Survive, Instinct
Tone: Polarize, Stabilize, Challenge

15:00	15:00
16:00	16:00
17:00	17:00
18:00	18:00
19:00	19:00
20:00	20:00
21:00	21:00

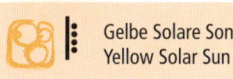 Gelbe Solare Sonne / Yellow Solar Sun

Tag | Day

Dreamspell

Long-count

24 Montag / Monday 7/15

146

Weisser Elektrischer Weltenüberbrücker: Tod, Ausgleichen, Möglichkeiten
···
Ton: Aktivieren, Binden, Dienen

White Electric Worldbridger: Death, Equalize, Opportunity
Tone: Activate, Bond, Service

101

| | Roter Planetarer Drache
Red Planetary Dragon |

07:00
08:00
09:00
10:00
11:00
12:00
13:00
14:00
15:00
16:00
17:00
18:00
19:00
20:00
21:00

25 Dienstag / Tuesday 7/16

147

Blaue Selbstexistierende Hand: Vollendung, Wissen, Heilung
Ton: Definieren, Messen, Form

Blue Selfexisting Hand: Accomplishment, Know, Healing
Tone: Define, Measure, Form

102

| | Weisser Spektraler Wind
White Spectral Wind |

07:00
08:00
09:00
10:00
11:00
12:00
13:00
14:00
15:00
16:00
17:00

Ideal fürs neue Zuvuya Agenda Jahr 2022 Ein persönliches Maya Reading für dich oder zum Verschenken !

26 Mittwoch / Wednesday 7/17

148

Gelber Oberton Stern: Ästhetik, Verschönern, Kunst
—
Ton: Ermächtigen, Befehlen, Strahlkraft

Yellow Overtone Star: Elegance, Beautify, Art
Tone: Empowerment, Order, Radiance

103

| | Blaue Kristallene Nacht
Blue Crystal Night |

07:00
08:00
09:00
10:00
11:00
12:00
13:00
14:00
15:00
16:00
17:00
18:00
19:00
20:00
21:00

27 Donnerstag / Thursday 7/18

Roter Rhythmischer
Mond: Universelles Wasser, Reinigen, Flow
Ton: Organisieren, Balancieren, Gleichheit

Red Rhythmic Moon:
Universal Water, Purify, Flow
Tone: Organize, Balance, Equality

 Gelber Kosmischer Same / Yellow Cosmic Seed

7:00
8:00
9:00
10:00
11:00
12:00
13:00
14:00
15:00
16:00
17:00
18:00
19:00
20:00
21:00

28 Freitag / Friday 7/19

Weisser Resonanter
Hund: Herz, Lieben, Loyalität
Ton: Kanalisieren, Inspirieren, Einstimmung

White Resonant Dog:
Heart, Love, Loyalty
Tone: Channel, Inspire, Attunement

 Rote Magnetische Schlange / Red Magnetic Serpent

07:00
08:00
09:00
10:00
11:00
12:00
13:00
14:00
15:00
16:00
17:00
18:00
19:00
20:00
21:00

29 Samstag / Saturday 7/20

Blauer Galaktischer
Affe: Magie, Spielen, Illusion
Ton: Harmonisieren, Modellieren, Integrität

Blue Galactic Monkey:
Magic, Play, Illusion
Tone: Harmony, Model, Integrity

 Weisser Lunarer Weltenüberbrücker | White Lunar Worldbridger

08:00
10:00
12:00
14:00
16:00
18:00

30 Sonntag / Sunday 7/21

Gelber Solarer Mensch:
Freier Wille, Beeinflussen, Weisheit
Ton: Pulsieren, Erkennen, Absicht

Yellow Solar Human:
Free Will, Influence, Wisdom
Tone: Pulse, Realize, Intention

 Blaue Elektrische Hand / Blue Electric Hand

Januar KW 4

VISION

....

Wie weit wollen wir springen?

Stell dir eine riesige Halle vor, gefüllt mit Tausenden von Konzertbesuchern. Auf einmal geht der Strom aus, keine Musik mehr, kein Licht, absolute Dunkelheit. Die Menge gerät in Panik und will hinaus ans Licht.

In dieser Situation zündet ein einzelner Mensch, der weiss, wo der Ausgang ist, sein Feuerzeug an und führt die verängstigte Menge sicher wieder nach draussen, ins Licht, in die Freiheit.

Wenn ein Mensch sich entscheidet, seiner einzigartigen Mission zu folgen, sich auf seine persönliche «Heldenreise» zu begeben, dann ist das gleichzeitig die Entscheidung, sein inneres Feuer scheinen zu lassen und anderen Menschen, die noch im Dunkeln tappen, ein Licht zu sein, dem sie folgen können.

Unsere Agenda soll ein Werkzeug sein, das dir hilft, ebenfalls zu erkennen, wer du wirklich bist und welch unglaubliches Potential und Licht in dir steckt, das entdeckt und entzündet werden möchte.

Wenn dir unsere «Zuvuya Agenda 2020» dabei geholfen hat und du ein zauberhaftes Jahr mit viel Flow und zahlreichen magischen Momenten erlebt hast, dann hoffen wir natürlich, dass du beim nächsten «Ride» auf den Wellen der Zeit erneut dabei bist.

Und ja, «Sharing is caring» oder auf gut deutsch: Geteilte Freude ist doppelte Freude!

Daher unsere Bitte an dich, über dieses wichtige Thema mit anderen Menschen zu sprechen, ihr KIN auszurechnen und sie ebenfalls einzuladen, auf den Zauberteppich aufzusteigen.

Denn dann geschieht das, was unser «Zuvuya Agenda Team» erreichen möchte, nämlich, dass wir gemeinsam von Jahr zu Jahr eine grössere Welle auslösen können, die immer mehr Menschen dazu inspiriert, das Bestmögliche aus ihrem einzigartigen Leben zu machen.

Je mehr Menschen ihrer «Seelenspur» folgen, umso grösser wird das Licht auf diesem Planeten. Und irgendwann wird es soviel Licht auf dieser Erde geben, dass die Dunkelheit verschwinden und das sichtbar wird, was die Maya in ihrer Prophezeihung «Quinto Sol» (fünfte Sonne) genannt haben. Dies ist das «Goldene Zeitalter», in welchem wir wieder in Frieden und Harmonie miteinander auf dieser Erde leben (und täglich einen heissen Cacao miteinander geniessen werden).

In diesem Sinne
Let's surf again!

....

How far do we want to jump?

Imagine a huge hall filled with thousands of concert visitors. Suddenly the power goes out, no more music, no light, absolute darkness. The crowd panics and wants to get out into the light.

In this situation a single person who knows where the exit is lights his lighter and leads the frightened crowd safely out again into the light, into freedom.

If a person decides to follow his unique mission, to go on his personal «hero's journey», then this is at the same time the decision to let his inner fire shine and to be a light to other people who are still groping in the dark, whom they can follow.

Our agenda is to be a tool that helps you also to recognize who you really are and what incredible potential and light there is in you to be discovered and ignited.

If our «Zuvuya Agenda 2020» has helped you with this and you have experienced a magical year with lots of flow and magical moments, then of course we hope that you will be there again at the next "Ride" on the waves of time.

And yes, «Sharing is caring» or «Shared joy is double joy»!

Therefore our request to you to talk about this important topic with other people, to calculate their KIN and to invite them to climb the magic carpet as well.

Because then will happen what our «Zuvuya Agenda Team» wants to achieve, namely that together we can trigger a bigger wave from year to year that inspires more and more people to make the most of their unique lives.

The more people follow their «soul path», the greater the light on this planet. And at some point there will be so much light on this earth that the darkness will disappear and what the Maya called «Quinto Sol» (fifth sun) in their prophecy will become visible.

This is the «Golden Age» in which we live again in peace and harmony with each other on this earth (and will enjoy a hot cacao daily with each other).

In this sense
Let's surf again!

«Ayum Hunab Ku. Evam Maya E Ma Ho»
Möge sich Harmonie und Frieden in unserem Geist ausbreiten.

«Ayum Hunab Ku. Evam Maya E Ma Ho»
May harmony and peace spread in our minds.

A   B   C

G   H   I

D   E   F

J   K   L

M N O

S  U

P   Q   R

V   W   X

Y   Z

Tanja | Rote Erde   **Martin | Gelber Stern**   **Onaquel | Gelber Samen**

Das sind wir!
Gemeinsam haben wir die Zuvuya Agenda 2020 auf die Welt gebracht. Egal ob Plakat, Logo oder Agenda – wir suchen und finden für alles eine kreative, innovative grafische Lösung.

Sie finden uns unter: www.moser.ch

Moser Graphic Design
seit 1998

Notizen

Notizen | Notes

Notizen | Notes

Notizen | Notes

IMPRESSUM

LITERATUR | literature
- Der Maya-Faktor, José Argüelles
- Erde im Aufstieg, José Argüelles
- Dreamspell – die Reise des Zeitschiffs Erde 2013, José & Lloydine Argüelles
- 28 Meditationen über das Gesetz der Zeit, José & Lloydine Argüelles
- Chroniken der Kosmischen Geschichte, Band 1, José Argüelles & Stephanie South
- Surfer der Zuvuya, José Argüelles
- Time & the Technosphere, José Argüelles
- Accessing Your Multidimensional Self, Stephanie South
- The serpent and the jaguar, Birgitte Rasine
- Mayan Caledar Astrology, Kenneth Johnson
- Practical Guide to the Tzolkin, Mariela Maya

Erhältlich über den Buchhandel

MAYA WEBSITEN
Deutsch
- www.zuvuya-agenda.ch
- www.vimeo.com/zuvuya
- www.blaubeerwald.de
- www.canamay-te.de
- www.mayaweg.at
- www.maya.at
- www.neuezeit.info
- www.flow260.com

Englisch
- www.lawoftime.org
- www.13moon.com
- www.calendartruth.info
- www.1320frequencyshift.com
- www.galacticspacebook.com
- www.newtimecourse.com
- www.timewaves.org
- gmwa-foundation101.teachery.co
- www.bridgingworlds.net
- www.mayankin.com

MEDIEN | NETZWERKE | FAIRTRADE
Medien | Networks | Fairtrade
Deutsch
- www.zeitpunkt.ch
- www.spuren.ch
- www.salve-gesund.de
- www.tattva.de
- www.sein.de
- www.kenfm.de
- www.filmefuerdieerde.org
- www.bluepingu.de
- www.myblueplanet.ch
- www.faircustomer.ch
- www.mynewenergy.ch
- www.wecollect.ch
- www.vivaconagua.ch
- www.universalsounds.ch
- www.pachamamafestival.ch
- www.aquariurs.ch
- www.gaia.com
- www.campax.org/de
- www.wemakeit.com
- www.kristallmensch.net
- www.koenigin-samurai.de
- www.init.earth
- www.biovision.ch
- www.erdfest.org/de
- www.nicasolar.org
- www.uhuru.ch
- www.intunemusic.de

Englisch
- www.highexistence.com
- www.resonance.is
- www.well.org
- www.oneworldindialogue.com
- www.vday.org/homepage.html
- www.onebillionrising.org
- www.gaia.com
- www.globalgiftproject.org
- www.futurism.com
- www.fuprosomunic.org
- www.maya-portal.net
- www.payitforwardfoundation.org
- www.thefourpillars.net/
- www.tortuga1320.com
- www.13months28days.info
- www.wemoon.ws
- www.calendartruth.info

BEZUGSQUELLE | Points of sale
- www.shop.zuvuya-agenda.ch
- www.elodia.ch
- www.blaubeerwald.de
- www.lawoftime.org
- www.syntropia.de

IMPRESSUM
1. Auflage, 4. Jahrgang,
Limited Edition (1'600 Expl.)

Verlag | Publisher Company
Zuvuya Flow Verlag
Druck | Print shop
FontFront.com, Rossdorf
printed in EU
Inhalt | Content u.r.s. josé zuber
Lektorat | Proof reading
Rob Men, Julia Wuillemin-Probst
Maya Zeichen | Seals
u.r.s. josé zuber
Illustrationen | Illustrations
Moser Zuvuya Team
Herausgeber | Publisher
u.r.s. josé zuber
Gestaltung| Layout | Design
Moser Graphic Design
Cover Moser Graphic Design

Urheberrecht | Copyright
Alle Rechte bei:
Zuvuya Flow Verlag
u.r.s. josé zuber
Haus der Wunder
Allmendstrasse 83
4500 Solothurn

urs@zuvuya-agenda.ch

Sämtliche Inhalte unterliegen der CC-BY-SA Lizenz

ISBN Nummer
- 978-3-9525136-2-0